The Advisor's Guide to Group Life and AD&D Insurance

By Thomas C. Kirner and Peter Silkowski

The Advisor's Guide to Group Life and AD&D Insurance is an entirely unique reference enabling you to master group concepts while managing specific real-world issues for your clients.

This one-of-a-kind guide takes you through group term life from selection to administration and is the only, single reference:

- Covering group term life pricing with detailed expertise
- Examining enrollment practices
- Delivering insights into the group products concepts
- Dedicating extensive analysis to voluntary coverage
- Explaining risk factors influencing the rating process
- Identifying specific elements within the plan that affect pricing
- Making it easy to research issues related to group term life
- Presenting numerous, relevant examples to help you explain key concepts
- Fully analyzing the practical aspects of what actually goes on with group term life in the real world

The Advisor's Guide to Group Life and AD&D Insurance enables you to clearly explain the derivation and driving factors behind rates. This exclusive, expert insight into the pricing process is only one of many unique elements delivered by the authors **Thomas C. Kirner**, CLU, FLMI, GBDS, and **Peter Silkowski**, GBDS—two of the foremost authorities in this field.

If you have any involvement or interest in group term life, the information contained in this resource will prove invaluable, including:

- How section 79 works
- How underwriting rating works and what drives pricing
- ERISA compliance for voluntary coverages regulatory issues, including how USERRA works
- What topics matter most to producers

To place additional orders for *The Advisor's Guide to Group Life and AD&D Insurance* or any of our products, or for additional information, contact Customer Service at **1-800-543-0874**.

The Advisor's Guide to Group Life and AD&D Insurance

Thomas C. Kirner, CLU, FLMI, GBDS
Peter Silkowski, GBDS

ISBN 978-1-936362-88-2

This publication is designed to provide accurate and authoritative information in regard to the subject matter covered. It is sold with the understanding that the publisher is not engaged in rendering legal, accounting or other professional service. If legal advice or other expert assistance is required, the services of a competent professional person should be sought. – From a Declaration of Principles jointly adapted by a Committee of The American Bar Association and a Committee of Publishers and Associations.

THE NATIONAL UNDERWRITER COMPANY

Copyright © 2013

The National Underwriter Company
5081 Olympic Blvd.
Erlanger, KY 41018

Printed in the United States of America

About Summit Business Media

Summit Business Media is the leading B2B media and information company serving the insurance, financial, legal and investment advisory markets. Summit strives to be "The Next Generation of Business Information" for executives and practitioners by providing breaking news and analysis, in-depth practice management strategies, business-building techniques and actionable data. Summit services the information needs of its customers through numerous channels, including digital, print, and live events. Summit publishes 16 magazines and 150 reference titles, operates 20 websites and hosts a dozen conferences, including the world's largest mining investment conference held each year in South Africa. Summit's Marketing Data division provides detailed information on millions of benefits plans, agents and advisors in the U.S.

Summit employs more than 300 employees in ten offices across the United States. For more information, please visit www.summitbusinessmedia.com.

About The National Underwriter Company

For over 110 years, The National Underwriter Company has been the first in line with the targeted tax, insurance, and financial planning information you need to make critical business decisions. Boasting nearly a century of expert experience, our reputable Editors are dedicated to putting accurate and relevant information right at your fingertips. With Tax Facts, Tools & Techniques, National Underwriter Advanced Markets, Field Guide, FC&S®, and other resources available in print, on CD, and online, you can be assured that as the industry evolves National Underwriter will be at the forefront with the thorough and easy-to-use resources you rely on for success.

The National Underwriter Company
Update Service Notification

This National Underwriter Company publication is regularly updated to include coverage of developments and changes that affect the content. If you did not purchase this publication directly from The National Underwriter Company and you want to receive these important updates sent on a 30-day review basis and billed separately, please contact us at (800) 543-0874. Or you can mail your request with your name, company, address, and the title of the book to:

The National Underwriter Company
5081 Olympic Boulevard
Erlanger, KY 41018

If you purchased this publication from The National Underwriter Company directly, you have already been registered for the update service.

National Underwriter Company Contact Information

To order any National Underwriter Company title, please

- call 1-800-543-0874, 8-6 ET Monday – Thursday and 8 to 5 ET Friday

- online bookstore at www.nationalunderwriter.com, or

- mail to The National Underwriter Company, Orders Department, 5081 Olympic Blvd, Erlanger, KY 41018

Dedication

To Ann, for the support and help over the years.

– Tom Kirner

Acknowledgements

We would like to acknowledge all those who have helped make this endeavor possible.

Many authors have preceded us who gave us insights. We appreciate their dedication to this subject area and we have liberally footnoted these authors' works. We also owe thanks to all those with whom we worked over the years and from whom we learned. Tom Kirner would like to thank in particular, Olin Sawyer, FSA, Joseph Fullerton, William Sproul, Patricia Owens, and Stephen McConnell. Their patience and guidance in understanding employee benefits was invaluable. Pete Silkowski would like to express gratitude for all those who taught him about group insurance in his 30 years in the business. Your influence is seen in the words of this book.

Finally, we must recognize the good folks at Summit Business Media/The National Underwriter Company, who supported this work and were instrumental in making this happen including, Kelly Maheu and Rebecca von Gillern.

Thomas C. Kirner, CLU, FLMI, GBDS

Peter Silkowski, GBDS

September 15, 2012

Preface

This book has been written with the intention of assisting practitioners in the group insurance arena with a deeper understanding of group term life and AD&D insurance. We have spent our careers in this business and know the level of nuance and change involved in this arena. We believe there are subtle differences in the product, risk selection, and regulation that can cause unintentional consequences if not appropriately addressed. Deeper understanding of these nuances and subtleties may also create opportunities. Therefore, we have tried to craft a comprehensive book on what we feel are the most important aspects and attributes of group term life/AD&D.

We have written this book to appeal to readers of many experience levels and backgrounds. It is our hope that those new to group life/AD&D and even those unfamiliar with the essentials of the group insurance business will find it both useful and helpful. We believe, however, that the book may find its greatest value as a reference, allowing practitioners to easily check on issues, aid in understanding, and ultimately better serve employers and employees.

About the Authors

Thomas C. Kirner, CLU, FLMI, GBDS has over 30 years of experience in the group insurance and reinsurance business and is currently working on authoring books on group ancillary benefits. He has managed in multiple functional operations including: underwriting, claims, sales, marketing, finance, and administration, for group: Disability, Life, Medical, and Dental coverage. Tom is also an experienced Continuing Education instructor. He has developed content for over 30 CE programs which were successfully delivered to thousands of Producers nationwide. He is a contributing author of National Underwriter's GBDS (Group Benefits Disability Specialist) professional designation and has authored several online continuing education modules used in the Life/Health industry.

Active in industry organizations, Tom was a member of the Disability Committee of the Group Underwriters Association of America and is a frequent speaker at industry meetings. Tom received a BS from the US Naval Academy, and an MA in Management from Webster University. He attended the Disability Institute at the Wharton School, University of Pennsylvania, and Executive Development programs in sales, marketing, and product development from Columbia University and the University of Michigan.

Peter Silkowski, GBDS owns and operates Silkowski, Consulting, LLC providing training and advisory services to the group insurance industry. He began his group insurance career in 1980 at Connecticut General (now CIGNA) as a benefits administrator and then underwriter for products including Life, Disability, Medical, Dental, Prescription Drug, and Vision Care. Pete joined The Hartford in 1986 as a Senior Underwriter for group national accounts (jumbo clients) and later became Product Manager for the Group Medical business. From 1992 to 2005, Pete developed, delivered and led internal training for Group Underwriting. Pete leveraged that experience in 2005 to serve as catalyst for launching Hartford's Vault program to help educate and train Hartford's distribution partners who market, sell and service group disability products. Pete holds a BA in History from Trinity College in Hartford, CT and is a contributing author to National Underwriter's GBDS (Group Benefits Disability Specialist) professional designation.

About the Developmental Editor

Rebecca von Gillern is a senior developmental editor with the Professional Publishing Division of the National Underwriter Company, Summit Business Media. She manages the editorial development of the Advisor's Guide and the Tools & Techniques series of investment and planning products. She also develops other financial services content for the company. Rebecca has been developing content for the higher education and business-to-business markets for the past sixteen years.

She began her career with Thomson Learning, where she developed and revised federal and state taxation publications. At Thomson she also developed product in the disciplines of accounting, business communication, communication, introduction to business, management, marketing, and the sciences. She is a graduate of the University of Southern Mississippi.

About the Editorial Director

Diana B. Reitz, CPCU, AAI, is the editorial director of the Professional Publishing Division of The National Underwriter Company. As such she is responsible for the overall integrity of all division publications. She previously was the Director of the Property & Casualty Publishing Department of the Professional Publishing Division.

Ms. Reitz has been with The National Underwriter Company since 1998, when she was named editor of the Risk Financing and Self-Insurance manuals and associate editor of the *FC&S Bulletins®*. She also is coauthor of the National Underwriter publication, *Workers Compensation Coverage Guide*, and has edited and contributed to numerous other books and publications, including *The Tools & Techniques of Risk Management and Insurance, Claims* magazine, and *National Underwriter Property & Casualty* newsweekly.

Prior to joining The National Underwriter she was with a regional insurance broker, concentrating on commercial insurance. She is a graduate of the University of Maryland and St. Francis College.

About the Director of Product Development

Kelly B. Maheu, J.D., is the director of product development and content acquisition for the Professional Publishing Division of Summit Business Media. She is responsible for acquiring expert authored content and working closely with Summit's editorial, sales, marketing, and technology teams to develop professional online and print reference libraries.

Kelly began work at Summit in 2006 as an editor for Fire, Casualty and Surety Service (FC&S). A graduate of the University Of Cincinnati College Of Law, Kelly worked in the legal and insurance fields for LexisNexis®, Progressive Insurance, and a Cincinnati insurance defense litigation firm prior to joining Summit. Kelly holds a BA from Miami University, with a double major in English/Journalism and Psychology.

Kelly has edited and contributed to numerous books and publications including the Personal Auto Insurance Policy Coverage Guide, Cyberliability and Insurance, The Tools and Techniques of Risk Management for Financial Planners, Claims Magazine, and ProducersWEB.

TABLE OF CONTENTS

Chapter 1

History of Group Life and AD&D

While it may not seem pertinent to most group insurance professionals, the history and tradition of Group Life and Accidental Death & Dismemberment (AD&D) insurance provides insight into the evolution of the products and perspectives on their continued evolution. As the British historian, Albert Toynbee said, "'History' is a Greek word which means, literally, just 'investigation.'"[1] If we investigate the past, we are bound to find some insight for the present and trends for the future. Then we may find that the expression "what is old is new again" is sometimes applicable.

Group insurance as an employee benefit began in the early twentieth century. Even the earliest programs included group term life insurance, the subject of this book. Prior to the development of group life insurance, families of workers who died on the job were reliant upon "pass the hat" insurance. Employers frequently contributed to these collections. This system, however, failed to adequately meet the needs of employees and their families.

Fraternal and mutual benefit organizations sometimes helped to meet these needs. Yet, large gaps still existed. Thus arose a need for some form of insurance.

The introduction of a formal insurance program served to directly relieve the employer of any burden. Substituting a known fixed cost for the vagaries of unanticipated contributions was an attractive option, which was made even more sensible from a business standpoint when businesses became subject to corporate income tax in 1909.[2] Companies could deduct business expenses from income and thus reduce their tax burden. Employer contributions to group life plans are still deductible as an ordinary business expense today.

Emergence of Group Term Life and AD&D Products

The first group term life insurance program was underwritten by The Equitable Life Assurance Society of New York in 1910. This policy was written on the 121 employees of the Pantasote Leather Company. However, the first truly notable group term life policy was issued to Montgomery Ward and Company in 1912. It covered nearly 3,000 employees.[3] By 1919, at least 29 companies were writing this kind of policy.[4]

In its genesis in late nineteenth and early twentieth-century America, group insurance was viewed as quite controversial. According to The American Life Convention 1906-1952, a study of the history of life insurance, at the time the biggest concerns which insurance experts expressed were that group coverage:

- Had too many pitfalls and was too great a risk for the average insurer to take on.

- Was discriminatory without the submission of medical evidence.

- Would destroy the idea of individual responsibility. Young men, who should be thinking about life insurance policies would say that the corporation would insure them so they need not worry about life insurance.

- With the lower rates of term coverage it would become more difficult to sell the advantages inherent in any other form of insurance.[5]

None of these dire consequences ever came to pass. Group risk, just like individual life insurance risk, was spread across many lives. The insurer could also raise rates if mortality was greater than expected, as most group life was and still is written on an annual renewal term policy. The use of reinsurance also allowed insurers to spread the risk. Today, group term life insurance is a consistent profit maker for insurers. The concerns about discrimination were simply unfounded. Worries about people being irresponsible about the need for life insurance were unrealized.

Data published by the American Council of Life Insurers (ACLI) clearly show that both group and individual life insurance purchases have grown over time, as will be illustrated later in the chapter. Further, while group term life insurance rates are attractive compared to traditional whole life insurance products, the individual life industry itself began pushing the sale of individual term life and its lower costs relative to traditional whole life products.

Accidental death & dismemberment (AD&D) insurance is an additional benefit paid in the event of death due to an accident or certain types of injury.[6] AD&D was originally issued as an additional benefit on life insurance policies against death in travel-related accidents.[7] By 1904, AD&D riders were developed to cover all types of accidents in addition to travel-related accidents.[8] While its first use in group policies is difficult to pin down, AD&D is clearly one of the earliest forms of group coverage to be developed.[9] The reasons for its early adoption and popularity with employers and employees are easy to understand:

- AD&D is relatively inexpensive.

- It pays a significant benefit in the event of a covered loss.

- Individuals could easily see themselves seriously injured due to an accident.[10] Before the advent of worker safety laws, the prevalence of on-the-job accidents was far greater than it is today.

Life insurance on employees' dependents began as a benefit offering early in the twentieth century. While the exact date of first usage is difficult to ascertain, we can determine that by 1944 dependent life insurance was becoming popular.[11] So much so, that by 1945, the state of California felt the need to enact legislation regulating dependent group life programs.[12]

Many states enacted restrictions on the amounts of insurance available for group dependent life. This is due partly to the theory that employees having large amounts of insurance on dependents presented a moral hazard. Legislators feared that employees would engage in untoward or fraudulent activity in order to collect the group life proceeds. Today, state regulation has eased, although some states still restrict the amounts to a relatively modest benefit.

Retiree life, as a group term life insurance product, developed a bit later. By 1950, it was noted as "one of the most important problems being considered in the group insurance field."[13] Why it was a problem is undoubtedly the high mortality risk of older people.

A century ago, one's chances of living much beyond the normal working age were slim and little attention was paid to the possibility. In 1900, at birth the average boy in America could expect to live only 46.3 years. In 1900 girls' life expectancy at birth was 48.3 years.[14]

Charging a sufficient premium to cover this retiree risk on an annual renewal basis must have been a challenge. Moreover, providing group life benefits to employees after their active service was not widely considered by employers, much less put into practice. A combination of a modest face amount and higher rates made the product viable, and it continues in use to this day.

Growth of Group Term Life and AD&D

The early growth of group life insurance is notable. By 1930, there were approximately 18,000 group life insurance policies in force.[15] Clearly, employers saw the value of providing group life insurance. Fairly consistent growth in the number of policies continued throughout the twentieth century. By 2011, LIMRA reported that there were over 477,000 group life policies in force.[16]

Each year, the American Council of Life Insurers (ACLI) publishes its *ACLI Life Insurers Fact Book*, which presents data on the growth of life insurance. In 2010, it reported that over 109 million certificates were in force. This was a marked decrease from the high of 159 million certificates in 1999. However, the face amount (the dollar amount of life insurance protection) in force actually grew over the same period.

Figures 1.1 and 1.2 present tables taken from the *ACLI Life Insurers Fact Book 2011*. They depict purchases of individual, group, and credit life insurance in the United States over a substantial period. You will note a steady rise in sales of group term life insurance until its zenith in 2001. Then, the 2001 recession caused a decline in sales. These bounced back a bit, but then suffered a significant decline in the latest recession. Obviously, reduced employment due to high unemployment rates and underemployment coupled with pressure on employers to lower costs, including benefit costs, has had a negative effect on the sales of group life insurance. However, as illustrated by Figures 1.1 and 1.2, the concern that group term life would eliminate the desire for individual life policies seems not to have occurred.

Figure 1-1. Life Insurance Purchases by Year

Policies and certificates in thousands/Amounts in millions

Year	Individual		Group		Total	
	Policies	Face amount	Certificates	Face amount	Policies/Certificates	Face amount
1940	17,872	$10,039	285	$691	18,157	$10,730
1945	16,212	13,289	681	1,265	16,893	14,554
1950	20,203	22,728	2,631	6,068	22,834	28,796
1955	21,928	37,169	2,217	11,258*	24,145	48,427*
1960	21,021	59,763	3,734	14,645	24,755	74.408
1965	20,429	90,781	7,007	51,385+	27,436	142,166+
1970	18,550	129,432	5,219	63,690+	23,769	193,122
1975	18,946	194,732	8,146	95,190+	27,092	289,922+
1980	17,628	389,184	11,379	183,418	29,007	572,602
1985	17,637	911,666	16,243	319,503*	33,880	1,231,169*
1986	17,116	934,010	17,507	374,741+	34,623	1,308,751+
1987	16,455	986,984	16,698	365,529	33,153	1,352,513
1988	15,796	996,006	15,793	410,848	31,589	1,406,854
1989	14,850	1,020,971	15,110	420,707	29,960	1,441,678
1990	14,199	1,069,880	14,592	459,271	28,791	1,529,151

Figure 1-1. Life Insurance Purchases by Year (Cont'd)					
1991	13,583	1,041,706	16,230	573,953+	29,813	1,615,659+
1992	13,452	1,048,357	14,930	440,143	28,382	1,488,500
1993	13,664	1,101,476	17,574	576,823	31,238	1,678,299
1994	13,835	1,057,233	18,390	560,232	32,225	1,617,465
1995	12,595	1,039,258	19,404	537,828	31,999	1,577,086
1996	12,022	1,089,268	18,761	614,565	30,783	1,703,833
1997	11,734	1,203,681	19,973	688,589	31,707	1,892,270
1998	11,559	1,324,671	20,332	739,508	31,891	2,064,179
1999	11,673	1,399,848	26,912	966,858	38,584	2,366,706
2000	11,820	1,593,907	21,537	921,001	33,357	2,514,908
2001	14,059	1,600,471	26,036	1,172,080	40,095	2,772,551
2002	14,692	1,752,941	24,020	1,013,728	38,713	2,766,669
2003‡	13,821	1,772,673	21,946	1,050,318	35,767	2,822,992
2004‡	12,581	1,846,384	25,872	1,101,599	38,453	2,947,983
2005‡	11,407	1,796,384	23,112	1,039,878	34,519	2,836,262
2006‡	10,908	1,813,100	18,378	1,022,080	29,287	2,835,180
2007‡	10,826	1,890,989	19,962	1,102,654	30,788	2,993,643
2008‡	10,207	1,869,554	18,392	1,073,273	28,599	2,942,827
2009‡	10,139	1,744,357	19,051	1,155,824	29,190	2,900,181
2010‡	10,123	1,673,216	18,498	1,135,354	28,621	2,808,570

Sources: ACLI tabulations of National Association of Insurance Commissioners (NAIC) data, used by permission; LIMRA International.

Notes: NAIC does not endorse any analysis or conclusions based on use of its data. Data represent direct business and exclude revivals, increases, dividend additions, and reinsurance acquired. 1940–73 data exclude credit life insurance. Beginning with 1974, data include long-term credit insurance (life insurance on loans of more than 10 years' duration). Data represent U.S. life insurers and, as of 2003, fraternal benefit societies.

*Includes Servicemen's Group Life Insurance of $27.8 billion in 1965, $17.1 billion in 1970, $1.7 billion in 1975, $45.6 billion in 1981, $51 billion in 1986, and $166.7 billion in 1991.

‡ Includes fraternal benefit societies.

Figure 1-2. Life Insurance In Force in the United States, by Year (millions)

Year	Individual		Group		Credit		Total	
	Policies	Face amount	Certificates	Face amount	Policies[1]	Face amount	Policies/ Certificates	Face amount
1900	14	$7,573	—	—	—	—	14	$7,573
1905	22	11,863	—	—	—	—	22	11,863
1910	29	14,908	—	—	—	—	29	14,908
1915	41	20,929	*	$100	—	—	41	21,029
1920	64	38,966	2	1,570	*	$4	66	40,540
1925	94	65,210	3	4,247	*	18	97	69,475
1930	118	96,536	6	9,801	*	73	124	106,413
1935	114	88,155	6	10,208	1	101	121	98,464
1940	122	100,212	9	14,938	3	380	134	115,530
1945	149	129,225	12	22,172	2	365	163	151,762
1950	172	182,531	19	47,793	11	3,844	202	234,168
1955	192	256,494	32	101,345	28	14,493	252	372,332
1960	195	381,444	44	175,903	43	29,101	282	586,448
1965	196	539,456	61	308,078	63	53,020	320	900,554
1970	197	773,374	80	551,357	78	77,392	355	1,402,123
1975	204	1,122,844	96	904,695	80	112,032	380	2,139,571
1980	206	1,796,468	118	1,579,355	78	165,215	402	3,541,038
1985	186	3,275,539	130	2,561,595	70	215,973	386	6,053,107
1990	177	5,391,053	141	3,753,506	71	248,038	389	9,392,597
1991	170	5,700,252	141	4,057,606	64	228,478	375	9,986,336
1992	168	5,962,783	142	4,240,919	56	202,090	366	10,405,792
1993	169	6,448,885	142	4,456,338	52	199,518	363	11,104,741
1994	169	6,448,758	145	4,443,179	52	189,398	366	11,081,335
1995	166	6,890,386	147	4,604,856	57	201,083	370	11,696,325

Figure 1-2. Life Insurance In Force in the United States, by Year (millions) (Cont'd)

Year	Individual		Group		Credit		Total	
	Policies	Face Amount	Certificates	Face Amount	Policies[1]	Face Amount	Policies/ Certificates	Face Amount
1997	162	7,872,561	142	5,279,042	47	212,255	351	13,363,858
1998	160	8,523,258	152	5,735,273	46	212,917	359	14,471,448
1999	162	9,172,397	159	6,110,218	46	213,453	367	15,496,069
2000	163	9,376,370	156	6,376,127	50	200,770	369	15,953,267
2001	166	9,345,723	163	6,765,074	48	178,851	377	16,289,648
2002	169	9,311,729	164	6,876,075	42	158,534	375	16,346,338
2003‡	176	9,654,731	163	7,236,191	40	152,739	379	17,043,661
2004‡	168	9,717,377	165	7,630,503	39	160,371	373	17,508,252
2005‡	166	9,969,899	167	8,263,019	40	165,605	373	18,398,523
2006‡	161	10,056,501	177	8,905,646	37	150,289	375	19,112,436
2007‡	158	10,231,765	180	9,157,919	36	149,536	374	19,539,219
2008‡	156	10,254,379	148	8,717,453	31	148,443	335	19,120,276
2009‡	153	10,324,455	113	7,688,328	25	125,512	291	18,138,295
2010‡	152	10,483,516	109	7,830,631	23	111,805	284	18,425,952

Sources: ACLI tabulations of National Association of Insurance Commissioners (NAIC) data, used by permission; Spectator Year Book.
Notes: NAIC does not endorse any analysis or conclusions based on use of its data; Data represent direct business for policies/certificates and net business for face amounts. Beginning in 1959, data include Alaska and Hawaii. 1994-97 data for individual amount and group certificates were revised. Individual and group categories include credit life insurance on loans of more than 10 years' duration; credit category is limited to life insurance on loans of 10 years' or less duration. Totals represent all life insurance (net of reinsurance) on residents of the United States, whether issued by U.S. or foreign companies.
* Fewer than 500,000.
‡Includes fraternal benefit societies.
[1] Includes group credit certificates.

Figures 1.1 and 1.2 depict life insurance in force in the United States over an extended period of time. Similar patterns developed for both group and individual policies. We can see that individual life continued to prosper as group life grew. We do see some falling off of the number of individual policies in force after their high-water mark in 1955. However, individual face amounts continued to grow and indeed continue to grow to this day.

One plausible reason for this shift in policy numbers and face amounts is the decline of the old debit system of life insurance sales. The debit system was one in which relatively small amounts of life insurance were sold to families, principally on the working man. Many of the workers were blue collar and had relatively few other ways to purchase additional insurance beyond anything the employer offered on a group basis. One characteristic of the debit system was that life insurance agents visited the families in person on a weekly or monthly basis to collect the relatively small premiums. This system became too costly to maintain over time and fell into disuse.

The Bureau of Labor Statistics (BLS) also reports on employee benefits and states that in 1999, 56 percent of workers (part time and full time) participated in employers' life insurance programs. As of its survey data in 2011 (see Figure 1-3), that number increased to 59 percent. It seems that the latest economic environment has caused a slowing in the growth of group life insurance. Nevertheless, the program is available through many employers and retains its popularity.

Figure 1-3. Life Insurance Benefits:
Access, Participation, and Take-Up Rates (National Compensation Survey, March 2011)

Characteristics	Civilian[2]			Private Industry			State and Local Government		
	Access	Participation	Take-Up Rate	Access	Participation	Take-Up Rate	Access	Participation	Take-Up Rate
All workers	61	59	97	58	56	97	80	78	97
Worker Characteristics									
Management, professional and related	78	76	98	77	76	98	81	78	97
Management, business, and financial	85	84	98	85	84	99	-	-	-
Professional and related	75	74	98	73	72	98	80	77	97
Teachers	75	73	98	-	-	-	79	77	97
Primary, secondary, and special education school teachers	82	81	98	-	-	-	86	84	98
Registered nurses	72	71	98	-	-	-	-	-	-
Service	38	36	95	31	29	94	75	73	97
Protective service	72	69	96	54	49	90	84	83	98
Sales and office	60	57	96	58	55	96	81	79	98
Sales and related	48	45	92	48	44	92	-	-	-
Office and administrative support	66	65	97	64	62	97	81	79	98

Figure 1-3. Life Insurance Benefits: Access, Participation, and Take-Up Rates (National Compensation Survey, March 2011) (Cont'd)									
Characteristics	**Civilian[2]**			**Private Industry**			**State and Local Government**		
	Access	Partici-pation	Take-Up Rate	Access	Partici-pation	Take-Up Rate	Access	Partici-pation	Take-Up Rate
Construction, extraction, farming, fishing, and forestry	53	51	96	49	46	95	-	-	-
Installation, maintenance, and repair	68	66	97	66	64	97	-	-	-
Production, transportation, and material moving	65	63	97	64	62	97	76	75	99
Production	71	69	97	71	69	97	-	-	-
Transportation and material moving	59	57	97	58	56	96	-	-	-
Full-time	76	74	97	73	71	97	90	88	98
Part-time	15	14	91	14	13	91	23	21	94
Union	85	83	98	83	81	98	86	85	98
Nonunion	57	55	96	55	53	96	74	72	97
Average wage within the following categories:									
Lowest 25 percent	28	26	92	25	22	91	62	60	97
Lowest 10 percent	15	14	91	13	12	90	46	44	95
Second 25 percent	64	62	96	61	59	95	84	82	97
Third 25 percent	75	73	97	71	69	97	85	84	98
Highest 25 percent	83	82	98	81	80	99	89	87	97
Highest 10 percent	87	85	98	85	84	99	89	86	97

Figure 1-3. Life Insurance Benefits: Access, Participation, and Take-Up Rates (National Compensation Survey, March 2011) (Cont'd)

Characteristics	Civilian[2]			Private Industry			State and Local Government		
	Access	Partici-pation	Take-Up Rate	Access	Partici-pation	Take-Up Rate	Access	Partici-pation	Take-Up Rate
Goods-producing industries	72	70	97	72	70	97	-	-	-
Service providing industries	59	57	97	55	53	96	80	77	97
Education and health services	69	67	97	62	61	98	80	77	97
Educational services	77	75	98	68	67	99	79	77	97
Elementary and secondary schools	77	75	98	-	-	-	78	77	98
Junior colleges, colleges and universities	83	80	96	86	85	99	82	77	94
Health care and social assistance	63	61	97	61	60	97	83	80	97
Hospitals	85	84	98	-	-	-	89	85	97
Public administration	82	80	98	-	-	-	82	80	98
1 to 99 workers	42	40	96	41	39	96	64	62	97
1 to 49 workers	38	36	95	37	35	95	63	61	96
50 to 99 workers	55	54	97	55	53	97	66	64	98
100 workers or more	78	76	97	76	74	97	82	80	97

Figure 1-3. Life Insurance Benefits:
Access, Participation, and Take-Up Rates (National Compensation Survey, March 2011) (Cont'd)

Characteristics	Civilian[2]			Private Industry			State and Local Government		
	Access	Partici-pation	Take-Up Rate	Access	Partici-pation	Take-Up Rate	Access	Partici-pation	Take-Up Rate
500 workers or more	85	84	98	86	84	99	85	83	97
Geographic Areas									
New England	60	58	97	58	56	98	72	69	95
Middle Atlantic	60	59	99	56	55	98	84	83	99
East North Central	66	63	96	64	61	97	78	74	95
West North Central	63	61	97	60	58	97	78	77	99
South Atlantic	61	59	97	57	55	97	83	80	97
East South Central	69	66	96	64	62	96	85	80	94
West South Central	61	58	95	58	54	94	76	75	98
Mountain	61	58	95	57	54	95	84	82	98
Pacific	55	53	97	51	49	97	76	75	99

1. The take-up rate is an estimate of the percentage of workers with access to a plan who participate in the plan, rounded for presentation.
2. Includes workers in the private nonfarm economy except those in private households, and workers in the public sector, except the federal government.
3. The percentile groupings are based on the average wage for each occupation surveyed, which may include workers both above and below the threshold. The percentile values are based on the estimates published in the "National Compensation Survey: Occupational Earnings in the United States, 2008."
NOTE: Dash indicates no workers in this category or data did not meet publication criteria. For definitions of major plans, key provisions, and related terms, see the "Glossary of Employee Benefit Terms" at: www.bls.gov/ncs/ebs/glossary20092010.htm.

Source: Bureau of Labor Statistics, US Department of Labor, News Release, Tuesday July 26, 2011

The obvious question is: Are we seeing a decline in the importance of group term life that is permanent, or once employment returns to more normal levels, will the group term life insurance business again resume its growth?

There are forces that argue both sides of this question. Those for a resumption of growth include:

- The fact that most individuals today have limited access to life insurance other than through work.

- The workplace is a convenient place for individuals to purchase insurance.

- The group life insurance industry has invested a lot of time and energy to develop the voluntary life insurance market (as we'll see in Chapter 12) and will work hard to receive a return on that investment.

Forces that argue against the return to a normal group life growth pattern claim that:

- the rise of the Internet as a distribution channel for life insurance allows individuals easy access to many life insurance options at reasonable costs;

- the economy, especially job growth (a key component of the growth of group life), is expected to lag for years;

- the continued unabated rise in the cost of employee health insurance makes it increasingly difficult for employers to offer ancillary benefits such as group life.

Time will provide the answer to this quandary.

Reasons for Growth

As early as 1915, the advantages of a group life insurance program were being touted:

> "The employer, by taking out this form of protection, binds his [sic] employees more closely to him, and inculcates something of a cooperative spirit…but all [employers] have the same general purpose, viz., the elimination of the loss that is connected with frequent changes in the working personnel."[17]

Employee recruitment and retention are still key reasons for offering group term life and AD&D today. In some industries, a group life program is viewed as a standard part of the employee's total compensation package.

The fact that employers could reduce their taxable income by the cost of the life insurance certainly helped contribute to the growth of group life and AD&D insurance.

The growing industrialization of the United States has also been cited as a factor.[18] As more and more people of working age in the United States were leaving farms and congregating in cities where the jobs were, the need for more formal modes of financial protection, including life insurance, increased. People could no longer rely on a subsistence form of farming to get by. Moreover, an increasing social consciousness regarding industrial workers and their well-being worked its way into the American political psyche. Legislators who may have previously opposed the expansion of group life coverage began to reverse their views.

The organized labor movement went hand-in-glove with increased industrialization. A 1949 Supreme Court decision gave labor unions the right to negotiate with employers on behalf of their members. Unions pushed for increased employee benefits, including life insurance. Employers who offered union members benefits were inclined to offer nonunion employees similar benefits.

During both World War II and the Korean War, the government imposed wage controls on private business. With so many working-age men in the military, competing for employees became a concern for private industry employers. One way in which they could compete for workers was by offering them more and more generous employee benefits. Group term life insurance and AD&D providers enjoyed the effects of this impetus. After the wars and with the booming economy, benefit packages continued to increase in value.

Life insurance went through many sharp adjustments during the period immediately following the end of World War II. The very structure of the business began to be materially affected by the upsurge in "fringe benefit" programs then being set up in large numbers by employer-employee groups.[19]

Insurance carriers made changes in their group term life programs that helped to spur the industry's growth. First, they greatly modified underwriting so that larger and larger amounts of face value, or benefit levels, were available without any medical underwriting. These higher "guaranteed issue" amounts made the coverage more meaningful. Simultaneously, improvements in mortality and a highly competitive market forced insurers to charge ever lower rates for group life and AD&D. One industry wag has termed this phenomenon the "race to zero." Indeed lower rates and higher face amounts undoubtedly combined to make group term life a very attractive proposition. In conjunction with all this, carriers started to promote voluntary products or employee-pay-all life coverage. This allowed employees to continue to get group rates but released the employer from many direct costs of the program as they sought to limit benefits in the face of escalating health care costs.

While today the growth of employee benefits in general seems stalled due to recent rising health care costs and lower employment, it seems clear that the need for group life insurance provided through the place of employment will continue.

Funding of Group Term Life and AD&D

Initially, group life and AD&D were employer-pay-all programs offered as incentives to increase employee loyalty. Soon after World War I, a growing trend toward contributory plans emerged, which required employees to bear part of the cost of group life programs.[20] This trend continues today, with more and more of the cost of group benefits being shifted to employees.

The BLS reports that in 2011, 95 percent of basic life programs did not require employee contributions. However, this does not take into account the widespread use of supplemental life and voluntary life programs. The BLS in its report for 2011 also stated that 60 percent of life programs provided a benefit that was one times basic annual earnings. Notably, a lot of group term life insurance is not part of the basic life data collected by BLS. Many industry observers have noted the rise of supplemental and voluntary programs with the employee-pay-all feature. By some estimates, as much as a quarter of new group term life sales today are voluntary.

Early Precedents and Continued Evolution

Prior to the first group insurance policy being issued, there were precedents established that can still be found in group coverage policies to this day. Several precedents of interest follow.

- By the 1870s, most companies were beginning to grant 30-day of grace of premium payments.[21]

- The writing of substandard risk policies was pioneered in 1865 by Guy Phelps and the company he founded, Connecticut Invalid Life Insurance Company. The new organization expanded its business to other areas but always remained at the forefront of substandard risk underwriting. The company later became known as Connecticut General and is now part of CIGNA.[22]

- The writing of substandard risk was pioneered by Connecticut General [now CIGNA]. which was organized in 1865 by Guy Phelps. At first called "Connecticut Invalid Life Insurance Company", the new organization soon ceased to restrict its business to substandard risk, but always remained at the forefront in this field of underwriting.[23]

- In the early days of group insurance, a firm with less than 50 employees could not be covered, but in recent times the minimum has been lowered to as few as ten.[24] Some carriers, through the use of a trust mechanism, write policies for groups with as few as two employees.

In the 100-year period since group life coverage was initially offered on a formal basis, the product has gone through a dramatic transformation. Despite continuing change, the principles upon which group life and AD&D coverage were founded remain intact. Group life and AD&D insurance provide protection from premature death for employees and a burial payment for retirees. This book will examine the culmination of all these developments in today's group life and AD&D world. Before embarking on this examination, it is important to recognize the efforts of the thousands of insurance workers, insurance organizations, our stable government institutions, a free market system, and caring employers, who through history have helped to make this transformation possible.

Key Takeaways

- Group term life and AD&D have long histories as employee benefits.

- In its genesis in the late nineteenth and early twentieth centuries, group insurance was viewed as controversial.

- The growth of voluntary markets has helped life programs grow by shifting the cost from employers to employees.

- While life sales growth has slowed in the past decade, sales remain healthy and the market for future sales remains strong.

- Improving mortality and competitive pressures have made rates for group term life and AD&D extremely attractive.

- In the early days of group insurance, a firm with less than 50 employees could not be covered, but in recent times, the minimum has been lowered to as few as ten.

- Wage controls during World War II and the Korean War propelled the popularity of fringe benefits, as employers competed for workers in a tight labor market.

- Employers who offered union members benefits were inclined to offer nonunion employees similar benefits.

- The fact that employers could reduce their taxable income by the cost of the life insurance contributed to the growth of group life and AD&D insurance.

Endnotes

1. Szasz, Ferenc M., "Quotes About History," *History News Network, http://hnn.us/articles/1328.html* (accessed June 11, 2012).

2. Bucci, Michael, "Growth of Employer Sponsored Group Life Insurance," *Monthly Labor Review* (October 1991), p. 26.

3. Ibid., p. 25.

4. Gudmundsen, John, *The Great Provider* (South Norwalk, CT: Industrial Publications Company, 1959), p. 77.

5. Buley, R. Carlyle, *The American Life Convention 1906–1952* (New York, NY: Appelton-Century-Crofts, Inc., 1953), pp. 421 and 690.

6. Beam, Burton T., *Group Benefits: Basic Concepts and Alternatives,* Tenth Edition (Bryn Mawr, PA: The American College Press, 2004), p. 543.

7. Maclean, Joseph B., *Life Insurance,* Ninth Edition (New York, NY: McGraw-Hill, 1962), p. 242.

8. Magee, John H., *Life Insurance,* Third Edition, (Homewood, IL: Richard D. Irwin, Inc., 1958), p. 140.

9. Ashman, Carl R., *Group Insurance Handbook,* Third Edition, (Homewood, IL: Richard P. Irwin Inc., 1965), p. 151.

10. *Unintended Exposure: The Surprising "Big Gamble" Employees Take Everyday: The Hartford's Disability Literacy Study* (Hartford, CT: The Hartford Financial Services Group, 2005), p. 3.

11. Gregg, Davis Weinert, *An Analysis of Group Life Insurance* (Philadelphia, PA: University of Pennsylvania Press, 1950), p. 173.

12. *The National Underwriter,* Life Edition (August 18, 1944), p. 3.

13. Gregg, op. cit., p. 181.

14. Gudmundsen, op. cit., p. 133.

15. Bucci, op. cit., p. 27.

16. LIMRA's U. S. Group Life Sales & In Force Survey, Second Quarter 2011 by Anita Potter.

17. Blanchard, Ralph H., *Life Insurance* (New York, NY: D. Appleton & Company, 1915, pp. 37 and 309.

18. Beam, op. cit, p. 10.

19. Gudmundsen, op. cit., p. 102.

20. Gregg, op. cit., p. 359.

21. Gudmundsen, op. cit., p. 74.

22. Ibid, 74.

23. Ibid, p. 74.

24. Gudmundsen, op. cit., p. 110.

Chapter 2

The Purpose and Need for Group Life and AD&D Insurance

Most financial planners tout the importance of life insurance as part of a sound and balanced financial portfolio. While the purposes and situations for people are as varied as individuals themselves, the overall need for life coverage is universal.

This chapter will address the need for life insurance with an emphasis on group life insurance. Some mortality statistics will be shown to remind us of the need for final and other expenses. The gap between what is considered adequate coverage for an individual versus what generally is in force on individuals will be examined. The hope is to demonstrate the vital role that life insurance protection provides in American society and to provide the producer with material useful in selling more life insurance. Other insurance professionals may find the information useful in deepening their appreciation of the group life products they support.

As human beings, we are aware that we will die someday. For most of us, the date is an uncertainty. We generally assume we'll die in old age, surrounded by family. Or, perhaps we envision dying in our sleep at age 105. It is the uncertainty of when our end comes that makes life insurance so valuable.

Risk of Premature Death

For too many of us, reality is different than our hopes for longevity. It is true that longevity in the United States has increased, but people do die prematurely. According to the Centers for Disease Control and Protection (CDC), the death rate is now 45 percent lower than in 1960, declining from 1,339.2 per 100,000 standard population in 1960 to 741.0 in 2009.[1] Figure 2-1 shows that while the number of deaths have increased, the death rate has decreased significantly since 1935.

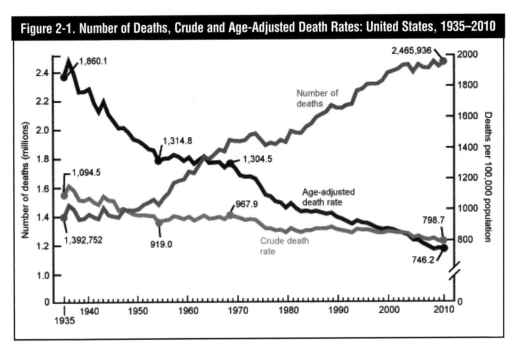

Figure 2-1. Number of Deaths, Crude and Age-Adjusted Death Rates: United States, 1935–2010

Notes: 2010 data are preliminary. Crude death rates on an annual basis are per 100,000 population; age-adjusted rates are per 100,000 U.S. standard population. Rates for 2001–2009 are revised and may differ from rates previously published.
Source: CDC/NCHS, National Vital Statistics System, Mortality.

Nevertheless, people of working age do suffer premature death. The National Vital Statistics Report's January 11, 2012 publication documents that 25 percent of all deaths in 2010 were among individuals ages 25–65, prime working years. (The year 2010 is the latest year of full data as of this writing.) While most people erroneously believe that it is unforeseen injury that causes most premature deaths, CDC reports that only 5 percent of all deaths were due to unintended injury in 2007. The reality is that most premature deaths are caused by disease, as indicated by Figure 2-2.

Premature death from the three leading causes—heart disease, cancer, and stroke—may be partially avoidable through lifestyle changes, but a large percentage of people are unwilling to make the necessary adjustments. Obesity, for example, is known to be a contributing factor to premature disease. According to the CDC, about one-third of U.S. adults (33.8 percent) are obese. People know that healthy living helps prevent many chronic diseases. Yet, in 2011, only 20.4 percent of adults engaged in aerobic activity and muscle strengthening, and 19.3 percent of adults still smoked.[2] It appears many Americans know the risk factors contributing to premature death, yet they continue to indulge in bad habits. That American workers are subject to premature death is borne out statistically, as shown in Figure 2-3.

Figure 2-2. The Leading Causes of Death	
Cause of Death	Number of Deaths –2010
Heart disease	616,067
Cancer	562,875
Stroke (cerebrovascular diseases)	135,952
Chronic lower respiratory diseases	127,924
Accidents (unintentional injuries)	123,706
Alzheimer's disease	74,632
Diabetes	71,382
Influenza and pneumonia	52,717
Nephritis, nephrotic syndrome, and nephrosis	46,448
Septicemia	34,828

Source: *Health, United States, 2010* (Hyattsville, MD: National Center for Health Statistics).

While mortality rates seem relatively low (and in fact they are), older workers have a much higher mortality rate. According to the Bureau of Labor Statistics, 28.1 percent of the labor force was comprised of workers aged 55 and older in 2010; this is exactly the point in age when mortality rates drastically increase. Further indications from the most recent recession indicate that a large number of retirement-aged individuals are continuing to work. *USA Today* reported that older workers are snaring an outsized share of job gains in the economic recovery as they put off retirement amid shrinking nest eggs, changes in Social Security benefits, and improved health.[3] Older workers, many of whom still have financial responsibilities such as mortgages, car loans, and saving for retirement (whenever that might happen), need life insurance protection.

Statistically, it is clear that there exists a very real risk of premature death for a worker. A worker with no financial dependencies (family, relatives, or debts) probably has little need for life insurance other than sufficient funds for a burial. But, most workers DO have families and relatives (like aged parents) who rely on the worker, and most workers also have significant debt in the form of car loans, credit card balances, and mortgages. Considering the complexities of surviving financially in 21st century America, obtaining life insurance protection is a sound move.

Figure 2-3. Exposure, Mortality Rates by Central Age, Based on Lives – 2006 Report						
Central Age	Exposure (Lives)		Monthly Mortality Rates Per Thousand (Lives)		Mortality Rates as a Percentage of 1996 Study	
	Male	Female	Male	Female	Male	Female
17	38,589	30, 031	0.181	0.050	289%	166%
22	528, 549	486, 904	0.055	0.019	66%	55%
27	1,0238,0204	1, 071, 297	0.049	0.017	63%	36%
32	1, 478, 613	1, 138, 591	0.051	0.024	66%	34%
37	1, 596, 163	1, 182, 346	0.063	0.037	58%	65%
42	1, 570, 768	1, 211, 833	0.095	0.052	63%	76%
47	1, 351, 461	1, 104, 950	0.143	0.083	66%	64%
52	1, 070, 074	923, 639	0.225	0.134	73%	95%
57	737, 877	606, 430	0.366	0.205	54%	82%
62	438, 585	326, 377	0.549	0.326	70%	84%
67	157, 502	101, 554	0.931	0.507	77%	64%
72	69, 780	38, 573	1.794	1.022	74%	90%
77	34, 292	17, 183	3.315	2.148	76%	103%
82	14, 215	7, 510	6.302	3.895	60%	99%
87	5, 004	2, 882	10.975	7.951	87%	91%
Total	10, 329, 676	8, 250, 098	0.184	0.096	-	-

Source: *Group Life Mortality and Morbidity Study*, The Society of Actuaries (August, 2006).

Workers Are Inadequately Protected from Premature Death

Study after study indicates that most workers are inadequately protected.

- MetLife does an annual survey of employee benefits. MetLife's 2010 survey indicated that 42 percent of employees have life insurance coverage of only two times household income or less, and 53 percent of those believe it is adequate.[4]

- Studies show that life insurance coverage is at its lowest point in more than five decades. Almost half of Americans with household incomes between $50,000 and $250,000 do not have life insurance, and those with insurance have only enough to cover 3.6 years of income, leaving their families significantly underinsured.[5]

- In 2004, LIMRA estimated that life insurance sales would increase $9.5 trillion if the 48 million underinsured households bought the amount of life insurance coverage they said they needed. By 2010, this sales opportunity had nearly doubled in size as life insurance ownership hit an all time low. At this point, half of U.S. households (58 million) said they needed more life insurance coverage—a sales potential of as much as $17.5 trillion.[6]

- The percentage of American households without *any* life insurance coverage has increased from 22 percent to 30 percent between 2004 and 2011.[7]

In conclusion:

- There is a need for life insurance, and many people are inadequately insured.

- The percentage of Americans without any life insurance has increased steadily in the past 7 years. In fact, life insurance coverage is at its lowest point in five decades.

- The unfulfilled need represents a great opportunity for insurance professionals who sell and service life insurance.

Why People Don't Purchase Life Insurance

The reasons people don't purchase adequate life insurance amounts or any insurance at all have been documented by the Life and Health Insurance Foundation for Education (LIFE). The excuses consumers give include:

1. It's too expensive.

2. I just haven't gotten around to it.

3. I prefer to put my money elsewhere.

4. I worry about making an incorrect decision.

5. The coverage provided through my employer is sufficient.

Let's examine the facts behind each of these resistances to buying.

It's Too Expensive

Group term life insurance is not expensive. The average *annual* premium is $198 for over $70,000 of coverage.[8] Compare this with the average cost of family health insurance, which cost an average of $15,073 per year in 2011.[9] Individual life insurance costs vary greatly by the type of coverage purchased. For a 45-year-old, a permanent cash-value life insurance policy with a level premium paid to age 100 would cost approximately $300 per month, while a 20-year term life insurance policy would be less than $50 per month for the same person.[10]

Group term life insurance is a relative bargain. It is true that many workers find their home budgets stretched to the breaking point, especially in the current economic environment. Yet, research shows that American families spend almost $800 a year for cell phone coverage,[11] and $900 a year for digital TV cable service.[12] To protect the family's financial health and viability, a cost of around $200 per year does not seem unreasonable.

I Just Haven't Gotten Around to It

Most insurance products are "sold not bought." Or, in the words of Steve Jobs, "It's not the consumer's job to know what they want."[13] The Hartford found that 84 percent of consumers rely on insurance agents to sell them life insurance.[14] The implication is that group producers should engage their clients' employees to explain the value of life insurance. This is not only a service to the employees but also to the client/employer.

As employers shift more of the cost of group benefits onto their employees, it is becoming increasingly important for producers to be able to sell employees on the importance of enrolling in voluntary group life. Producers are becoming experts at the "second sale," where marketing to the employees is vital to the success of the group plan as well as providing a valuable service to sometimes ill-informed employees.

I Prefer to Put My Money Elsewhere

Clearly, buying the latest iPod version is more attractive to most consumers than purchasing an intangible like life insurance. So, too, the escalating employees' share of health care costs does make other insurance purchases more difficult to consider. However, this does not mitigate the need for life insurance. For a little more than $1 per day, the average worker can purchase almost $150,000 of group term life insurance. An old saying goes something like, "No family of a deceased person ever complained about the deceased having too much life insurance." What workers need is someone to help them understand the financial risk of not having life insurance and how at an affordable cost, the worker and family can be made financially secure.

I Worry about Making an Incorrect Decision

According to the 2005 Life Literacy Study by The Hartford, only 22 percent of workers surveyed stated they fully understood their life insurance program at work. Clearly, the majority of workers need help in understanding their insurance needs and what is available to them. It appears that employers think their insured workforce is more knowledgeable about life insurance than they actually are. We will outline some ways to help workers feel more comfortable in making decisions about life insurance.

The Coverage Provided Through My Employer Is Sufficient

We have already shown the need for life insurance among workers. This need may be filled by a variety of sources that include employee benefit programs and individual products sold by producers. Many employers offer a very modest noncontributory basic life program whose primary purpose is to assure the decedent's family has enough to afford a decent funeral arrangement. If an employee believes this to be sufficient, he or she may be unknowingly underinsured. By educating the employee about the financial risk of being underinsured, the producer can make a voluntary life program even more appreciated.

Adequate Coverage Amounts

How much life insurance is adequate is the fundamental question each employee must ponder before making a decision. Sometimes these decisions are so challenging that they prevent a decision from being made altogether and no insurance is purchased.

Consider a 40-year-old making $50,000 a year in salary who dies but who intended to work until age 65. Assuming there would have been no increases to salary in that 25-year period, losses of $1,250,000 in anticipated income would result. If we apply the standard rule that life insurance should cover 3.6 times the insured's annual income, or $180,000, this employee would clearly be underinsured. A different rule of thumb is that insurance should cover 6 to 8 times an employee's annual income, or between $300,000 and $400,000 in force for the aforementioned 40-year-old.[15]

The reader can find a calculator to determine life insurance needs at many insurers' websites. The calculator allows the user to plug in factors such as salary, various debt amounts, and the number of dependents for which the calculator will recommend an appropriate coverage amount. One such calculator is available at the LIFE Foundation's website at www.lifehappens.org.

Other methods of figuring an adequate amount of life insurance involve the actual calculation of future income needs of a worker's family should the worker suffer premature death. The following are some examples of typical income needs in current dollars:

- Final expenses (medical and burial)

  - The average cost of a funeral in 2009 was $7,755 according to the National Funeral Directors Association's 2010 survey.[16]

  - There could be individuals who don't need life insurance, by having great wealth. However, most of us or rather our families and survivors will face the expense of burial. In the case of a prolonged terminal illness, there may be medical bills as well, even for medically insured individuals. Thus having life insurance, even if only a small amount for just final expenses, makes sense.

- Mortgage

  - The median mortgage debt per family in the United States is $107,000.[17]

  - Having a large outstanding debt such as a mortgage would be a real burden for a surviving family. This is especially true today where so many homeowners' equity positions are "under water." Having sufficient life insurance to cover the cost of paying off or keeping up with an outstanding mortgage can be a real financial lifesaver for the surviving family. Even in the event the family does not own a home, the family that rents is in a financial strain with the death of a loved one. Rent needs to be paid, and unless the surviving head of household can easily increase his or her earning power, having life insurance to assist on paying rent can be a real blessing.

  - Nonmarried individuals who are homeowners leave their survivors with a financial burden the survivors may never have anticipated unless there is sufficient life insurance to pay off the mortgage. Frequently, even insurance professionals assume nonmarried workers have no "financial dependents." In a recent *USA Weekend* edition, a blurb appeared on different categories of people who might not need life insurance. Included was the "Unattached"— those without dependents. The article stated, "The purpose of life insurance is to provide for people who depend on you financially. If you're single and no one falls into that category, why pay for unnecessary coverage?"[18] However, a single "unattached" with a mortgage (and perhaps a car and/or student loan), may be leaving relatives, who would not normally "depend" financially on the unattached worker a big legacy financial burden. Life insurance is intended to mitigate these types of burdens.

- Living expenses

  - The IRS publishes its estimate of living expenses (for food, clothing, cleaning supplies, and so on) at over $16,000 per year for a family of four.[19]

  - A relatively young worker who dies prematurely can leave a family in a huge financial hole. Living expenses don't stop, yet the deceased's income has. Figuring out a way to pay ongoing living expenses for 20 or more years can be daunting. Plus, as we all know, the cost of food, gas, and utilities tends to increase over time. Life insurance in adequate amounts is one of the only ways a worker can protect his or her family.

- Education

  - The average annual tuition (plus expenses) at a private nonprofit four-year college is about $35,000.[20]

  - Many Americans dream of a college education for their children and/or grandchildren. Many Americans take advantage of special savings programs to help plan for this. Premature death can easily put a college education out of reach. Life insurance can help make the dream a reality.

- Retirement (spouse)

  - Median income for a family unit aged 65–69 is $35,257.[21]

  - The consequences of failing to save enough for retirement will be the need to continue working past traditional retirement age. Losing income due to a working spouse's death would leave the surviving spouse in dire straights. Having adequate life insurance is a hedge against one spouse dying before retirement and thus losing that spouse's income.

  - The need for life coverage has become all the more evident with the many baby boomers who have found they need to continue working late in life.

- Taxes

  - Federal, state, and local taxes as a percentage of workers' wages has increased significantly in the last 30 years. Fortunately, group life benefit payments to beneficiaries are not taxable as income.

An insurance producer working with a client can help the client estimate these and other future expenses and determine the full life insurance need for the insured employee population.

Helping Clients Decide

Group term life insurance is the primary topic of this book. A producer most likely can't assist each worker individually. Fortunately, there are resources available to assist the producer and worker in determining how much insurance is adequate. As previously mentioned, online insurance calculators are offered by many insurance companies, and many are free of charge. Most workers have access to the Internet, and those who do not can find access at their local library.

A word of caution is in order. Even if workers know how much life insurance is needed and have a desire to purchase an adequate amount, the group term life underwriter may be unwilling to issue the amount necessary for risk reasons. As we'll discuss in Chapter 5 "Benefits and Plan Design" and Chapter 6 "Risk Selection," there are usually limitations on coverage amounts. For cost reasons, the employer may be unwilling to pay for such amounts. Some employers may not even offer group life as part of their benefits program. For many, a fully adequate life insurance program will come through a combination of coverages that includes an individual life policy.

Advantages of Group Term Life and AD&D Insurance

Using group term life and AD&D as a way to fill the employees' life insurance gap is a great strategy. Besides simply providing additional life insurance at a reasonable cost, group life and AD&D can offer a number of advantages including:

- Group benefits are a key way to attract and retain employees.

- Most employers believe that providing benefits is important to retaining employees.[22] One of the original reasons for the development of group life insurance was so the employer could avoid "passing the hat" as was mentioned in Chapter 1. This need is not going away—ever. Group term life and AD&D are cost effective ways of providing valuable benefits to employees and their families.

- A majority of employees feel benefits are important to their feeling of loyalty to a particular employer.[23]

- Employees value benefits. Employers can use benefits such as group term life and AD&D to increase the feeling of loyalty an employee has. This is another of the reasons group life insurance was developed to begin with.

- Employees are increasingly looking to employers for help in planning for the employee's financial future.[24]

- Employees realize the need to be financially responsible. Often they are not sure how to get help. An employer that provides some basic financial planning tools and solutions such as life and AD&D coverage is bound to make employees more loyal.

- For employees with health problems, group life insurance, with its guaranteed-issue amounts, may be the only life insurance protection the employee can get.

- As the working population gets older, in part due to the baby boom generation working longer, there are bound to be even more employees with health issues. Providing some level of group term life insurance on a guaranteed-issue basis can be a comfort to these older employees.

- For the employer, the cost of a group term life program is tax deductible as an ordinary business expense, subject to complying with IRS rules (covered in Chapter 10).

- Group insurance is affordable and deductible for employers. This makes it a financial win for both employers and employees.

- For the employee, the employer-paid portion for life insurance is provided tax free for the cost of the first $50,000 of face amount. (This will be explained further in Chapter 10.)

- As will be covered, a basic amount of life insurance can be provided at no cost to employees and with no taxable income to employees.

- The employee may be able to obtain life insurance on his/her dependents if the employer's group plan includes dependent life.

- For those employees wanting life insurance for their dependents, a group dependent life program may be the most convenient and affordable way of obtaining it.

- Retirees can access affordable life insurance from an employer who provides retiree life insurance.

- Group retiree life insurance programs may provide valuable benefits that retirees may not be able to get elsewhere.

- Voluntary and supplemental group term life and AD&D insurance can be offered to employees at little or no cost to the employer other than the cost of administering the plans.

- These programs are a great way for the employer to provide even more financial tools to employees at no cost to the employer. The rise in popularity of these programs is a testimonial to their effectiveness, both for employers and employees.

- Most group plans have a waiver-of-premium provision that continues coverage at no cost for an employee who becomes disabled.

- Getting life insurance once disabled can be difficult at best and impossible at worst. The waiver-of-premium provision protects employees from this financially threatening situation.

- All group insurance plans offer some form of conversion privilege where an employee whose group coverage is terminating can convert to an individual life policy without being required to submit evidence of good health.

- This is another provision, along with waiver of premium, that may seem insignificant but can be a great aid to an employee in time of need.

The Market of Group Life and AD&D Insurance

There is a strong market for group term life with a large number of participating carriers. Figure 2-4 lists the various carriers with their share of the market.

There is a wide selection of reputable and highly-rated group carriers from which to choose. Producers and their clients can take comfort in the fact that such extensive competition keeps life prices in line and a great value.

In summary, the need for life insurance almost speaks for itself. Group term life insurance is a good way to fill part of this need. It is affordable. It can be issued regardless of an individual's health status. It helps an employer demonstrate the employer's concern for and appreciation of employees. Group term life insurance forms a solid foundation of a worker's financial well-being.

Figure 2-4. Group Term Life Carriers	
Company	**2010 Total Premiums Collected (in millions)**
MetLife	$6,515
Prudential	2,961
The Hartford	1,420
Minnesota Life	1,193
Unum	1,110
CIGNA	1,078
Aetna	942
The Standard	764
Lincoln Financial Group	575
Sun Life Financial	557
ING Employee Benefits	493
Reliance Standard	410
WellPoint	331
Dearborn National	329
Mutual of Omaha	308
Guardian Life	303
Principal Financial Group	280
Liberty Mutual	175
Assurant Employee Benefits	168
United Healthcare	143
USAble Life	102
OneAmerica	92
Union Labor Life	41
CUNA Mutual	14
Harleysville Life	11
Kansas City Life	10
Consumers Life	10
Symetra Life	10
Mutual of America	8
Nationwide	8
New York Life	7
Trustmark	3

Source: *2010 U.S. Group Life Market Survey Summary Report* (Stamford, CT: Gen Re Research, 2011) p. 10.

Key Takeaways

- Workers underestimate the danger of premature death (before retirement).

- Workers often assume premature death is the result of an accident, when in reality, it is disease or sickness that causes most premature deaths.

- Most workers have dependents and debts and need the protection of an adequate amount of life insurance.

- Life insurance, especially group term life insurance, is a cost-effective means of purchasing life insurance.

- Many employers have life insurance programs. However, a thorough review of the employer's program may indicate room for improvement and is a valuable service to the employer.

- Although considered a "mature" market, selling group life still presents opportunity for producers.

- The percentage of Americans without life insurance has increased in the past 7 years. In fact, life insurance coverage is at its lowest point in five decades.

- For those employees wanting life insurance for their dependents, a group life program that extends to dependents may be the most convenient and affordable way of obtaining it.

- Employers can use benefits such as group term life and AD&D to increase the feelings of loyalty in employees.

- Group life benefit payments to beneficiaries are not taxable as income.

Endnotes

1. Arialdi M. Miniño, M.P.H., Death in the United States, NCHS Data Brief, No 64, (Hyattsville, MD: National Center for Health Statistics. July 2011).

2. Health, United States, 2011. In Brief (Hyattesville, MD: National Center For Health Statistics, January 2012).

3. Paul Davidson, "Older Workers Capture More New Jobs," USA Today (April 4, 2012).

4. 8th Annual Study of Employee Benefits Trends (New York, NY: MetLife, Inc., April 12, 2010).

5. The LifeJacketSM Study 2011: 7 Key Insights to Help Close the Coverage Gap (Richmond, VA: Genworth Financial, Inc., August, 2011).

6. "LIMRA: Sales Potential for Underinsured Life Insurance Doubles in Six Years," http://www.limra.com/newscenter/NewsArchive/ArchiveDetails.aspx?prid=200 (Windsor, CT: LL Global, September 6, 2011).

7. Matthew Sturdevant, "Gamers with Benefits," Hartford Courant (November 14, 2011).

8. 2010 U.S. Group Life Market Survey Summary Report, http://genre.com/sharedfile/pdf/GLMS201103-en.pdf, (Stamford, CT: Gen Re Research, 2011).

9. Employer Health Benefits 2011 Annual Survey, http://ehbs.kff.org/pdf/2011/8225.pdf (Chicago, IL; The Kaiser Family Foundation, September, 2011).

10. Marvin H. Feldman, "Dollars for Pennies Apiece," www.lifehappens.org (accessed January 3, 2012).

11. Press Release (Westlake Village, CA: J. D. Power and Associates, October 4, 2006).

12. Julianne Pepitone, "Why Cable Is Going to Cost You Even More," CNNMoney.com, (January 9, 2010).

13. "Steve Jobs Quotes," All Famous Quotes (http://allfamousquotes.weebly.com/steve-jobs-quotes.html) (accessed May 24, 2012).

14. Connecting the Disconnect: The Hartford's 2005 Life Insurance Literacy Study (Hartford, CT: The Hartford Financial Services Group) p. 6.

15. Stephan R. Leimberg and Robert J. Doyle Jr., Life Insurance Planning, 4th Edition, (Cincinnati, OH: The National Underwriter Company, 2007) p. 19.

16. Press Release (NFDA, October 6, 2010), NFDA website (http://www.nfda.org/news-a-events/all-press-releases/2192-nfda-releases-results-of-2010-general-price-list-survey.html#.TvSf_yUJ3CI.email) (Accessed May 23, 2012).

17. Statistical Abstract of the United States, (Washington, D.C.: U.S. Census Bureau, 2012) Table 1172, p. 734.

18. Jeff Wuorio, "Think It Over: Do You Really Need Life Insurance?" USA Weekend (March 23–25, 2012).

19. "National Standards: Food, Clothing and Other Items," IRS website (http://www.irs.gov/businesses/small/article/0,,id=104627,00.html).

20. "The Average Cost of a U.S. College Education," U.S.News & World Report website (http://www.usnews.com/opinion/articles/2010/08/24/the-average-cost-of-a-us-college-education) (August 24, 2010).

21. Income of the Aged Chartbook, 2010 (,Washington, D.C.:, Social Security Administration, April 2010) p. 4.

22. 8th Annual Study of Employee Benefits Trends (New York, NY: MetLife, Inc., April 12, 2010), p. 7.

23. Ibid., p. 8.

24. Ibid., p. 15.

Chapter 3

Regulation of
Group Life Insurance

This chapter provides a general background of the regulations affecting Group Term Life and Accidental Death & Dismemberment (AD&D) insurance at both the state and federal levels. Because several federal discrimination laws affect employee benefits in general, these too will be reviewed. By having a good understanding of these regulations, producers can ensure that their clients avoid running into legal complications.

The complexities of insurance regulations are compounded by the fact that they stem from both state and federal levels. Because many employers have employees in several states, the extent of each state's regulatory jurisdiction is a matter of some concern.[1] Federal laws which come into play with all group insurance, and specifically on group life insurance, include the Employee Retirement Income Security Act of 1974 (ERISA), the Age Discrimination in Employment Act (ADEA), the Uniformed Services Employment and Reemployment Rights Act (USERRA), the Family Medical Leave Act (FMLA), and the Internal Revenue Code (IRC). Fortunately, all group insurers are well versed in the applicable laws impacting group life policies, and they do all that they can to ensure their clients are in compliance.

State Regulation

State regulation of insurance is the norm. The McCarran-Ferguson Act of 1945, a federal law, exempted the "business of insurance" from the federal level. The result was that states were given the sole right to regulate insurance, and they do so to this day. Federal regulations that have an impact on group life/AD&D plans are generally focused on regulating employers and labor practices as part of labor law.

State regulation of insurance was firmly established long before the McCarran-Ferguson Act. As was noted in Chapter 1, states established regulations soon after the first group life policy was issued. Many of the state regulations initially were designed to prevent fraud or misuse of the plans. For example, during the Great Depression, several state legislatures enacted group insurance laws that restricted the amount of coverage that could apply to dependents. The idea was to reduce the motivation for potential criminal acts. The fear was that employees would buy high amounts of dependent life coverage and then murder their dependents to collect the proceeds.

In more recent history, state insurance regulations have been driven largely by concern with consumer protection. Consumer protection issues related to group insurance have taken on even more importance as employers continue to shift the cost of group life/AD&D coverage to employees.

Most states have significantly more regulations governing group medical and dental plans than group life and AD&D coverage. However, many states continue to monitor the need for further group life regulations. The most notable areas of state regulation for group insurance occur in the following areas: group size, policy provisions, dependent life amounts, eligibility as a dependent, eligible groups, and number of options.

Group Size

The first notable state regulation on group life insurance was concerned with the size of the group. States have continued to regulate minimum group size to this day, although some states do permit groups as small as two employees. In response to restrictions on group size, and to reduce the costs of administration, some group life insurance companies underwrite policies for small employers—those having fewer than ten employees—as part of a multi-employer insurance trust. The insurer will establish, or situs, the trust in a state in which policies for small groups may be written. Then small employers in other states are permitted to join the trust. In these cases, the employer is not actually issued the policy. The policy is issued to the trustee. The trustee is some third party, frequently a bank that operates as trustee.

Policy Provisions

With the National Association of Insurance Commissioners' (NAIC) recommendation in 1957, many states have adopted regulations concerning provisions that must appear in a group life policy. Not all states have adopted the same provisions, but collectively, the various state provisions form the basis for the policy provisions found in most group term life contracts. Provisions adopted by the majority of states for life and AD&D coverage include the following:

- A 31-day grace period must be granted for late/nonpayment of a premium before the policy can be cancelled.

- A two-year incontestability provision states that misstatements on the group policy application cannot be used to void the coverage after two years.

- A copy of the application must be included with the issued policy.

- If evidence of insurability is required, the stipulations must be stated.

- There must be a provision specifying how a misstatement of age will be addressed. Either the premium will be adjusted or the death benefit will be adjusted for the correct age.

- A provision must be made for beneficiary designation.

- Employees covered by the policy must receive a certificate of coverage.

- In the event of employee or policy termination, a conversion right must be granted under specific conditions. This includes a provision that if an employee has been covered by the policy for a specific number of years, the conversion privilege must be offered.

- If the employee dies during the conversion period, the employee is deemed to have converted.

To make policy issue and administration a bit easier, most group life insurance companies have adopted all of these provisions in all of the states in which they operate. In other words, this language is just about universal or "boiler plate." Because of this, one sees relatively little variation in the basic provisions of a group term life policy, so the sale itself is less about policy language and more about price and other aspects, as will be covered in Chapter 13.

Dependent Life Amounts

Many states have placed restrictions on the amount of life insurance that can be sold under a group policy on the life of a dependent. However, fewer states have restrictions on dependent life amounts in the current environment than have historically existed. Rather, today it may be said that group term life insurers' underwriting guidelines and protocols have become more restrictive and self-regulating than is required by law.

Eligibility as a Dependent

Many states have passed legislation requiring domestic partners and civil union partners to be included as dependents. As more states adopt these requirements, many group term life insurers have simply made domestic partners eligible in all jurisdictions.

Eligible Groups

As a general rule, most states prohibit the formation of a "group" solely for the purpose of acquiring insurance. What constitutes a group can vary from state to state. Most group term life policies are issued to what are called employer-employee groups, that is, through an employer. As mentioned earlier, group insurers do commonly use multiple-employer trusts for groups under ten lives. In addition, insurers will issue policies to labor unions as part of a trust agreement.

Limited Number of Options

Some states limit the number of options available to employees in a group life plan. The intent is to reduce potential confusion caused by too many choices. In these instances, group insurers must comply.

State Departments of Insurance

States also regulate other aspects of the business of insurance, including the licensing of producers and insurance companies. Each state has its own Department of Insurance (DOI) whose function is to oversee the conduct of the insurance business in its state. The DOI is responsible for ensuring that all regulations are enforced.

States charge a premium tax on all group insurance policies issued in their states to fund DOI operations. The tax varies from state to state, but averages 2 percent of collected premiums. Collection may be administered by the DOI or Department of Revenue Services.

DOIs are most interested in protecting consumers from unsound insurance practices, both on the part of producers and insurers. They oversee the products insurers sell and monitor insurers' financial soundness. For added protection, states also establish guarantee funds from the insurance taxes collected. The funds are used to help cover consumer losses in the event an insurer goes insolvent and cannot meet its statutory financial commitments to policyholders or covered employees.

DOI activities involved in regulating producers and insurers include the following:

- For producers:

    - Developing educational requirements and examinations for being licensed as a producer.

    - Licensing producers.

    - Establishing and enforcing standards of professional conduct for producers.

- Establishing and monitoring continuing education (CE) requirements.

- Hearing and investigating complaints against licensed producers.

- For insurers:

  - Establishing criteria to be admitted in the state as a licensed insurer, including surplus requirements.

  - Establishing procedures for filing and gaining approval of policy language and insurance forms to be used.

  - In some states, requiring insurers to file rates in addition to policy forms.

  - In some states, setting requirements on commissions to be paid on a policy.

  - In some states, establishing minimum loss ratios (of expected claims to collected premiums) on insurance products to keep profits for insurers at a reasonable level.

  - Establishing minimum requirements for claim reserves.

  - Requiring insurers to file an annual "statutory accounting" of all insurance activities in the state.

As a result of state regulation, coupled with industry practices, the provisions of most group life and health insurance policies are relatively uniform from company to company.[2]

Federal Regulation—ERISA

When insurance professionals think about group insurance and federal regulation, they immediately think of the Employee Retirement Income Security Act (ERISA) of 1974. While ERISA does not regulate insurance companies directly, it is a part of labor law, which affects employers and the benefit plans they offer to employees. The law is administered by the U.S. Department of Labor. ERISA regulations primarily focus on retirement plans and health plans, but they do affect other benefits, including group term life. Employers often offer a basic life plan that is noncontributory along with a voluntary or supplemental life plan for which the employer does not contribute to the cost. The basic life plan—a benefit for employees paid for by the employer—falls under ERISA regulation. (Note: several types of "groups" are exempt from ERISA requirements, including government plans, church plans, workers' compensation plans, unemployment compensation plans, and statutory state disability plans.)

Group voluntary programs are exempt from ERISA requirements provided they meet the following criteria:

- The employer does not contribute to the cost.

- The coverage/participation is voluntary.

- The only administrative function provided by the employer is to collect premiums through payroll deduction.

- No consideration is received by the employer other than compensation for administrative services performed.

There are differences of opinion as to how ERISA, in fact, affects voluntary life programs. We will explore voluntary plans in depth in Chapter 12.

ERISA has 3 major components: a written plan, fiduciary responsibility, and reporting.

Written ERISA Plan

What is a "plan"? Many individuals may think the group term life insurance policy issued by an insurance company is the "plan." However, this is not necessarily the case. To meet the requirements of ERISA, a plan must be in writing, must include the name of at least one fiduciary, and must meet some specific requirements.

> "A plan must have at least one fiduciary (a person or entity) named in the written plan, or through a process described in the plan, as having control over the plan's operation. The named fiduciary can be identified by office or by name. For some plans, it may be an administrative committee or a company's board of directors."[3]

While the insurance company-issued group term life/AD&D policy may not be a plan document, most insurance carriers as a general rule include a Summary Plan Description (SPD) as part of the group policy, which becomes the "written plan." The Summary Plan Description (SPD) is a basic descriptive document, which in plain language must provide an explanation of the plan that is comprehensive enough to apprise participants of their rights and responsibilities under the plan. It also informs participants about the plan features and what to expect of the plan. Among other things, the SPD must include basic information such as:

- plan name, address, and contact information;

- the plan benefits;

- an explanation of how to qualify for the benefits;

- the duties of the plan and/or employee.

More specific information must also be provided, including:

- the plan's claims procedure (either in the document or as a separate attachment);

- a participant's basic rights and responsibilities under ERISA (model language is provided in the SPD rules);

- information on any applicable premiums, cost-sharing, deductibles, co-payments, etc.;

- any caps (annual or lifetime) on benefits;

- procedures for using network providers (if PPO/HMO) and composition of network;

- conditions regarding precertification;

- a description of plan procedures governing qualified medical child support orders;

- notices and descriptions of certain rights under the Health Insurance Portability and Accountability Act (HIPAA) and other health coverage laws.

This document is given to employees within 90 days after they are covered by the plan. SPDs must also be redistributed every 5th year and provided within 30 days of a request. The SPD must be current within 120 days.[4]

While some of these requirements clearly are intended for health plans, rather than life insurance, the above is an all inclusive list.

Fiduciary Responsibility

The "fiduciary" is anyone exercising discretionary authority over the plan and its participants (the covered employees). Typically, one associates the term "fiduciary" as the Plan Sponsor who is usually the employer and who exerts financial control over the plan. Insurance carriers who exercise claims adjudication, as a general rule, consider themselves as having fiduciary responsibilities. Fiduciary liability is limited by ERISA to plan benefits and legal costs. However, to gain this limited liability, fiduciaries must be prudent in carrying out their duties, which include:

- acting solely in the interest of plan participants and their beneficiaries and with the exclusive purpose of providing benefits to them;

- carrying out their duties prudently;

- following the plan documents (unless inconsistent with ERISA);

- holding plan assets (if the plan has any) in trust;

- paying only reasonable plan expenses.[5]

ERISA Reporting

Reporting under ERISA can be somewhat complicated. There are several different documents and reports that must be filed/submitted to various parties. There are slightly different requirements for "small groups" of fewer than 100 lives. Providing an SPD that follows the rules covered above ensures compliance with ERISA guidelines concerning proper notice to plan participants.

The Summary Plan Description is the "written plan" and must adhere to the rules covered above. Generally, insuring a group term life plan with an insurer who provided an SPD is a good way to ensure compliance. Also, since most state law requires covered employees receive a certificate of coverage, the ERISA requirements concerning notice to plan participants can easily be met.

Anytime the SPD or plan undergoes a major change, participants must be notified within 210 days after the plan year in which the change occurred. The plan year is not necessarily a calendar year. Rather, it is the year beginning from the plan establishment date, policy effective date, or anniversary date. However, more group insurance policies are effective as of January 1 than any other date.

The mechanism for this change notification is called a Summary of Material Modifications. "material modifications" means "any plan change that eliminates benefits; reduces benefits payable; increases premiums, deductibles, coinsurance, or co-payments; reduces the service area covered by an HMO, or establishes new conditions or requirements (such as preauthorization) for obtaining services or benefits."[6] Again, notice how the requirements are primarily directed at health insurance.

An annual report using a Form 5500 is generally required. It must be filed with the IRS within 210 days of the end of the plan year. The form itself contains the reporting requirements. The form is filed using the ERISA Filing Acceptance System (EFAST).[7] Plan participants can also receive a copy of the form upon written request.[8]

The information needed to complete the Form 5500 is provided by the insurer. Most insurers will complete a Form 5500 and send it to the policyholder (employer), who reviews it and then sends it on to the IRS. It is imperative for the insurer to complete the retrospective accounting on a timely basis in order to ensure that the policyholder is able to file the Form 550 information within the 210-day timeframe.

A Summary Annual Report is also provided to plan participants. It simply contains a narrative of information provided in the Form 5500.[9] The Annual Report (Form 5500) and Summary Annual Report are not required for plans covering fewer than 100 lives.

Federal Regulation—ADEA

The Age Discrimination in Employment Act (ADEA) of 1967 (amended in 1978, 1986 and 1990) "forbids discrimination when it comes to any aspect of employment, including hiring, firing, pay, job assignments, promotions, layoff, training, fringe benefits, and any other term or condition of employment."[10] The law protects workers age 40 and over. This means the employer (and thereby the insurer) cannot arbitrarily reduce or terminate life insurance coverage for older workers. The law was designed to protect older employees from being terminated from employment or from losing coverage under a group plan solely on account of age.

ADEA is civil rights law rather than insurance law. Compliance is an employer responsibility. However, insurers create and provide ADEA-compliant schedules to their policyholders to make compliance pro forma for employers.

The law does permit the employer to pay "equal costs" for benefits for older workers as for younger workers. Under the ADEA, an employer that spends the same amount of money, or incurs the same cost, on behalf of older workers as on behalf of younger workers may—if specified conditions are met—provide certain fringe benefits to older workers in smaller amounts or for shorter time periods than it provides to younger workers. This is known as the "equal cost" defense. It is the employer's obligation to prove that all aspects of this defense have been met.[11]

As a response, insurance companies issuing group term life plans have developed "age reduction schedules" that have been actuarially justified to meet the equal cost requirement. In most cases, these reductions apply to workers age 65 and over. A typical schedule is shown in Figure 3-1.

Figure 3-1. Group Term Life Insurance Benefit Reductions	
Age	*Percentage Reduction*
65 – 69	65%
70 – 74	45%
75 – 79	30%
Over 79	20%

Source: Beam, Burton T., *Group Benefits: Basic Concepts and Alternatives*, 10th Edition (Bryn Mawr, PA: The American College Press, 2004), p. 51.

The purpose of an age reduction schedule in group term life insurance is to keep overall costs reasonable for the employer and to control risk for the insurer. The ADEA age reduction schedule keeps the plan fairer for younger employees by protecting the financial integrity and viability of the plan, yet providing older employees with coverage.

Federal Regulation—Uniformed Services Employment and Reemployment Rights Act (USERRA)

The purpose of USERRA is to protect the rights of activated National Guard personnel and Military Reservists recalled to active duty. The law has multiple provisions affecting employers. Here we will focus only on the details of the law that affect group term life and AD&D insurance. More information regarding USERRA may be found at http://www.dol.gov/compliance/guide/userra.htm.

There are two USERRA provisions that affect employers and thus life insurers. One provision requires the employer to offer an extension of group term life and AD&D if the employer offers extensions of these benefits to other individuals taking similar-length leaves of absence. This provision is cited below:

> "To the extent that an employer offers other non-seniority benefits (e.g., holiday pay or life insurance coverage) to employees on furlough or a leave of absence, the employer is required to provide those same benefits to an employee during a period of service in the uniformed services. If the employer's treatment of persons on leaves of absence varies according to the kind of leave (e.g., jury duty, educational, etc.), the comparison should be made with the employer's most generous form of leave. Of course, you must compare periods of comparable length. An employee may waive his or her rights to these other non-seniority benefits by knowingly stating, in writing, his or her intent not to return to work. However, such statement does not waive any other rights provided by USERRA."[12]

The next provision requires the employer to reinstate coverage for group term life and AD&D upon the individual's return to work. A returning service member is entitled to accrued seniority, as if continuously employed. This applies to rights and benefits determined by seniority as well. This includes status, rate of pay, pension vesting, and credit for the period for pension benefit computations.[13]

Federal Regulation—Family Medical Leave Act (FMLA)

FMLA requires employers to allow employees to take a leave of absence in the case of specific health or family issues as addressed in the Act. It is beyond the scope of this text to go into details of this Act other than how they apply to group term life and AD&D.

Employers with 50 or more employees within a 75-mile radius are required to comply with FMLA. The law allows an employee to take an unpaid leave of up to 12 weeks in any 12-month period for the birth or adoption of a child or to address a serious medical condition of his/her own or of an immediate family member (spouse, child, or parent).[14]

Some states have broadened FMLA laws, including those covering smaller employer groups. Coordination between the federal requirements and the state mandate is required and increases the complexity of FMLA administration for the employer.[15]

Employers are not required to continue group life and AD&D during the leave, although employers may continue such coverage if allowed under the plan. If an employee is paying all or part of the premium prior to the leave, the employee will continue to pay his or her share during the leave period.[16]

FMLA requires the employer to take an employee back who has been on an approved FMLA leave of absence if the employer still has the employee's previous (or equivalent) job. Included in this provision is the requirement to restore all benefits the employee had prior to the leave of absence:

"Upon return from FMLA leave, an employee must be restored to the employee's original job, or to an equivalent job with equivalent pay, benefits, and other terms and conditions of employment. An employee's use of FMLA leave cannot result in the loss of any employment benefit that the employee earned or was entitled to before using FMLA leave, nor be counted against the employee under a "no fault" attendance policy. If a bonus or other payment, however, is based on the achievement of a specified goal such as hours worked, products sold, or perfect attendance, and the employee has not met the goal due to FMLA leave, payment may be denied unless it is paid to an employee on equivalent leave status for a reason that does not qualify as FMLA leave.

An employee has no greater right to restoration or to other benefits and conditions of employment than if the employee had been continuously employed."[17]

Federal Regulation—Tax Code

Group term life insurance coverage is also affected by the Internal Revenue Code (IRC). According to the Department of the Treasury, "Any fringe benefit you provide is taxable and must be included in the recipient's pay unless the law specifically excludes it."[18] However, Section 79 of the IRC allows employers to provide up to $50,000 face value of life insurance with no income tax consequences provided specific conditions are met. This is an important exclusion. As it is often misunderstood, it will be covered in great detail in Chapter 10.

Key Takeaways

- Group Term Life and AD&D are regulated at both the state and federal levels, so producers must be aware of both.

- Each state's Department of Insurance has a wide range of responsibility in overseeing and enforcing group insurance regulations.

- State regulation generally specifies the policy provisions to be used.

- Insurers must file policy language in advance of marketing the policy provisions.

- Changes to previously approved policy language must be approved by the state in which the policy is to be issued.

- ERISA, a federal regulation, has numerous requirements that a group term life and AD&D plan must meet. Complying with ERISA is an employer responsibility. However, insurers generally ensure the group life and AD&D plans they sell will be in compliance.

- ADEA limits the age reduction schedules that can be used by employers in group term life plans. Insurers make every attempt to ensure that any age reduction schedules they include with the plans they sell are in compliance with ADEA.

- Both USERRA and FMLA require employers to reinstate an employee in the group term life and AD&D plan upon the employee's return from an approved leave.

- The Internal Revenue Code (IRC) also has an impact on group term life plans. Chapter 10 provides a complete discussion of this topic.

Endnotes

1. Beam, Burton T., Jr., and John J. McFadden, *Employee Benefits,* Eighth Edition (New York, NY: Kaplan Publishing), p. 126.

2. Ibid., p. 132

3. *Understanding Your Fiduciary Responsibilities Under a Group Health Plan* (Washington, D.C.: U.S. Department of Labor Employee Benefits Security Administration, October 2008), p. 1.

4. Ibid., p. 9.

5. Ibid., p. 2.

6. Ibid., p. 9.

7. Ibid., p. 11.

8. Beam, Burton T., *Group Benefits: Basic Concepts and Alternatives,* 10th Edition (Bryn Mawr, PA, The American College Press, 2004), p. 63.

9. Ibid., p. 64.

10. "Age Discrimination," *Equal Employment Opportunity Commission (EEOC) website, http://www.eeoc.gov/laws/types/age. cfm* (accessed June 15, 2012).

11. "Section 3 Employee Benefits," *Compliance Manual (Washington, D.C: U.S. Equal Employment Opportunity Commission, 2000).*

12. "USERRA Frequently Asked Questions," *Military.com*, *http://www.military.com/benefits/content/military-legal-matters/userra/userra-frequently-asked-questions.html* (accessed June 15, 2012), Question 11.

13. Ibid., Question 12.

14. Kirner, Tom and Pete Silkowski, *Group Benefits Disability Specialist Handbook* (Erlanger, KY: The National Underwriter Company), p. 4-12.

15. Ibid., p. 4-12.

16. Ibid., p. 4-12.

17. "Fact Sheet #28: The Family and Medical Leave Act of 1993," *United States Department of Labor website*, *http://www.dol.gov/whd/regs/compliance/whdfs28.htm* (accessed June 15, 2012).

18. *Publication 15-B - Employer's Tax Guide to Fringe Benefits*, (Washington, D.C.: Department of Treasury, Internal Revenue Service, 2012), p. 2.

Chapter 4

Types of Life Insurance

This chapter explores the various forms and features found in life insurance policies. While this book is about Group Term Life and Accidental Death & Dismemberment (AD&D) insurance, other forms of life insurance will be introduced in the chapter. A producer who engages a new client may encounter one of these other forms of life insurance and therefore should be familiar with them. The differences found between group and individual life insurance and between permanent and term life insurance will be highlighted.

Reasons for the Many Forms of Life Insurance

There are several reasons why there are so many different forms of life insurance. One important reason is that an individual's needs for life insurance protection can change over time. Insurance Companies have responded with different types to fill changing needs. For example, a young new parent with limited means may need a large amount of life insurance. Low term life rates can make a large amount affordable, especially for a family just starting out. As time goes by and the young parents become financially established, the savings element and constant premium rates inherent with a whole life policy may be more appealing.

Another reason for multiple forms of life insurance is that insurance companies need and want to differentiate themselves. Many life insurance companies have done so by offering variations of life insurance. It is not uncommon for a person to have both an individually owned life insurance policy and coverage under a group life plan. This, in itself, has contributed to the evolution of life insurance products as insurers seek ways to differentiate themselves with their direct competitors and from other distribution avenues.

Because there are so many different varieties of life insurance, many consumers are concerned about making an incorrect life insurance choice. A variety of choices is great for consumers, but it can be intimidating. Here the producer plays a key role in advising clients about how different products can fit the needs of individual employees and their families.

The first obvious distinction is between individual insurance and group insurance. Individual life insurance is most likely what many people think about when they do think about life insurance. Individual life predates group insurance by about 100 years.

There are a great many life insurance companies, both individual and group. In fact, there were 917 life insurance companies in operation in the United States at the close of 2010. Individual policies make up the majority (57 percent) of life insurance in force, which contrasts with group life insurance at 39 percent. [1] Additional life insurance statistics are provided in Figure 4-1.

Figure 4-1. Life Insurance in the United States

	Life Insurance		Average Annual Percent Change
	2000	2010	2000/2010
PURCHASES			
Face amount (millions)			
Individual[1]	$1,593,907	$1,673,216	0.5
Group	921,001	1,135,354	2.1
Credit	166,326	68,355	-8.5
Total	2,681,234	2,876,925	0.7
Policies (thousands)			
Individual	11,820	10,123	-1.5
Group (certificates)	21,537	18,498	-1.5
Credit	20,045	10,988	-5.8
Total	53,402	39,609	-2.9
IN FORCE			
Face amount (millions)			
Individual	$9,376,370	$10,483,516	1.1
Group (certificates)	6,376,127	7,830,631	2.1
Credit	200,770	111,805	-5.7
Total	15,953,267	18,425,952	1.5
Policies (thousands)			
Individual	162,550	151,787	-0.7
Group (certificates)	156,274	109,462	-3.5

Source: adapted from information from the National Association of Insurance Commissioners (NAIC) ACLI tabulations.
[1] Policies issued by fraternal benefit societies are considered individual business.

It is interesting to note from Figure 4-1 that while individual life insurance policies *in force*, 151,787,000, and the face amounts of those policies, $10,483,516,000,000, exceed group insurance certificates (a measure of individuals covered) in force, 109,462,000, and the face amounts of those policies, $7,830,631,000,000, the current trend is that group insurance *sales* in certificates, 18,498,000, is exceeding individual policies sold, 10,123,000.

Contrasts between Group and Individual Life Insurance

Figure 4-2 Contrasts the main differences between individual and group life insurance.

Figure 4-2. Characteristics of Individual and Group Life InsurancePolicies	
Individual	*Group*
• Anyone can purchase	• Must meet plan eligibility to enroll
• Access via a number of channels such as an agent, mass marketer, direct mail, association, or other various channels • Owned by the individual	• Access via employment • Owned by the employer (plan sponsor)
• Policy flexibility	• Limited plan design
• Can get large amounts	• Amount limited by employer/insurer
• Medical underwriting	• Liberal medical underwriting
• Can change the policy	• Only employer can change the policy
• Can continue coverage	• Conversion or portability
• Coverage not contingent upon employment • Rates generally higher than group	• Coverage contingent upon remaining with the employer who offers coverage • Rates generally less than individual
• Issued a policy • Coverage not automatically reduced by age	• Issued a booklet/certificate • Coverage reduced by ADEA age reductions
• Term or permanent insurance options	• Typically term insurance only

Obtaining Coverage

A person can purchase individual life coverage in a variety of ways. The Internet has become a popular source for insurance shopping, since the consumer can easily compare a number of insurance companies, products, and rates. However, technology-based individual life insurance offerings are usually limited to term life at preset amounts. Consumers frequently get solicitations in the mail from organizations like AARP, AAA Auto Club, banks, and even credit card companies. However, the traditional method of working with an individual agent for a customized plan is still commonly used.

Group insurance, as its name implies, is offered to a group. Usually the group policy is issued to an employer, although other types of groups such as unions and associations are possible policyholders. While most any employer can work with a producer to find an insurance company for group life, an individual worker must be employed by the policyholder (employer) to be eligible for coverage. Further, the employee must be in what is called an "eligible class" of employees to participate in the program. (Eligible class or eligibility is discussed in Chapter 5.)

Plan Ownership

Ownership is very different between individual and group insurance plans. The insured or some interested person, such as the insured's spouse, owns the individual life insurance on the insured. This ownership conveys valuable rights. While these rights can vary with the type of plan, ownership is important.

In group insurance, by contrast, the owner of the master contract is the employer or plan sponsor. The insured employee is a participant in the plan. The group policy, governed by state statute, conveys certain rights to the covered employees. These rights may include the right to name a beneficiary, the right to convert coverage if the policy terminates, and the rights of appeal. However, these are not as broad as the rights of ownership that come with an individual life policy.

Plan Design

With individual life insurance, an agent is frequently assisting the consumer with the purchase. Once the agent is familiar with the consumer's specific needs and financial situation, the agent can propose a wide array of insurance types, costs, benefits, and riders. The agent can custom fit the individual life insurance program to the unique needs of the client as well as fill the client's other insurance needs, such as individual health, disability, auto, and homeowners insurance.

With group insurance, employees can accept only what the employer is willing to offer. There is not an agent to customize coverage or who is aware of each employee's specific needs and financial situation. Clearly, this is a disadvantage of group life insurance. However, some individuals see this as a plus. In a world in which consumers are bombarded and confused by seemingly endless choices, having a limited selection makes the purchase decision simpler.

Amounts of Coverage

An individual can apply for as much individual insurance as he or she feels is necessary. A person is assumed to have an "unlimited" insurable interest in his or her own life, so insurers presume that individuals will act prudently in determining the amount of coverage they need. By contrast, with group life insurance, the employer (with advice from the producer) will determine how much life insurance will be available. Frequently, the employer will offer options for the employee to purchase. The differing amounts are typically based on the employee's class and the selections offered by the underwriter to the group. This is especially true with supplemental and voluntary life insurance where schedules based on multiples of annual earnings are frequently used. However, the group life insurer's underwriter may well limit the amount of coverage provided. In order to pass regulatory nondiscrimination tests, the amounts offered may be limited.

With individual life insurance today, it is quite possible, especially with Internet sales, for a person to apply for and obtain a limited amount of life insurance with no requirement to prove good health. For large amounts of insurance, an individual may need to complete an application with health questions, and the underwriter may require a follow-up physical examination. The underwriter may even require the applicant to submit medical records. There can be a lengthy amount of back and forth between the applicant and the insurance company underwriter in this process.

Medical Underwriting

With group life insurance, the use of medical information is much less common. Generally speaking, group life insurance is "guaranteed" for the individual employee up to an established guaranteed issue (GI) limit. This means that as long as the individual is in an eligible class and under the GI limit, the individual is not medically underwritten. For amounts of employee life insurance exceeding the GI limit, the underwriter may require "evidence of good health." The applicant will fill out what is called a "personal health statement" sometimes called a "short form medical application," to answer a limited number of health questions. If a medical condition is disclosed on the application, the underwriter may subsequently require that an Attending Physician's Statement (APS) be completed. (Evidence of good health is discussed further in Chapter 5.)

Making Changes

Once the policy is issued, the individual owner has the right to make changes, such as increasing or decreasing benefit amounts, adding features, or even terminating the policy. With group life insurance, which is generally issued on a one-year renewable term basis, only the employer can make policy changes. (Note: The underwriter may have authorized a multi-year rate guarantee stating that premium rates will not change as long as certain stated conditions are met.) Employers usually engage the services of a producer who specializes in group insurance to help them find the insurer who best suits their price point, benefits, and needed services. The producer plays a pivotal role in helping the employer select the carrier for the group life plan. The amount of group insurance to be offered to employees is a choice of the employer. However, some group life programs do permit the employee to select supplemental amounts that have been preapproved by the insurer, such as a multiple of earnings. In these cases, employees may be able to change amounts of insurance during the annual enrollment period. (Supplemental group life insurance is discussed further in Chapter 5.)

Continuing Coverage

Generally, as long as the individual owner pays the premium, the insurance company cannot cancel a privately owned policy prior to its agreed-upon expiration. With term insurance, this will be some stated period of time, such as 5, 10, or even 20 years. In addition, the insured may have the option of converting the term life insurance to some form of whole life insurance without medical evidence of good health under specific conditions. With whole life insurance, the insurer cannot ever cancel the policy as long as the premiums are paid.

With group life insurance, the employer can cancel the policy outright at any time with no warning to employees, although such occurrence is rare. Most often, the employer cancels coverage with one group insurer to immediately take on new coverage with a successor carrier. If the employer terminates the policy outright or if employees lose coverage on account of an employer's change in carrier, there will be a conversion privilege that permits the employee to convert the terminating group coverage to a form of individual insurance. (Conversion privileges will be covered more fully in Chapters 5 and 13.)

An individually insured person may be able to drop life coverage by informing his or her own agent or the individual life insurance company. An employee can opt out of the employee-paid portion of the group insurance plan by informing the employer policyholder that he/she no longer wishes to participate. Generally speaking, the employer is the one with the right to continue or terminate group coverage on an employee via the relationship with the employee. Termination of employment usually means termination of coverage under the group plan. However, as was mentioned, in some instances the individual may have the right to "convert" or continue coverage through a mechanism called "portability." (Chapter 5 addresses the continuation of group life insurance coverage by an individual employee and the employee's dependents.)

Rates

Individual insurance is rated and priced depending upon the type and amount of coverage age, and the health of the applicant. In contrast, group insurance is underwritten on an aggregate basis. The employees are lumped together for the purpose of determining risk selection, benefits, rates, and services. The health of the individuals, if such information is requested at all, is not usually a factor in the development of the rates for basic group coverage. Evidence of good health only comes into play with an application for coverage above the GI limit. In general, group rates are usually less expensive than individual rates.

Proof of Coverage

The individual employee in group insurance is not issued the master policy, but is instead issued a "certificate of coverage." The terms are per the agreement between the employer and the insurer and cannot be changed by the employee, with the possible exception of opting for supplemental amounts based on a multiple of earnings at annual enrollment. In comparison, a person who buys individual coverage is issued his or her own, personalized policy.

Coverage Reductions

When an individual purchases an individual life insurance policy, the amount of coverage is generally fixed. The amount usually won't change unless the individual decides to purchase additional amounts or has purchased a type of term life insurance called "decreasing term." With decreasing term, the amount will reduce over time according to some fixed schedule published in advance. The individual may also purchase a type of life insurance in which he or she has the option to increase amounts of life coverage at set predetermined times and preselected amounts.

By contrast, the group plan participant who stays employed and covered by the plan may well face a reduction of insurance coverage as he or she approaches retirement age. The amount of life insurance reduction is determined by the reduction schedule provided by the group insurance underwriter. Such schedules typically comply with the reduction amounts acceptable under the Age Discrimination in Employment Act (ADEA).

Summary of Pros and Cons

There are pros and cons of both individual and group types of life insurance from a consumer standpoint. Figure 4-3 outlines the major pros and cons. These pros and cons are primarily the result of their different characteristics.

Figure 4-.3 Pros and Cons of Individual and Group Life Insurance Policies	
Individual	*Group*
Pros:	Pros:
• Flexible	• Easier access
• Custom-tailored	• Simple underwriting
Con:	Cons:
• Stricter underwriting	• Inflexible
	• Costly at older ages

For example, according to The American Council of Life Insurers (ACLI) 2010 Fact Book, as of the end of 2009 there was $10 trillion of face amount in force. In contrast with group insurance for which there was $7.7 trillion of face amount in force.

Contrasts between Permanent and Term Life Insurance

Another major distinction in types of life insurance is permanent versus term. Permanent insurance is insurance that has no specific ending point; as long as the policyholder pays the premium, it stays in force. That contrasts with term insurance, which, as its name implies, covers the person for a specific span of time (the "term"). Term insurance can apply to both individual and group insurance.

After the expiration of the term (which in individual policies is stated in years such as 10 or 15) the individual term policy may be renewed at the option of the insurer if the covered person wishes. However, the price may increase at renewal, because the insured is now older and represents a greater risk.

Most group life insurance is term. In fact, of the $10 billion of group life insurance in force in 2011, 90 percent of it was group term life.[2] Unlike an individual policy, the term of coverage for the employees under the policy is only for as long as the policyholder keeps the coverage in force and the employees wishing to participate in the plan are eligible.

Figure 4-4 outlines the major differences between permanent and term life insurance.

Figure 4-4. Characteristics of Permanent and Term Life Insurance Policies	
Permanent	**Term**
• Stays in force as long as premiums are paid (or until age 120)	• Specifies limited length of insurable period (the "term")
• Has higher premiums initially, but allows flexible premium options afterward, including no premium	• Has generally lower premiums, which are based on age and health (in individual coverage) (not a building cash value); pays the highest death benefit for the lowest cost
• Can accumulate cash values on a tax-deferred basis	• Has no lasting financial value
• Is rare in group coverage	• Is the most common type of group life coverage

As has been mentioned, term insurance lasts for a specific period of time—the term, as opposed to permanent insurance, which stays in force so long as the premium is paid. The disadvantage of individual term life insurance is that at its end, even if it has been a long term of 20 years, the insured's need for life insurance may still exist, and the insured may have to apply for a new policy. Since the insured is now older, the new term insurance will be much more costly. It may even cost more than the permanent insurance would have cost 20 years prior. Further, the person's health may have declined, which could result in even higher costs or denied coverage.

In contrast to individual term insurance, group term insurance is purchased for the duration of the rate guarantee provided by the insurer to the policyholder, assuming no major changes occur in the plan during the rate guarantee. At the end of the rate guarantee, the insurer has the option of whether or not to offer renewal terms to the policyholder. In the vast majority of cases, the incumbent carrier does offer the policyholder a renewal.

Permanent insurance will have a higher initial cost for a given amount of life coverage compared to term. But permanent life insurance has two major advantages. The first and biggest advantage is permanent's ability to build a "cash value" over time. This affords the holder of permanent insurance a range of financial options, including:

- having premium payments stop (in reality paid by the accumulated cash value);

- taking a loan against the policy's cash value;

- taking the cash value at some point in time with the tax advantage of having only the accumulated cash value minus the premiums paid taxable as income.

The other significant advantage is that once the premium is set for the policy, it is generally a level premium; that is, it remains unchanged over the life of the policy. This contrasts to term coverage, which at the term's expiration, the policyholder will typically see a premium increase upon renewal of the policy.

The major advantage of term over permanent insurance is that the initial premiums for term are lower. However, at advanced ages, the cost of term life insurance can get fairly expensive. Term insurance is often dubbed "pure" protection as it does not have any sort of residual value to the policyholder at the end of the term.

The Various Forms of Individual Life Coverage

Because many forms of individual life insurance are sold in the workplace as part of worksite marketing, the producer who specializes in group insurance may come across various individual insurance types. These individual life insurance forms include whole life, universal life, variable whole life, variable/universal life, and term life. Brief descriptions of these major types of individual life insurance follow.

Whole Life

Whole life, sometimes called "ordinary life," is permanent life insurance. Premiums are generally paid throughout the insured's life. Many policies allow for the premium to be "paid up" after a certain period of time, after which the owner is no longer required to make premium payments. Premiums are "level," that is, they do not change over the life of the policy. Cash values accumulate.

Universal Life

Universal life is a combination of permanent whole life insurance and term insurance. While premiums are "level," the owner can elect to make larger premium payments so that cash values can build faster.

Variable Whole Life

Variable whole life combines permanent whole life insurance with a "side fund" that is invested in securities. This presents the owner with the opportunity to have a death benefit and a cash value that builds based on stock market performance.

Variable/Universal Life

This is a hybrid permanent life insurance product that combines elements of universal and variable life. It offers a variety of investment options, flexible premium payments, and a guaranteed death benefit.

Term Life

With term life, the owner purchases a death benefit for a set term. Usually, the death benefit is level as are the premiums, although some products do include a decreasing death benefit. The product, while not permanent, may include a renewal option. However, the cost will generally increase upon renewal.

The Various Forms of Group Life Coverage

Group life insurance also comes in many different forms. However, as previously noted, the vast majority of group life is term insurance. Other group life insurance forms include group term life, accidental death & dismemberment (AD&D), specialty products, and permanent. Brief descriptions of these major types of group life follow.

Group Term Life

Group term life is the most common type of group life insurance. Generally, it is issued on an "annually renewable term" basis. That is, the term is one year or longer, if longer terms are offered by the insurer. Generally, the employer is "allowed" to renew upon expiration of the one-year term or rate guarantee. Rates and some other aspects may be changed by the insurance carrier upon renewal. However, market pressures have made group term life very competitive, so unless the program is running at a very high loss ratio, the employer can expect the incumbent carrier to offer renewal on similar terms. Group term life may also be issued on the lives of employees' dependents.

Accidental Death & Dismemberment (AD&D)

AD&D is a subset of group term life. It differs from group term life in that the benefit is paid only in the event the death is due to an accident. In addition, a partial benefit may be payable for certain specific losses (such as the loss of a leg) due to an accident.

Specialty Products

Some very specialized life insurance offerings are sometimes sold to companies for very specific reasons. Two examples of specialty products are COLI and BOLI.

- Corporate Owned Life Insurance (COLI) is purchased by the employer on the lives of select employees with the employer as beneficiary. The death benefits are used to fund the overall employee benefit program.

- Bank Owned Life Insurance (BOLI) is purchased by a bank, usually on the lives of the bank's officers, as a way to increase the assets of the bank at no risk to the bank.

Permanent Group Coverages

Like their individual counterparts, permanent group life programs offer cash values that increase over the life of the policy. Unlike individual coverages, the employer may contribute to the cost of the program. The types include group whole life and group universal life. Permanent group life represents only 10 percent of group life insurance in force and only 8 percent of new group sales, but these programs are popular with some employers.

Key Takeaways

- There are many different types of life insurance. In the group market, the vast majority of programs are group term life.

- Life insurance products have evolved over time to meet the changing needs of consumers and because insurers have tried to differentiate themselves in the market.

- A producer may come across many other forms of group life insurance as he or she calls on new clients.

- In today's environment, group insurance is virtually all term insurance.

- Individual life insurance predates group insurance by about 100 years.

- Key differences between individual and group life policies include the degree of flexibility/customization, the need for medical underwriting, and premium rates.

- Key differences between permanent and term life insurance involve the length of coverage, the premium rates, and the ability to accumulate cash value.

- The various forms of individual life coverage include whole life, universal life, variable whole life, variable/universal life, and term life.

- The various forms of group life coverage include group term life, AD&D, specialty products, and permanent life.

Endnotes

1. *ACLI Life Insurers Fact Book 2011* (Washington, D.C.: American Council of Life Insurers), p. 66.
2. Potter, Anita, *U.S. Group Life Insurance, 2011 Second Quarter Review* (Windsor, CT: LL Global, October 7, 2011).

Chapter 5

Group Life and AD&D Contract Provisions

The information in this chapter can be used to instruct new learners about how group life and Accidental Death & Dismemberment (AD&D) benefits work and as a reference and guide for seasoned insurance professionals. Life coverage is one of the oldest group products. Carriers have developed provisions intended to differentiate themselves, many of which have been copied by the competition. As a result, the same benefit may exist under various names, depending on the carrier. This chapter will identify many of the various names under which the benefits are known by the carriers.

While the focus of this chapter will be on how the benefits work, an emphasis will be placed on the underwriting and pricing implications of the benefits. The spectrum of benefits offered by group carriers is wide. This examination will concentrate on the most common provisions and the most customary fashion of how the benefits work.

The benefits are described in two legal documents which are generated by the insurer:

- The contract, which is the legally binding agreement between the policyholder (Plan Sponsor/employer) and the insurer. It details the benefits to be provided to employees and dependents and how the plan is to operate in all aspects.

- The booklet/certificate, is the legally binding agreement between the policyholder (Plan Sponsor/employer) and the insured employees (and their covered dependents if dependent coverage is chosen by the policyholder). It details the benefits to be provided to employees and dependents as well as the duties and responsibilities of the insurer and insureds in the operation of the plan. The language is required to be straightforward by most states' Department of Insurance so that employees and the policyholder can clearly understand the language.

We'll examine provisions in major categories by the way they affect potential benefit payments, as outlined in Figure 5-1, and by the way they affect plan administration, as outlined in Figure 5-2.

Figure 5-1. Contract Provisions Affecting Benefit Payments

Eligibility	Benefit Amounts	Definitions	Commencement of Coverage	Termination of Coverage and Exclusions	Extensions of Coverage
Minimum Weekly Hours	Schedule of Benefits	Employee and Dependent	Effective Date of Coverage	Termination of Coverage	Waiver of Premium
Beneficiary	Guaranteed Issue	Active Full Time Employee	Deferred Effective Date	Life Suicide Exclusions	Coverage Continuation
Evidence of Good Health	Accelerated Death Benefits	Disabled	Enrollment	AD&D Exclusions	Conversion Privilege
Contributions	ADEA Age Reductions	Physician	Changes in Amounts of Coverage		Portability
	Minimum and Maximum	Earnings			Assignment

Figure 5-2. Contract Provisions Affecting Plan Administration

Premium	Policy Termination	Rate Guarantee	Renewal Notification	Amending the Contract
Grace Period	Termination of Policy	Significant Changes in Census	Minimum Advanced Notice	Approval Process
Billing Method and Payment Frequency				

Eligibility

Eligibility for group life and AD&D term coverage applies the same requirements as other group coverages, such as medical or dental. Since dependent coverage can be offered, eligibility for dependents must be described in the contract also.

The employer as policyholder or plan sponsor decides which types of coverage are to be offered to the employees under the group plan. The plan can be as simple as basic life only or can include various supplemental and dependent coverages, as listed below:

- Basic Life

- Supplemental Life

- Supplemental AD&D

- Dependent Supplemental Life

- Dependent Supplemental AD&D

The eligibility waiting period is the length of time an employer wants a new employee to be continuously employed and at work before the employee is eligible for coverage. It can be as short as the date of hire or as long as one or more years. It can be expressed in days, months, or years.[1] In industries that have traditionally high turnover, a long waiting period might make sense to avoid the administrative hassle of enrolling an employee only to have that person leave.[2] Examples of eligibility waiting periods are provided in Figure 5-3.

As a general rule, the eligibility waiting period is not a major factor in rating and pricing, unless there is something very unusual in the waiting period. For example, underwriters may consider adjusting rates related to the eligibility waiting period if the employer had employees working overseas or in a high risk environment (especially related to potential acts of terrorism). It is important, regardless, to provide the underwriter with the eligible census to price the covered population, especially if the eligibility waiting period is long and the employer has high turnover.[3]

It is the employer's decision whether or not to offer dependent life and dependent AD&D on the plan. Dependent life eligibility is customarily tied to the employee's eligibility for coverage, so if the employee is not covered then neither are his or her dependents until such time as the employee becomes covered. Some insurers, however, do allow eligible dependents to enroll for Life and/or AD&D coverage without the employee being covered.

The employee is expected to work continuously and uninterrupted during the eligibility waiting period. Vacation days, Paid Time Off (PTO), and normal sick days usually are not considered interruptions. An example of an interruption is time off as the result of a disabling condition.

In most situations, the eligibility waiting period is the same for basic life, supplemental life, and AD&D. However, there can be different eligibility waiting periods by line of coverage if the policyholder so desires. This may occur under collective bargaining agreements or in situations where the employer is using the life plan as an attractive fringe benefit.

Figure 5-3. Sample Eligibility Waiting Periods		
Coverage	Same for All Lines	Different Waiting Period by Line
Basic life	First day of the month coinciding with or next following 30 days of employment	Date of hire
Basic AD&D	First day of the month coinciding with or next following 30 days of employment	Date of hire
Supplemental life	First day of the month coinciding with or next following 30 days of employment	First day of the month coinciding with or next following 60 days of employment
Supplemental AD&D	First day of the month coinciding with or next following 30 days of employment	First day of the month coinciding with or next following 60 days of employment
Dependent supplemental life	First day of the month coinciding with or next following 30 days of employment	First day of the month coinciding with or next following 60 days of employment
Dependent supplemental AD&D	First day of the month coinciding with or next following 30 days of employment	First day of the month coinciding with or next following 60 days of employment

Minimum Weekly Hours

The employer, with underwriter approval, determines the minimum number of hours an employee must work each week in order be considered an active full-time employee. Minimum hours typically range from 20 to 40 per week and vary by industry and employer. It is not uncommon for a policyholder to have different minimum weekly hour requirements applying to different classes of employees. Occasionally, part-time employees are identified as a separate class and may have a minimum weekly hour requirement ranging between 15 to 25 hours per week.

It is important that the contract is explicit about weekly minimum hours when an employer has employees who work nontraditional schedules. For example, a class of employees may work three 12-hour shifts, have three days off, and then work another series of three 12-hour shifts. The hours would have to be averaged over a period of time, such as a month, to determine if weekly minimum hours are met. The key is that this accounting be spelled out in the contract.

The weekly minimum hours usually appears in the Schedule of Benefits, as illustrated in Figure 5-4. It is incumbent upon the policyholder to track employee eligibility relating to minimum hours for billing and claim purposes. In the event of a claim, the insurer will verify the claimant's eligibility that was reported to the insurer all along by the policyholder.

Figure 5-4. Sample Weekly Minimum Hours	
Weekly Minimum Hours:	
Class 1	30 hours
Class 2	Not less than 35 hours per week averaged over a month

Enrollment

On noncontributory coverage, the employee is automatically enrolled in the plan. If dependent coverage is non-contributory, eligible dependents will also be automatically enrolled in the plan. Some carriers require an enrollment card to capture employee and dependent information on noncontributory coverage for ease in claims administration.

On rare occasions, an employee may opt out of noncontributory coverage due to religious reasons or philosophical beliefs, or because of imputed income as a result of IRS Section 79 (see Chapter 10). On these rare occasions, the underwriter must ensure that such employees sign documentation stating that they understand they are knowingly giving up their right to "free" life coverage.

On contributory coverage, the employee is required to actively enroll. The enrollment "window" begins as soon as the employee fulfills the eligibility waiting period and lasts for 31 days afterward. If the employee fails to enroll within the 31-day enrollment window, the employee will be considered a "late entrant" if he or she attempts to enroll subsequently.

Dependent enrollment is customarily contingent upon employee enrollment. Insurers usually require the employee to be enrolled for coverage before dependents can be considered eligible.

To enroll, an employee must complete forms, including an authorization of payroll deductions for the premium cost if the plan is contributory or voluntary. The employee is not considered enrolled until all the required enrollment documentation has been completed and received by the policyholder. If evidence of insurability is required (due to coverage limits or due to the employee being a late entrant), the employee will not be enrolled until such time as the evidence of good health is received and approved by the insurer.

Contributions

Basic life insurance is typically offered on a noncontributory basis. Basic AD&D insurance is also typically noncontributory. Dependent life can be offered on a noncontributory basis, but in today's environment, dependent life is usually offered on a contributory basis as part of the supplemental life plan.

The term "contributory" can cause confusion in the group arena. It refers to the premium contribution level required of the employee for coverage. Many insurance professionals equate contributory to mean 100 percent "employee pay all" of the premium and use the term "voluntary" as a synonym. While this nomenclature works in most cases, it does not encompass the technical meaning of contributory" where employee contributions can range from 1 percent to 100 percent of the premium cost. Voluntary plans, almost by definition, are employee-pay-all plans.

Supplemental life, supplemental AD&D, dependent life, and dependent AD&D are typically offered on a contributory basis, mostly as employee-pay-all plans. However, there are instances where the employer contributes a portion of the cost in supplemental plans.

Knowing the employee contribution level is important to the underwriter in evaluating and gauging employee participation levels in contributory supplemental life plans. The underwriter can expect slightly higher participation in a plan where the employer contributes towards the cost of the premium versus an employee-pay-all plan.

Beneficiary Designation

Employees have the right to designate whomever they want as beneficiaries of their life and AD&D death (dismemberment claims are paid to the employee) claim proceeds. Married employees typically name their spouses and/or children as beneficiaries. Some states prohibit the policyholder from being named as beneficiary. Some states require the current spouse to receive 50 percent of life claim proceeds, even if the spouse is not the designated beneficiary.

The employee is the beneficiary of dependent life proceeds. Most carriers request that the employee update the enrollment card on file to reflect the addition (by birth or adoption) of a new covered dependent.

Employees have the right to change their beneficiaries whenever they want. In order for such a change to be officially recognized, employees must complete the required forms and submit them to the policyholder's benefits administrator. The insurer may or may not be providing beneficiary administration services. If the insurer is not providing beneficiary record services, the employer or a third-party plan administrator would need to maintain the recordkeeping.

Evidence of Good Health

Carriers have a variety of names they apply, including evidence of good health, evidence of insurability, medical evidence, proof of insurability, or simply evidence. Evidence of good health is a fundamental life/AD&D contract provision and is a vital risk management mechanism that the underwriter uses to control plan risk. The purpose of evidence is to limit selection against the plan, wherein a late entrant or a person with a higher potential for claim now wants to enroll in the plan or if already enrolled, to increase the amount of coverage.

Evidence of good health comes in a wide range of methods and requirements. The evidence application to the insurer (versus the administrative application of) may require one or more of the following: personal health statement, lab work and/or X-rays, examination by a qualified medical practitioner, and an independent medical exam (IME). As more "flags" are noted by the medical underwriters in the application process, higher levels of evidence may be required.

Personal Health Statement

All applicants begin with completing and submitting a personal health statement or statement of health. Applicants respond to a series of questions and provide details of health history related to the questions. The statement of health application may vary by state, since some states regulate the nature and type of questions the insurer can ask.

Lab Work and/or X-rays

If there are questions about health history revealed in the statement of health, the insurer may require the applicant to submit to blood, urine, or other lab tests, which may include X-rays.

Examination by Qualified Medical Practitioners

An examination by a medical practitioner who is employed or contracted by the insurer may also include additional lab work. It is common for the medical practitioner to conduct an exam in the privacy of the applicant's home. Among other tests, the practitioner may take the applicant's temperature, blood pressure, heart rate, and weight and may interview the applicant about his or her statement of health.

Independent Medical Exam (IME)

If the medical data is unclear or inconclusive, a third party may be needed to help interpret the data. IMEs may also be used when a rejected applicant requests reconsideration. An independent third party is used to provide an objective and unbiased opinion regarding the applicant's health condition(s).

When Evidence of Good Heath Is Required

An evidence of good health is typically required:

- For late entrants, including the late entrant's dependents.

- For employees or dependents who cross the established guaranteed issue (GI) limit.

- At annual enrollment in a Section 125 plan where employees can increase their coverage by increments of one level or more (example: increasing from 1 × annual basic earnings (ABE) to 3 × ABE.

- When minimum participation requirements on a voluntary plan are not met.

An employee who is a late entrant is likely to have his or her dependent(s) subject to evidence as well.

Employees are generally not required to submit separate evidence applications for life and AD&D. Approval or denial of an evidence application is deemed applicable for both if AD&D applies.

Submitting evidence does not constitute coverage; coverage or an increase in coverage does not become effective until the insurer approves the evidence application. Some insurers will approve the evidence application and make coverage effective as of the approval date. Other insurers may delay the effective date until the first of the month to align with the billing cycle. The insured will be informed of the effective date of coverage by the insurer.

Carriers vary with regards to who bears the costs related to an evidence application. Generally, if the evidence is required on account of a situation out of the applicant's control, the insurer absorbs the costs. Crossing the GI limit or increasing levels of coverage are examples where the insurer usually pays. Late entrants are typically required to pay for the costs related to the evidence application.

Schedule of Benefits

The Schedule of Benefits is also referred to as the Plan of Benefits, Schedule of Insurance, or simply the Schedule. It describes the level of benefits for which an employee or dependent may be covered. The level of benefits may be subject to the GI limit. There are many schedules and variations of schedules that are available to accommodate a policyholder's needs. Schedules often vary by class. In order for the employer and employees to qualify for Section 79 premium exclusion on the first $50,000 of coverage, the schedule must conform to non-discrimination rules published by the IRS (see Chapter 10).

The Schedule of Benefits appears prominently in the employee's booklet/certificate as well as the policy. It is the section the employee usually looks at first in the booklet/certificate. A class of employee having a different Schedule of Benefits will often receive an amendment or rider attached to the booklet/certificate, which describes the class-specific Schedule. In some cases (and at policyholder request) an entirely separate booklet/certificate may be printed for different classes due to schedule differences.

Flat Benefits

Flat benefits that provide one set amount of coverage are popular with basic life and AD&D plans. Flat benefits can also readily apply to supplemental life or dependent life. The advantage of a flat benefit is that it is easy for employees to understand, since there are no calculations involved. It is also easy for the benefits administrator to compute the monthly premium, since all employees have the same amount of coverage. Figure 5-5 provides an example of a flat schedule.

Figure 5-5. Example of Flat Schedule			
Class	Class Description	Basic Life Amount per Employee	Basic AD&D Amount per Employee
1	Steamfitter	$25,000	$25,000
2	Driver	15,000	15,000
3	Warehouse employee	10,000	10,000

Earnings Schedules

Perhaps the most popular schedule type in group benefits is based on a multiple of earnings. A multiple is applied to the employee's salary or earnings to calculate the amount of coverage the employee can potentially receive. Earnings are defined in the Definitions section of the policy and are usually based on annual basic earnings (ABE) or basic annual earnings (BAE). Many plans allow employees to select the multiple that applies to their earnings. Figures 5.6 and 5.7 provide examples of earnings schedules. Figure 5-8 provides an example of combined flat and earnings schedules.

Figure 5-6. Earnings Schedule (Example 1)			
Class	Class Description	Basic Life Amount	Basic AD&D Amount
1	Site supervisors	3 times annual basic earnings, rounded to the next highest $1,000, if not an even multiple thereof, subject to a maximum of $150,000	3 times annual basic earnings, rounded to the next highest $1,000, if not an even multiple thereof, subject to a maximum of $150,000
2	Foremen	2 times annual basic earnings, rounded to the next highest $1,000, if not an even multiple thereof, subject to a maximum of $100,000	2 times annual basic earnings, rounded to the next highest $1,000, if not an even multiple thereof, subject to a maximum of $100,000
3	Laborers	1 times annual basic earnings, rounded to the next highest $1,000, if not an even multiple thereof, subject to a maximum of $50,000	1 times annual basic earnings, rounded to the next highest $1,000, if not an even multiple thereof, subject to a maximum of $50,000

Figure 5-7. Earnings Schedule (Example 2)			
Class	Class Description	Basic Life Amount	Basic AD&D Amount
1	Executives	Choice of 1, 2, 3, 4, or 5 times annual basic earnings, rounded to the next highest $1,000, if not an even multiple thereof, subject to a maximum of $300,000	Choice of 1, 2, 3, 4, or 5 times annual basic earnings, rounded to the next highest $1,000, if not an even multiple thereof, subject to a maximum of $300,000
2	Managers	Choice of 1, 2, or 3 times annual basic earnings, rounded to the next highest $1,000, if not an even multiple thereof, subject to a maximum of $200,000	Choice of 1, 2, or 3 times annual basic earnings, rounded to the next highest $1,000, if not an even multiple thereof, subject to a maximum of $200,000
3	All other employees	Choice of 1 or 2 times annual basic earnings, rounded to the next highest $1,000, if not an even multiple thereof, subject to a maximum of $125,000	Choice of 1 or 2 times annual basic earnings, rounded to the next highest $1,000, if not an even multiple thereof, subject to a maximum of $125,000

Figure 5-8. Example of Combined Flat and Earnings Schedule			
Class	Class Description	Basic Life Amount	Supplemental Life Amount
1	Employees with 10 or more years of service	$20,000	Choice of 1, 2, 3, 4, or 5 times annual basic earnings, rounded to the next highest $1,000, if not an even multiple thereof, subject to a maximum of $300,000
2	Employees with more than 5 but less than 10 years of service	15,000	Choice of 1, 2, or 3 times annual basic earnings, rounded to the next highest $1,000, if not an even multiple thereof, subject to a maximum of $200,000
3	Employees with less than 5 years of service	10,000	Choice of 1 or 2 times annual basic earnings, rounded to the next highest $1,000, if not an even multiple thereof, subject to a maximum of $125,000

Increment Schedules

Some plans are constructed to allow employees greater flexibility in choice and may not be tied to an employee's earnings. Plans with an increment schedule enable employees to elect a flat amount of coverage. Figure 5-9 provides an example of an increment schedule.

Figure 5-9. Example of Increment Schedule			
Class	Class Description	Basic Life Amount	Supplemental Life Amount
1	Branch managers	$20,000	A choice of $10,000 to $50,000 in increments of $10,000
2	Tellers	15,000	A choice of $10,000 to $30,000 in increments of $10,000
3	All other employees	10,000	A choice of $10,000 or $20,000

Dependent Life Schedules

Dependent life schedules can be offered on a noncontributory basis, but are more often offered on a contributory basis as part of the supplemental life and AD&D plan. There is a wide range of schedule types offered by insurers. Typically, there are separate schedules for spouses and children.

Dependent life amounts and schedules, particularly maximums, may be subject to statutory restrictions, depending on the state. To limit risk, some insurers restrict the maximum amount of coverage a spouse may have to no more than 50 percent of the employee's face amount, regardless of the situs state.

Schedules for dependent children are often substantially lower than those offered for spouses. The schedules are flat amounts since children aren't considered to have annual earnings. Many carriers categorize the children's schedule by ages, due to the mortality risk at given ages. Unless required by law to cover children from birth, many carriers begin covering dependent children at 14 or 15 days or older. Underwriters routinely offer to cover children from birth with a load to the rate. Figure 5-10 provides an example of a basic dependent life schedule.

Dependent children who are considered full-time students are usually eligible for coverage, provided they meet the contractual definition of "dependent." The cutoff age for covering students usually ranges from between 21 and 27 years. There may be a rate load for covering students beyond age 21.

Dependent AD&D typically applies to spouses and is usually only applicable as part of a supplemental AD&D policy. Figures 5.11 and 5.12 provide examples of supplemental dependent life and AD&D schedules.

Figure 5-10. Example of Basic Dependent Life Schedule					
Class	Spouse	Child from Birth to 14 Days Old	Child from 15 Days to 6 Months Old	Child 6 Months and Older to Age 19	Students to Age 23
1	$20,000	$200	$1,000	$4,000	$4,000
2	10,000	100	500	2,000	2,000

Figure 5-11. Supplemental Dependent Life and AD&D Schedule (Example 1)					
Supplemental Spouse Life	Supplemental Spouse AD&D	Child from Birth to 14 Days Old	Child from 15 Days to 6 Months Old	Child 6 Months and Older to Age 19	Students to Age 23
$25,000	$25,000	$500	$2,500	$5,000	$5,000

Figure 5-12. Supplemental Dependent Life and AD&D Schedule (Example 2)					
Supplemental Spouse Life	Supplemental Spouse AD&D	Child From Birth to 14 Days Old	Child from 15 Days to 6 Months Old	Child 6 Months and Older to Age 19	Students to Age 25
50% of the employee's face amount subject to a maximum of $50,000	50% of the employee's face amount subject to a maximum of $50,000	$1,000	$5,000	$10,000	$10,000

Retiree Life Schedules

Because of the absolute and imminent risk of death, retiree schedules are modest and limited. The employer may provide a noncontributory basic life plan of $5,000 to cover burial expenses. Retirees may also be offered a voluntary supplemental life plan with a choice of $10,000, $15,000, or $20,000. Once an amount is selected, no increases can be elected later.

Retirees are usually required to enroll within 31 days of their retirement date for supplemental life. After the 31-day eligibility window passes, they can no longer enroll. If they later cancel their supplemental plan, they cannot re-enroll at a later time.

Accidental Death & Dismemberment Schedules

Many insurers require the employee to participate in the life insurance plan before being able to enroll in the AD&D plan. AD&D schedules typically mirror the life schedule. The amount of AD&D coverage an insured has is commonly called the "principal sum." Loss of life is paid to the beneficiary. Loss of physical function due to a dismembering accident is paid to the employee.

Most carriers offer AD&D schedules for dependent spouses, but dependent children are rarely covered for AD&D.

AD&D differs from life coverage in that in addition to a death benefit, a principal sum may be payable to a living insured who has suffered a physical loss as a result of an accident. Losses from illness or sickness are not recognized as payable under AD&D unless directly caused by an accident.

Carriers vary in the type of accident losses covered as well as the principal sum payment. Figure 5-13 provides an illustrative list of typical accidental losses.

Figure 5-13. Typical Accidental Losses with Percent of Coverage	
Description of Accidental Loss	*Percent of Principal Sum*
Life	100%
Sight in both eyes	100%
Both arms or both legs	100%
Both hands or both feet	100%
Quadriplegia	70%
One eye	50%
One arm or one leg	70%
Speech	50%
Hearing in both ears	50%
Thumb and index finger	25%
Big toe	10%

Carriers will further refine their definition of accidental loss with descriptors such as:

- Loss of sight means total and irreversible loss.

- Loss of hearing means the ability to hear is total and cannot be restored.

- Loss of hand means completely cut off at the wrist. Loss of foot means completely cut off at the ankle.

- Loss of thumb and index finger is at the metacarpophalengeal joints.

Some carriers offer a common carrier or double indemnity benefit as an option the policyholder can add to the AD&D policy. An accidental loss (including loss of limb, etc.) in a licensed public transportation conveyance results in 2 or 3 times the principal sum.

Example of a Life and AD&D Benefit with Rounding

Assume the following schedule and employee information:

Basic Life	Basic AD&D
1 times annual basic earnings, rounded to the next highest $1,000, if not an even multiple thereof, subject to a maximum of $50,000	1 times annual basic earnings, rounded to the next highest $1,000, if not an even multiple thereof, subject to a maximum of $50,000

- Employee's annual basic earnings are $37,340.

- AD&D policy has double indemnity benefit.

- Employee dies in an airline crash.

The life and AD&D benefit would be calculated as follows:

Life benefit = 1 × $37,340 = $38,000 (rounded up to next highest thousand)

AD&D benefits = 2 × $37,340 = $75,000 (rounded up to next highest thousand)

Total amount payable to beneficiaries = $113,000 ($38,000 life + $75,000 AD&D)

Note that rounding is applied to the initial calculation after the multiple is applied to earnings. Each covered person has the rounding applied to the ABE times the earnings multiple. In most cases, roundings are to the next highest $1,000 (as illustrated above) or $500, if not an even multiple thereof. Rounding to the next highest amount represents minimal risk, so most underwriters are not overly concerned with the rounding language. Occasionally, roundings apply to the next lowest $1,000 or $500. Rounding can sometimes cause confusion. Some examples of rounding related to an employee's coverage amount are shown here:

Examples of Rounding Applied to an Employee's Coverage Amount

Assume the following information:

- Employee's Annual Basic Earnings = $33,550

- Schedule = 2 times Annual Basic Earnings, rounded to the next highest $1,000, if not an even multiple thereof, subject to a maximum of $100,000

The benefit would be calculated as follows: $2 \times \$33,550 = \$67,100$. With rounding applied, the amount of coverage is $68,000.

Assume the following information:

- Employee's Annual Basic Earnings = $42,660

- Schedule = 3 times Annual Basic Earnings, rounded to the next lowest $500, if not an even multiple thereof, subject to a maximum of $150,000

The benefit would be calculated as follows:

$3 \times \$42,660 = \$127,980$. With rounding applied, the amount of coverage is $127,500

Guaranteed Issue

The Guaranteed Issue (GI) is the maximum amount of life and/or AD&D coverage an individual can obtain without having to provide evidence of good health to the insurer. The guaranteed issue is also termed the "nonmedical maximum", but is most commonly referred to as the GI by insurance professionals. The GI is a fundamental contract provision and risk management mechanism that is included in most life and AD&D contracts with maximums greater than $50,000.

The guaranteed issue amount usually appears adjacent to the schedule of benefits in the booklet/certificate as it impacts the amount of coverage the insured individual could potentially have.

The underwriter applies the GI to a formula established in the insurer's underwriting guidelines. The factors in the formula are usually related to the overall life maximum, the number of lives, the monthly case volume, and/or the average amount of coverage per employee. The AD&D GI level typically applies separately from life. Some carriers apply a separate GI table to AD&D while others mirror the life GI amount. The GI formula for a dependent spouse is usually based on the dependent life maximum. A GI chart in the underwriting guidelines might appear as shown in Figure 5-14.

Figure 5-14. GI Chart		
Total Monthly Volume of Coverage	Combined Basic and Supplemental Maximum	Combined Basic and Supplemental Guaranteed Issue
$0 – $999,999	$150,000	$ 50,000
$1,000,000 – $2,999,999	250,000	150,000
$3,000,000 – 6,999,999	300,000	200,000
$7,000.000 – $14,999,999	350,000	250,000
$15,000,000 – $29,999,999	400,000	300,000
$30,000,000 – $49,999,999	500,000	350,000
$50,000,000 and over	750,000	500,000

Examples of GI Limits Applying on Coverage Amounts

Assume the following employee information and schedule:

- The GI on combined basic and supplemental life is $150,000.

- The GI on AD&D is $150,000.

- The GI on dependent spouse is $50,000.

- Employee elects 5 times ABE on supplemental life and 3 times ABE on AD&D.

- Employee's annual basic earnings are $43,860.

Class	Class Description	Basic Life Amount	Supplemental Life Amount	Supplemental AD&D Amount	Supplemental Life Dependent Spouse
1	Employees with 10 or more years of service	$20,000	Choice of 1, 2, 3, 4, or 5 times annual basic earnings, rounded to the next highest $1,000 if not an even multiple thereof, subject to a maximum of $300,000	Choice of 1, 2, 3, 4, or 5 times annual basic earnings, rounded to the next highest $1,000 if not an even multiple thereof, subject to a maximum of $300,000	50% of the employee's total life face amount subject to a maximum of $100,000

The life and AD&D benefit, assuming the employee and spouse were approved above their GI limits, would be calculated as follows:

Basic life = $20,000

Supplemental life = 5 × $43,860 = $220,000 (rounded up to next highest thousand)

Combined basic and supplemental life = $240,000 ($20,000 + $220,000)

Supplemental AD&D = 3 × $43,860 = $132,000 (rounded up to next highest thousand)

Supplement life on spouse = 50% × $240,000 = $120,000, but limited to $100,000 maximum

The amount over the GI limit for life coverage that is subject to evidence of good health is $90,000 ($240,000 − $150,000 GI). If the employee does not submit evidence or if the evidence application is not approved, the employee would be limited to $150,000 in life coverage ($20,000 basic + $130,000 supplemental).

Since the AD&D face amount is below the GI level, evidence of good health is not required. The employee would have $132,000 in supplemental AD&D coverage.

In this example, the amount of supplemental life for the dependent spouse is based on whether or not the employee's evidence of good health is approved and if the spouse's evidence of good health is approved. If the employee's evidence is approved, the spousal coverage would be 50 percent of $240,000, or $120,000, but subject the maximum coverage limit of $100,000 and the spousal GI limit of $50,000. The spouse would have to submit evidence for the amount above the spousal GI limit, or $50,000 ($100,000 − $50,000 GI). If the spouse does not submit evidence or if the spouse's evidence application is denied, the spouse would be limited to $50,000 of coverage.

If the employee's evidence is not approved, the spouse's coverage calculation would be 50 percent of $150,000, or $75,000. The spouse would be required to submit evidence for the $25,000 ($75,000 − $50,000 GI) in excess of the spousal GI. If the spouse does not submit evidence or if the evidence application is denied, the spouse would only qualify for $50,000 coverage.

Now, suppose an employee who was approved above the GI limit receives a salary increase and wants to maintain coverage at the same multiple of salary. For example, assume the employee was approved for $90,000 in coverage over the $150,000 GI level in 2012 and the employee's earnings increase in 2013 pushes the amount of coverage over the GI to $98,000. Must the employee submit evidence for the additional $8,000 over the GI?

Most carriers have a formula that involves a capped amount over a period of time. The formulas vary widely. For example, the formula might state that evidence will not be required for such increases in a two-year period provided the increases do not exceed the lesser of a 10 percent increase in face amount or $50,000.

Accelerated Death Benefits

A contract provision for an accelerated death benefit enables a terminally ill employee or dependent to receive a portion of proceeds from the group life plan while still alive. The purpose is to provide claim funds to a person who very likely has extraordinarily high medical expenses. This provision may also be referred to as a living benefits option or an accelerated benefit. The accelerated death benefit is not applicable to AD&D.

Most carriers include this provision as standard, whereas others offer the provision as an option the policyholder can add to the life contract. Carriers vary in the range of benefit they will advance to a terminally ill insured, but all carriers have these fundamental rules regarding payment:

- The claimant must provide medical information and physician prognosis of a life expectancy of less than 6–24 months in order to receive payment.

- The insured has a minimum amount of coverage, usually not less than $10,000.

- A minimum payout, usually ranging from $3,000 to $10,000.

- The premium payment must continue on the original face amount of the remaining un-accelerated coverage, unless the claimant is approved for waiver of premium.

- Payment is made to the employee only, including payments covering terminally ill dependents.

- The number of accelerated payments is usually limited to one per covered person.

The terminally ill insured can elect how much he or she wants to have in an accelerated life claim payment, subject to the carrier's minimums and maximums. Insurers allow between 50 percent and 80 percent of an insured's face amount to be accelerated subject to a maximum of $100,000 to $500,000.

Upon the death of the terminally ill insured, the balance of the remaining unaccelerated face amount is payable to the beneficiary as a "normal" claim. The amount of AD&D is typically not impacted on account of an insured taking an accelerated death benefit payment.

Example of Accelerated Death Benefit Payment to an Employee

Assume the following facts:

- A terminally ill employee with $20,000 basic and $130,000 supplemental life has qualified to receive an accelerated death benefit.

- The plan's accelerated death benefit allows up to 80 percent of the employee's total life benefit subject to a maximum of $300,000 and a minimum of $10,000.

- The employee decides to accelerate 70 percent of the life benefit to pay for medical expenses.

The employee's accelerated death benefit would be calculated as follows:

70% × ($20,000 + $130,000) = $105,000

The $105,000 falls below the Accelerated maximum, so the employee would receive this full amount. Upon death, the remaining $45,000 ($150,000 − $105,000) of the face amount would be payable to the beneficiary. While the employee is alive, the remaining $45,000 in coverage is subject to ADEA age reductions (discussed next).

Most carriers will not reduce a dependent spouse's life amount that is based on a percentage of the employee's amount because the employee receives an accelerated payment, unless required by law.

ADEA Age Reductions

The Age Discrimination in Employment Act (ADEA) of 1974 was enacted to prevent discrimination against older employees whose continued employment and rights to employment benefits could be lost due to age discrimination.[4] ADEA is a federal civil rights law rather than an insurance law. It is the employer's responsibility to be compliant, not the insurance company's. However, insurers have a vested interest in ensuring that life benefit schedules are compliant to ADEA to keep their policyholders from becoming embroiled in legal difficulties related to the plan.

The intent of ADEA is to protect older workers, although not at the expense of younger workers, particularly relating to group benefits. Employers are allowed to reduce benefit amounts or duration for older employees if the cost of providing benefits for older workers is equivalent to the cost of benefits for younger workers. [5]

The life/AD&D contract applies reductions to employees' face amount of coverage, based on age. Carriers offer different ADEA-compliant age reduction schedules, but they are all designed to achieve the same objective: to allow coverage to older employees without unduly impacting the financial integrity of the plan and to ensure compliance with ADEA on the part of the employer.

Carriers offer an array of compliant ADEA schedules from which the policyholder can choose, with underwriter approval. In addition, the manner in which the reduction schedules are applied can vary by carrier. Most carriers apply rounding based on the existing schedule. Figure 5-15 provides an illustrative list of typical ADEA reduction schedules.

Figure 5-15. Example ADEA Reductions

Age	Reduction Percentage Sample 1	Reduction Percentage Sample 2	Reduction Percentage Sample 3	Reduction Percentage Sample 4	Reduction Percentage Sample 5	Reduction Percentage Sample 6	Reduction Percentage Sample 7
65	35%	35%	40%	35%			
70	50%	40%	40%	35%	45%	50%	65% of original
75		40%	35%	35%	35%		45% of original
80		35%	25%	25%	25%		30% of original
85		40%	25%	25%	25%		
90		35%	25%	25%	25%		
95		55%	25%	25%	25%		

ADEA age reductions do not apply directly to dependent life/AD&D coverage. However, if a state regulation limits the maximum amount of dependent coverage to 50 percent (or other formula) of the employee's face amount, then a dependent's face amount would reduce in conjunction with the employee's age-reduced amount. Moreover, some insurers apply underwriting guidelines that limit the amount of dependent coverage to no more than 50 percent of the employee's face amount in any event.

Employees and dependents are allowed to convert to an individual policy the coverage they are losing on account of ADEA age reduction. Dependent children's schedules are rarely impacted by ADEA age reductions. ADEA age reduction schedules do not apply to retiree coverage.

Carriers adjust their ADEA schedules based on whether the reduction percentage applies to the original amount at each age bracket or if the reduction percentage applies to previously reduced amounts.

Example of the Application of an ADEA Reduction Schedule

Assume the following facts:

- The contract applies ADEA reduction progressively to previously reduced amounts.

- Rounding is to next highest $500.

- The plan follows Sample 1 in Figure 5-15.

- The employee has a flat $50,000 basic life and $50,000 basic AD&D coverage on the day before his 65th birthday.

The ADEA reduction schedule would be applied as follows:

- At age 65, the employee's Life and AD&D insurance coverage would be reduced respectively by 35% to $32,500 [(1 − 0.35) × $50,000].

- At age 65 until the day before his 70th birthday, the employee would have $32,500 of basic life and $32,500 of basic AD&D. The employee would have the option to convert the $17,500 ($50,000 − $32,500) lost because of the ADEA age reduction. The conversion is typically required within 31 days of the qualifying event, in this case within 31 days of the employee's 65th birthday.

- At Age 70, the employee's insurance coverage would be reduced another 50 percent to $16,500 (0.50 × $32,500,= $16,250 rounded up to next highest $16,500).

- On and after his 70th birthday, the employee would have $16,500 of basic life and $16,500 of basic AD&D. The employee would have the option to convert the $16,000 ($32,500 − $16,500) lost because of the second ADEA age reduction. The employee cannot at this time convert the $17,500 lost previously at age 65, since he will have gone past the 31-day conversion enrollment window.

Maximum Benefit

The maximum benefit is the maximum amount of coverage an insured individual can have as stated in the schedule of benefits. Each line of coverage will have a separate maximum, even if the maximum benefits are mirrored between policies. Usually, the life and AD&D maximums mirror each other. Maximum life insurance benefits are a matter of risk tolerance for the insurer. As such, they can vary greatly among carriers. Usually, insurers have strict maximum amounts of life insurance they will issue on any one person. Companies will not usually deviate from these maximums.

Maximums routinely vary by class. The maximum benefit is established by the underwriter according to formulas in the insurer's underwriting guidelines. If both basic and supplemental life are offered, the underwriter may establish an overall combined maximum.

The maximum benefit is usually related to the amount of volume exposure, annual premium, and/or number of lives by class or on the case. Many insurers tie their GI formula to the maximum benefit formula. The maximum benefit may also be tied to a formula established by the reinsurer which would be transparent to the policyholder.

If an employee's combined basic/supplemental coverage amount is capped by an overall maximum, the supplemental coverage amount is usually reduced first in order to have the employee's maximum set appropriately.

Example of Applied Maximum Coverage

Assume the following employee earnings and schedule:

- The employee's annual basic earnings are $93,800.

- Both Basic and Supplemental Life is employee-pay-all

Basic Life Amount	Supplemental Life Amount	Combined Basic & Supplemental Maximum
$25,000	3 times annual basic earnings, rounded to the next highest $1,000, if not an even multiple thereof, subject to a maximum of $300,000	$300,000

The maximum coverage would be determined as follows:

- Supplemental life coverage = $282,000
  282,000 (3 × $93,800, rounded up to next highest thousand)

- The basic plus supplemental life calculation yields $307,000 ($25,000 + $282,000) in combined coverage.

- Since the $307,000 exceeds the combined maximum, the supplemental life would be reduced by $7,000 to comply with the overall combined plan maximum. The employee would actually have $275,000 ($282,000 − $7,000) in supplemental life coverage and $25,000 basic life coverage.

Definitions

The definitions in the life/AD&D contract are essential for legal purposes, claim adjudication, and for risk management. Crisp, thorough definitions ensure smoother overall administration of the plan. Defined terms are customarily capitalized in the policy and booklet/certificate since they clarify and refine how policy provisions work. Carriers differ in the terms they use in contracts and how they define them. There are definitions that appear in all contracts that are critical in properly administering the plan.

Active Full-Time Employee and Actively at Work

An active full-time employee is a worker who is employed by the policyholder in the usual course of business on a continuous basis and who receives compensation for his or her work. It is a worker who routinely works an established minimum number of hours per week as set by the employer for the purpose of coverage eligibility. The employee must be performing the employee's usual material/substantial duties at the employer's place of business (or on business-related travel) to be considered actively at work.

Dependent

A dependent is a person related to the employee by blood or marriage. A dependent may be:

- A legal spouse (not legally separated).

- A domestic partner (as defined by the state).

- Biological, adopted, and step children up to the age of 18 or 19.

- Foster children and grandchildren up to the age of 18 or 19 who are solely dependent upon the employee for financial support.

- Handicapped children (no age limit).

- Children who are full-time students up to a specified cutoff age, usually from 21 to 27 years.

If an employee and spouse are both employed by the policyholder, they cannot be considered as both an employee and a dependent. And if they have children they want covered, each child can only be covered by one parent, not both parents.

Disabled

For employees, disabled means an impairing medical condition that prevents them from performing any occupation based on training, education, and experience. The disability must continue to last for 3, 6, 9, or 12 continuous months of the elimination or waiting period. Some carriers will not recognize the disability if it results from a self-inflicted injury. To tie into the accelerated death benefit, some carriers recognize an insured as being disabled if he or she has a life expectancy of 6–12 months or less.

Most carriers apply a "totally disabled" definition where the employee is unable to perform any occupation. A handful of carriers offer the choice of an "own occupation" definition for additional cost.

Earnings

Earnings are defined in contracts where the schedule applies a salary multiple to annual basic earnings to calculate the employee's amount of coverage. "Earnings" typically means the employee's average annual base salary or pay over the course of a year. The timeframe for determining the average is usually agreed upon by the policyholder and the insurer. The definition of earnings can be expanded to include commissions, bonus, or other variable pay. The amount in the employee's W-2 tax form is usually referenced when variable pay is included in the definition of earnings.

Physician

The term "physician" is defined since it is referenced and pivotal in GI, waiver of premium, accelerated death benefit provisions, and AD&D contracts. Physicians are essential in helping to determine health conditions related to the contract provisions. A physician must be a licensed practitioner who is practicing within the scope of his or her license. Physicians are often excluded contractually from diagnosing themselves or family members.

Retiree

If retiree coverage is part of the group life plan, the definition of retiree is included. A retiree is a former employee who has met the employer's qualifications as a retiree and who meets the minimum requirements to obtain life coverage. Retirees are rarely covered for AD&D.

Spouse

If dependent coverage is part of the group life plan, the definition of spouse is included. A spouse is the person who is legally married to the employee. This can include marriage via civil union and domestic partnership, depending on state regulations relating to coverage. Legally separated spouses or ex-spouses are usually not recognized as meeting the definition of spouse.

Student

A student is a dependent child (subject to a maximum cut-off age) who is financially dependent upon the employee and who attends (or is enrolled in) an institution of higher learning on a full-time basis. Usually, there is a minimum of 8 to 12 semester hours for which the student must be matriculated in order to qualify as a dependent student.

Effective Date of Coverage

The group policy refers to the effective date of coverage at both the policy level and at the individual insured's level. In order for the life/AD&D policy to be in effect to cover eligible employees and dependents, the following are required:

- The policyholder's application has been approved and accepted by the insurer.

- The monthly premium due has been received by the insurer within the timeframe prescribed in the policy.

- The policyholder complies with the administrative procedures and responsibilities outlined in the policy.

In order for life/AD&D coverage to be effective for employees, the following are required:

- The employee is in an eligible class.

- The employee has completed the eligibility waiting period.

- The required enrollment documentation has been completed and received by the policyholder within 31 days of completing the eligibility waiting period.

- The employee has had the required monthly premium contribution made.

- The evidence of good health (if required) has been approved by the insurer.

The effective date for dependent coverage usually occurs once the employee's coverage goes into effect, provided the dependent(s) has been enrolled within the 31-day enrollment window. When the employee acquires a new dependent, the employee must enroll the dependent for contributory coverage within 31 days of the date he or she is considered a dependent. If the enrollment takes place at a later date, the dependent is considered a "late entrant."

Decreases to the amount of an insured's coverage are effective on the date the applicable provision causing the decrease applies. For example, an ADEA age reduction is typically effective on the employee's birthday.

Deferred Effective Date

The deferred or delayed effective or active full-time requirement is a standard contractual provision that requires employees to be actively at work before coverage or increases in coverage can take effect. This includes increases in coverage due to an increase in annual basic earnings. The deferred effective date also applies to dependents who need to be able to engage in the normal activities of their age in order for coverage or increases in coverage to take effect.

Delaying the coverage effective date is a fundamental provision of any group life/AD&D contract. It is designed to limit anti-selection in that it screens out individuals who are too sick to work or engage in normal activities and who may have a potentially disabling condition. It limits employees or their dependents from trying to obtain insurance through employment solely because of a known dire medical condition.

If an employee is not actively at work on the date the coverage or increase in coverage would otherwise take effect, then the effective date will be delayed until the employee returns to work for one full day. Scheduled vacation or PTO days, weekends, or holidays ordinarily do not cause a delay in effective date if the coverage would otherwise have gone into effect.

If a dependent is confined in a hospital or other medical institution on the date their coverage or increase in coverage would otherwise take effect, then the effective date will be delayed until the dependent is no longer confined and is able to resume normal activities. Some insurers allow newborns to have coverage effective, despite being in the hospital, if it is a "normal" delivery or if the employee enrolled the newborn in advance.

Enrollment

For noncontributory life/AD&D coverage, enrollment is essentially automatic after the employee has completed the eligibility waiting period. Most insurers require the insured to complete an enrollment card and/or beneficiary designation as soon as is feasible.

For contributory coverage after the completed eligibility waiting period, the employee must decide whether or not to enroll since the employee must pay for some or all of the premium. The enrollment process requires the completion of a payroll deduction authorization request in addition to the enrollment card and beneficiary designation form. Until the documentation is completed and received by the policyholder, the employee (and dependents) is not officially enrolled in the plan.

Savvy benefits administrators suggest to employees that they complete and submit the required documentation right after hire, even before completing the eligibility waiting period. This averts the employee from forgetting to do the paperwork and thereby becoming a late entrant.

Eligible late entrants, whether in a traditional life/AD&D plan or as part of a Section 125 plan, are required to submit evidence of good health if they attempt to enroll after they have gone past the 31-day eligibility enrollment window.

Section 125 plans allow late entrants to enroll in the plan during the annual enrollment period. If the annual enrollment is an open enrollment, a late entrant may be able to enroll without providing evidence of good health.

A change in family status in a Section 125 plan allows an employee to enroll or to change benefit amounts during the plan year outside of the annual enrollment period if they have a qualifying event. Applicable family status changes include:

- Marriage

- Divorce

- New dependent

Evidence of good health is usually required to enroll or to increase benefits with a change in family status.

Carriers vary in their handling of change in family status or late entrant enrollment outside of Section 125 plans.

Termination of Coverage

After becoming covered, an employee's coverage will terminate at the earliest of the following events:

- The group policy is terminated.

- The employee is no longer in an eligible class or otherwise eligible for coverage.

- The employee's employment is terminated.

- The employee no longer wants the coverage and opts out.

- The premium due for the coverage has not been paid within the grace period.

After becoming covered, a dependent's coverage will terminate at the earliest of the following events:

- The group dependent policy is terminated.

- The employee is no longer in an eligible class or otherwise eligible for coverage.

- The dependent no longer meets the definition of dependent or is otherwise not eligible for coverage.

- The employee's employment is terminated.

- The employee or dependent no longer wants the coverage and the employee opts out.

- The premium due for the coverage has not been paid within the grace period.

Many carriers have contract language that extends coverage to the end of the month for both employee and dependents, provided the premium has been paid. For example, if an employee is terminated from employment on April 21, the employee's (and dependent's) coverage would continue until April 30.

Coverage Continuations

Carriers usually offer extensions on life/AD&D and dependent life coverage for certain situations that might otherwise cause insurance coverage to terminate. Such extensions are authorized by the underwriter. Some of the most common extensions are due to:

- Going from full-time to part-time employment status, in which case coverage continues to the last day of the first to third month following the month in which the change occurred.

- Being laid off due to a lack of work, in which case coverage continues to the last day of the first or second month following the month in which the layoff occurred.

- Taking an approved leave of absence [other than under the Family and Medical Leave Act (FMLA)] or sabbatical, in which case coverage continues to the last day of the first or second month following the month in which the leave commences.

- Taking an approved leave under FMLA (if included in the policy), in which case coverage can continue for up to 12 weeks from the date the leave commences.

- Taking a leave of absence due to injury or illness (not actively at work), in which case coverage can be continued for up to 12 continuous months from the initial date of the absence.

Many states mandate coverage extensions for employees who are activated and/or deployed Reservist/National Guard military personnel. Regulations vary by state.

Example 1: Extension Due to Layoff

Assume the following:

- The employee has basic, supplemental, and dependent life coverage through the employer.

- The plan for all lines allows for continuation of coverage after layoff to the last day of the month following the month in which the layoff occurred.

- The employee receives a pink slip on March 3.

In this example, all lines of the employee's coverage would be continued until April 30. Note, however, that the extension calls for the required premium to be paid and may be subject to benefit reductions stated in the policy. In addition, the extension terminates if the policy terminates.

Example 2: Extension Due to a Disabling Illness

Assume the following:

- A 62-year-old employee has basic, supplemental, and dependent life coverage through his employer.

- The employee becomes disabled due to illness.

- A standard Premium Waiver provision exists with an age 60 qualifying age.

- The employee's last day of being actively at work is March 4, 2012.

- The employee remains absent from work but exceeds the age to qualify for a waiver of premium (discussed next).

In this example, the employee's coverage continues until March 3, 2013, provided the required premiums are paid during the time period. The extension is subject to any benefit reductions stated in the policy. In addition, the extension terminates if the policy terminates.

Waiver of Premium

The waiver of premium provision provides continuation of coverage for employees who meet the contractual definition of disabled. It is also called a premium waiver or simply waiver. Coverage will be continued for the disabled employee and the employee's dependents coverage without premium cost for the duration of the disability, subject to approval by the insurer. Waiver coverage continues as long as the disabled person meets the contractual definition of disabled and/or the maximum waiver duration specified in the policy, even if the policy is cancelled by the policyholder and replaced by another carrier.

The waiver of premium rarely applies to AD&D coverage. The waiver applies only to disabled employees, not to disabled dependents. A waiver claimant can have dependent life coverage continued via the waiver provision, provided the dependents are already enrolled for coverage. A dependent who has a disability will continue to have dependent coverage the same as any other eligible dependent while the employee is on waiver. Qualifying for Waiver of Premium is usually not considered a qualifying event for change in family status.

There is a wide variety of waiver provisions available that are offered by group insurers. Richer versions will cost more. Insurers vary qualifications for waiver and duration of the waiver as a means of distinguishing their life contract from the competition. Below is an illustrative sampling of the most common waiver stipulations:

In order to qualify for a premium waiver, the employee must meet the following requirements:

- The disability begins prior to age 60. (Age 60 is standard, but the policy could specify 65, Social Security normal retirement age (SSNRA), or any age.)

- The insured is (Totally, 2 Year Own Occupation) disabled, according to the contractual definition.

- The insured remains continuously disabled for the specified elimination period (from 3, 6, or 9 months from the date the disability began) and remains disabled thereafter.

- The premium continues to be paid for the disabled person's coverage during the elimination period.

Waiver coverage continues until the waiver claimant:

- dies;

- no longer meets the definition of disabled;

- returns to active work (full- or part-time, as specified by policy);

- refuses to supply requested proof of loss to the insurer and/or refuses to be examined;

- attains some age limit associated with normal retirement age or a duration-of-time limit, such as:

- age 65 or SSNRA, if disabled prior to age 60;

- SSNRA, if disabled prior to age 60;

- 5 years, if disabled after age 60;

- SSNRA, if disabled prior to SSNRA;

- SSNRA, if disabled after age 60 but prior to SSNRA;

- 12 months, if disabled prior to age 65, SSNRA, or 70.

The amount of coverage while under the waiver provision is the amount in place on the date the employee's disability began. Such coverage is subject to contractual reduction provisions, such as ADEA age reduction.

Several important restrictions apply in most waiver-of-premium provisions:

- Waiver claimants cannot apply for portability coverage.

- Approval is not effective until approved by the insurer. The insurer may require proof of loss initially and once waiver is approved on an ongoing basis. The insurer determines the nature and level of proof of loss required.

- If the employee or covered dependent dies before being approved for waiver (typically during the elimination period), the insurer will pay a death claim to the beneficiary if the death occurs within one year of the last day worked.

- Proof of loss must be submitted within one year of the date last worked as an active full-time employee.

- If the policy terminates before the insured is approved for waiver, the face amount of coverage can be converted to an individual life policy. If the insured converts and is subsequently approved for waiver, the insurer will refund the conversion premiums that were paid.

- Insurers urge those who are awaiting waiver approval to convert in case the policy terminates altogether or, more than likely, the employer switches to another carrier.

The waiver applicant risks losing coverage since the application may not be approved and the employer's successor carrier will not recognize the applicant as eligible for coverage. (A successor carrier is not bound to pick up a prior carrier's pending waivers unless they meet the eligibility and coverage criteria of the successor carrier's policy.)

Conversion Privilege

The conversion privilege enables an insured who is losing some or all group life coverage to convert to an individual policy issued by the insurer. It is referred to as a "privilege" because the insured has the option to convert some or all of the face amount without being subject to evidence of good health.

The conversion privilege is standard in all group life contracts. It extends to both employee and dependent coverage. Many states have mandates regulating the conversion privilege as a means of ensuring those losing coverage have certain rights and access to continued life coverage. Conversion is not applicable to AD&D coverage.

The following events are the most common reasons for an insured person to convert:

- Employment ends.

- The employee's eligibility qualification status changes.

- The employee is going from full- to part-time employment.

- The employee is no longer part of an eligible class.

- The employee is unable to meet the actively-at-work requirement.

- The employee is losing a portion of coverage due to a change in class.

- The employee attains an age resulting in an ADEA age reduction.

- The employee retires.

In the event of the employee losing coverage, dependents can convert since their coverage is typically contingent upon the employee being covered. Dependents may also convert if they reach the contractual limiting age of the policy. Dependents can convert their coverage even if the employee chooses not to.

For many carriers, if the reason for loss of coverage is due to policy termination or termination of a class for coverage, the insurer requires the employee to have been continuously insured under the policy for not less than 5 years. In addition, conversion amounts are reduced by the amount for which the employee becomes eligible under another group policy within 31 days of coverage termination.

The insured employee or dependent must apply for conversion within 31 days of the qualifying event. Failure to apply within the 31-day election period means the conversion privilege is lost. If the employee dies within the 31-day conversion election period, the insurer will pay the beneficiary the full amount due had the conversion been made.

For reasons other than policy termination or termination of coverage for a class, the insured can convert any amount for which he or she was covered as of the date of the qualifying event. Those who convert can expect substantially higher premium rates than those that were paid under the group policy. However, many carriers allow the insured to increase the individual amount of coverage once insured under the individual conversion policy. It is estimated that only 1 or 2 percent of eligible employees actually take advantage of the conversion privilege. [6]

Example of Conversion

Assume the following:

- The employee's face amount of coverage was reduced from $50,000 to $32,500 due to an age 65 ADEA age reduction.

- The dependent spouse has coverage for 50 percent of the employee's amount, rounded up to the nearest $500.

- The spouse's coverage was reduced from $25,000 to $16,500.

The conversion could be:

- For all or some part of the $17,500 ($50,000 – $32,500) of lost coverage for the employee.

- For all or some part of the $8,500 [50% × ($25,000 – $16,500), rounded up to the nearest $500] of lost coverage for the spouse.

Portability

Portability is an optional provision that the employer can decide to add to the supplemental life contract, usually at additional cost. Portability typically does not apply to basic life or AD&D. Some carriers allow supplement dependent life to be ported. The provision enables employees who are terminating employment to "port" or carry their group insurance with them when the coverage might otherwise have ended. The insurer is now responsible for directly billing the employees who have ported.

To qualify for portability, the terminating employee must:

- be under age 65 or SSNRA;

- apply within 31 days of coverage termination.

Portability is similar to the conversion privilege in that evidence of good health is not required in order to port. The great advantage of portability lies in the fact that the employee will pay premiums at the group rate. Carriers who offer portability usually extend it to any dependent coverage that is also in effect for the employee.

Carriers apply various restrictions to the portability provision. Below is an illustrative sampling of those restrictions:

- The employee must have been continuously insured under the supplemental policy for not less than 6 (6 or 12) months.

- Retirees or disabled employees are not eligible to port coverage.

- Ported coverage can be continued for 3 (3 to 5) years or to age 70 (70 or 75).

- Waiver of premium is not included in the ported contract.

- An age reduction schedule may apply to ported amounts.

- A minimum of $5,000 (5,000 to $10,000) must be ported.

- Once an employee has selected a ported amount, the employee cannot opt up to a higher level for which he or she was previously eligible.

Employees (and dependents, if applicable) can port the full face amount of the supplemental life coverage they had in place on the day the employee's employment terminated.

Life Exclusions

Basic life contracts rarely contain any type of exclusion. A claim is payable due to death by any cause.

Because of the elective nature of supplemental life/AD&D, a suicide exclusion is a standard contract provision. The exclusion is a risk management mechanism designed to prevent a suicidal person from enrolling in coverage or increasing the amount of coverage in order to provide a beneficiary with a substantial benefit. No claim is payable on claims (or claim amounts) subject to the suicide exclusion.

Where not regulated by state mandate, the suicide exclusion applies for two years after the insured's initial effective date of coverage, after which full payment will be made to the beneficiary even in the event of suicide. If there is a subsequent increase in the amount of coverage, the suicide exclusion will be in effect for two years on the amount of the increase.

If a supplemental life/AD&D claim is denied on account of suicide, most carriers will pay to the beneficiary a refund of the premium contributions made for coverage under the supplemental plan.

AD&D Exclusions

Because individuals could harm themselves or engage in harmful behavior in order to collect an AD&D benefit, exclusions are imperative in the policy. Carriers vary in the types of exclusions stated in the contract, some of which may be standard for some carriers and optional for others. Below is an illustrative sampling of common AD&D exclusions. Benefits will not be paid when the death or dismemberment is the result of:

- an intentional self-inflicted injury, while sane or insane;

- an act of war, declared or undeclared;

- a medical treatment for illness or disease, except pyogenic infection resulting from an accidental wound;

- engagement in illegal activity;

- participation in a riot or civil disturbance;

- alcohol or drug intoxication or under the influence of drugs, unless prescribed by a physician;

- breaking applicable traffic laws or race car or stunt driving;

- working for pay or profit, because the employer would be responsible and worker's compensation would cover accidents at work;

- placing oneself in a foreseeably perilous situation.

Further, the AD&D loss typically has to occur within 365 days of the accident.

Assignment of Benefits

The assignment of benefits provision, sometimes called "absolute assignment," allows employees to assign their legal interest in the group life and AD&D policy to another person. The assigned person then has all the rights and privileges the employee had under the policy, including the right to name the beneficiary or to exercise the conversion privilege. Once the assignment has been made, only the assignee (person to whom the rights were given) can reverse or release the assignment. Such an assignment has been commonly used to avoid federal estate tax by removing the proceeds of an insurance contract from the insured's estate at death.[7]

Optional Benefits

In an effort to create marketplace distinctions and differentiators, carriers have developed an array of provisions that the employer can add to enhance the plan. Most of the options are offered as part of the AD&D contract and cover very specific loss situations. Most of the options have only modest price implications. Following is an illustrative sampling of optional benefits with brief descriptions.

Seatbelt and Airbag Benefit

When riding in a passenger vehicle driven by a licensed driver, an additional AD&D principal sum will be paid to a covered employee or dependent for losses relating to an accident in that vehicle if:

- the claimant was wearing a seatbelt;. or

- the airbag deployed.

The benefit is often from 5 percent to 15 percent of the principal sum and subject to a maximum of $10,000 to $25,000.

Repatriation Benefit

If death occurs outside the territorial boundaries of an insured's home state or country, an additional AD&D principal sum will be paid to the beneficiary (or person incurring the costs). The benefit is payable for reasonable costs for repatriation of the decedent's body to home, including preparation for burial or cremation.

The benefit is often from 5 percent to 10 percent of the principal sum and subject to a maximum of $3,000 to $5,000.

Education Benefit

An additional AD&D principal sum will be paid to the employee's dependents in the event of the employee's death. The benefit is payable to any dependent who is considered a student. For the purpose of this benefit, a student is defined as a dependent attending a post high school institution of higher learning or is in the 12th grade of high school and planning to attend an institution of higher learning within a year after the employee's death. The benefit per student is usually the lesser of 2 percent to 5 percent of the principal sum or $2,500 to $10,000. The benefit is payable in up to 4 annual payments. If there are no dependent students, the benefit will be paid to the beneficiary.

Felonious Assault Benefit

An additional AD&D principal sum is payable if the loss results from a felonious act of violence, such as robbery, burglary, kidnapping, hijacking, or murder. The amount of additional benefit is usually the lesser of 10 percent (to 25 percent) of the principal sum or $10,000 (to $25,000).

ERISA Conforming Instrument

Most group plans are established by the employer/plan sponsor under the auspices of ERISA. The ERISA conforming instrument outlines the rights and privileges that employees have in the group plan. It is called a conforming instrument because it fulfills an ERISA requirement of disclosure to employees.

Employee Proof of Coverage

The employee proof of coverage is a booklet/certificate detailing benefit provisions. It is issued to each covered employee. It is also termed the employee handbook, Summary Plan Description (SPD), or simply the certificate or cert. While many of these terms are used synonymously and interchangeably, they each have distinct legal ramifications. For example, a summary plan description has specific requirements under ERISA whereas some benefits administrators refer to a simplified, "folksy" booklet as a summary plan description.

Each booklet/certificate has a certifying page that states that the bearer is entitled to the benefits described therein. This certification can be used as proof of coverage in a court of law.

In today's electronic world, many insurers provide an e-copy to the policyholder who determines how to distribute the copies, via hardcopy printout, e-mail, or other electronic media. Certain states have regulations about the distribution of employee booklet/certificates.

Policy Provisions

Most insurers use a "policy of incorporation" or entire contract clause as their legally documented master contract rather than a separate policy issued to the employer and booklet/certificates to the employees. It consists of the booklet/certificate and policy provisions that are incorporated together to form the complete policy.

The policy provisions go only to the employer. The policy provisions describe the roles and responsibilities of the plan sponsor (policyholder) and the insurer in the operation of the plan and administration of the policy.

Since employees are not directly involved in the day-to-day administration of the group plan, it is not necessary for them to have a copy of the policy provisions. Figure 5-16 provides a summary of contract provisions affecting plan administration. Each of the terms contained in the summary are discussed below.

Figure 5-16. Contract Provisions Affecting Plan Administration

Premium	Policy Termination	Rate Guarantee	Renewal Notification	Amending the Contract	Discretionary Clause
Premium, billing method, and payment frequency	Termination of policy	Significant changes in census	Minimum notice of renewal	Approval process	Discretionary clause
Grace period	Notification of termination			Incontestability	

Premium

The contract provides a high level description of how premiums are to be calculated. Insurers offer two types of premium calculation and collection methods:

- The self-administered or self-accounting method, in which the employer calculates its own bill and submits the bill along with the calculated premium to the insurer. Carriers provide the policyholder with an administration manual, which details how to calculate the premium, along with forms and examples to assist in the process.

- The home office or direct billing method, in which the insurer creates the bill and sends it to the policyholder. The policyholder remits premium based on the insurer's bill. This option is typically reserved for smaller policyholders, since it requires more of the insurer's resources to administer.

The premium for the vast majority of group life plans is paid on a monthly basis, with payment due on the first day of the month for which coverage is provided. Quarterly or semiannual billing and premium payments can be accommodated. The insurer may load the rate or charge interest for quarterly or semiannual billing to make up for loss of cash flow and investment potential.

Grace Period

The policy of incorporation describes the grace period for submission of the premium payment, typically 31 days. If premium is not received within the stated grace period, then policy cancellation processes are begun by the insurer. Insurers occasionally extend the grace period for an additional 30 to 60 days beyond the standard 31-day grace period. This extension, or deferred premium arrangement, is usually offered to select policyholders. In exchange for extending the grace period, the policyholder agrees to pay an additional premium amount to make up for the loss of cash flow and investment potential.

Even if the policy is allowed to lapse or is terminated during the grace period, the policyowner is legally liable for the payment of any premium due during the portion of the grace period when the contract was still in force. [8]

Termination of Policy

The termination of policy provision entitles the insurer to terminate coverage after first providing 31 to 60 days of notice to the policyholder if certain situations occur, such as the:

- Policyholder's failure to meet its contractual or administrative duties.

- Policyholder's failure to provide appropriate information in order to operate the plan.

- Number of covered persons falling below a minimum based on underwriting guidelines or statutory requirements.

Some insurers authorize themselves to interrupt the rate guarantee if the policyholder is not acting in good faith or in the best interests of the plan.

Minimum Notice of Renewal

Most group insurers will not guarantee a renewal offer to the policyholder. In practice, however, not offering a renewal is rare. The contract will indicate the minimum notice that the insurer must provide to the policyholder to initiate renewal/rate action. This minimum notice is subject to statutory regulation. The minimum notice ranges from between 60 to 90 days. Policyholders who have multiple locations or who have challenges in communicating with their employees often request a minimum notification of 120 days, which underwriters are generally willing to accommodate.

Rate Guarantee

The initial rate guarantee is typically stated in the policy. Rate guarantees on group life are in effect from 2 to 5 years. Some carriers may marry the Life/AD&D rate guarantee to other lines of coverage they provide (e.g., medical) which might have only a one year rate guarantee. The policy describes reasons the rate guarantee may be suspended or renegotiated. The most common reasons are:

- an increase or decrease of more than 5 percent to 15 percent of the insured population;

- a change to the plan or a policy amendment;

- an addition or deletion of an affiliate or subsidiary;

- a material misrepresentation of data provided to the insurer in the request for proposal and bid process.

Amending the Contract

The policyholder can request changes to the contract at any time. However, before the request is processed, it first must be approved by the underwriter. Moreover, changes to the policy are not recognized and do not go into effect until an officer of the insurance company approves and authorizes them in writing. The policyholder is then asked to countersign the amendment, which becomes part of the master policy.

State or federal regulations may require the insurer to amend the contract language. In such case, the insurer will act unilaterally to comply with the law and amend the contract. The insurer will inform the policyholder about the amendment and any related rate change 31 to 60 days before the amendment is to go into effect.

Incontestability

Except for the nonpayment of premiums, the validity of the contract cannot be contested after it has been in force for a specified period, generally one or two years. During this time, the insurance company can contest the contract on the basis of policyowner statements in the request for proposal and application attached to the contract that are considered to be material misrepresentations. [9]

Discretionary Clause

A discretionary clause states that the insurer has the sole authority and discretion to interpret the language and provisions in the policy. The insurer's discretion applies as to how the contract language affects the benefit payments and the operation of the plan.

This clause has been challenged by several states' Department of Insurance because of the belief that an inherent conflict of interest exists between the entity that issues the policy (the insurer) versus the entity that interprets the policy (again, the insurer) and adjudicates the claims.

The ERISA conforming instrument describes the responsibilities of the employer/plan sponsor and the insurer in operating the plan. It will:

- state the plan sponsor, the sponsor's employer identification number, and the insurer;

- describe the employees' right to view and receive information about the plan, including assistance with questions;

- explain the role of plan fiduciaries, those responsible for operating the plan, who must act in the best interests of the plan and those who are insured under it;

- describe claim procedures, including timeframes in which a claim must be processed as well as the appeals process for a denied claim.

Key Takeaways

- Dependent life amounts and schedules may be subject to statutory restrictions.

- Holidays, scheduled PTO time, and vacation time typically do not cause interruption of the eligibility waiting period. Nor do they delay the effective date of coverage.

- ADEA compliance regarding group life plan design is an employer responsibility. However, underwriters have a vested interest in ensuring plan compliance.

- ADEA age reduction schedules do not apply to retiree coverage.

- ADEA age reductions do not apply directly to dependents, but dependent coverage amounts can be affected if they are based on the employee's face amount.

- Retirees are rarely covered for AD&D. Retirees are not eligible to continue coverage under portability.

- Waiver rarely applies to AD&D coverage.

- The conversion privilege enables a person who is losing coverage to convert to an individual policy without evidence of good health.

- If the employee dies within the 31-day conversion election period, the insurer will pay the beneficiary the amount the employee would have been entitled to convert.

- Insurers vary in the principal sum amounts for AD&D casualty losses as well as the contractual exclusions.

- Basic life benefits are payable for death from any cause. Supplemental life benefits are subject to the suicide exclusion.

- Insurers offer a wide variety of waiver of premium options from which the employer can select.

- A waiver of premium, upon approval, allows basic/supplemental life and dependent life coverage to continue without premium payment. Such waivers only apply to employees.

- Disabled employees are required to satisfy a 3-, 6-, or 9- month elimination or waiting period before qualifying for waiver of premium.

- Portability offers employees losing coverage on account of employment termination the ability to take basic/supplemental and dependent life coverage with them at group rates and without being required to provide evidence of good health.

- Annual enrollments are not always "open" enrollments. An open enrollment can occur during an annual enrollment in a Section 125 plan. This enables late entrants to enroll into the plan without providing evidence of good health.

- Insurers develop situation-specific benefit provisions as a means of differentiating themselves in the group life marketplace.

- A booklet/certificate is issued to each employee in one form or another. The policy provisions detailing plan operation and administration as well as the responsibilities of the plan sponsor/employer and the insurer are issued to the plan sponsor/ employer. Together they comprise the entire master contract.

- The insurer can terminate the policy if the policyholder fails to meet the policyholder responsibilities outlined in the contract.

- The standard premium grace period is 31 days.

- A policyholder's failure to pay the required premium with the grace period can result in cancellation of the policy.

- Insurers amend group contracts unilaterally in order to comply with state and federal regulations.

Endnotes

1. Kirner, Tom and Pete Silkowski, *Group Benefits Disability Specialist Handbook* (Erlanger, KY: The National Underwriter Company), p. 8-8.

2. Ibid.

3. Ibid.

4. Ibid., p. 4-14.

5. Ibid., p. 4-15.

6. Beam, Burton T., Jr., and John J. McFadden, *Employee Benefits,* Eighth Edition (New York, NY: Kaplan Publishing), p. 163.

7. Ibid., p. 159.

8. Ibid.

9. Ibid., p. 160.

Chapter 6

Life and AD&D Risk Selection

This chapter discusses the factors an insurance company underwriter takes into consideration on a Group Life and Accidental Death & Dismemberment (AD&D) case when evaluating whether to accept the risk, and if so, how those factors will affect pricing and plan structure. The underwriter may add charges, restrictions, limitations, and conditions in order to make the risk of a case acceptable. An understanding of this process will help the producer in assessing whether his or her client represents a good risk for the insurer. This will help the Producer in understanding the rates a particular insurer may charge and any restrictions, limitation, or conditions the underwriter may place in the proposal or renewal on the case under consideration. The information is also generally useful to other group insurance professionals in understanding the considerations and processes the underwriter utilizes when evaluating potentially new customers as well as renewing existing clients.

Risk Selection Considerations

Seeking only the most attractive industries with the youngest employees is not what sound underwriting and risk selection are about for group life and AD&D. There are a myriad of factors to consider in determining if a prospective policyholder is the right risk to put on the books at a particular point in time. Careful consideration also needs to be given to renewing an existing policyholder.

The risk selection process is, in large part, driven by the insurer's objectives. An insurer who is in growth mode and who is willing to price below-needed rates in order to garner and expand market share certainly has a different objective than the insurer whose emphasis is measured growth with solid near-term profits. These considerations also vary by what the insurer may consider as its target markets. An insurer who mainly targets small employers (fewer than 100 employees) will approach a large case of 5,000 lives differently than an insurer whose target market is cases over 1,000 lives.

The group life underwriter takes a holistic approach to evaluating the risk with the following questions in mind:

- Can a long-term relationship be established with the policyholder?

  - Group life/AD&D rates are extremely competitive and below-needed rates are often quoted and sold. It may take several renewal cycles for the insurer to recoup the acquisition costs and to get the rates to an appropriate, self-sustaining level.

- Will we ever have a chance to make a profit on this case?

  - If the policyholder is strictly shopping rates and has a history of changing insurers frequently, the likelihood that the insurer will have the lowest rate on future bid situations is low. If the needed rate cannot be achieved over time, the chances for the case to operate at a profitable level are significantly diminished.

If the answer to both of these questions is "no," the underwriter must have other compelling reasons for agreeing to take on the risk. For instance, the underwriter may agree to take on a less-than-ideal case in order to establish a relationship with a new producer or to make inroads into a new market. These are often termed as "business decisions" by underwriting management.

No one factor drives the risk selection decision. Rather, all the factors are weighed together to help the underwriter answer the above questions and justify his or her decision. Moreover, underwriters understand that when higher risk cases are selected for the aforementioned "business reasons," it does not reflect negatively on their skills, knowledge, or judgment.

Risk Selection Process

The case underwriter considers all aspects of the risk before deciding to quote on a prospect or to renew an existing client. The decision of whether to quote/renew is married to the contract provisions, service arrangements, and rates the underwriter offers. If any aspect of these cannot be structured to the underwriter's satisfaction, the underwriter may decline to quote/renew. We'll examine key elements in the risk evaluation and selection process.

Eligible Groups and Ineligible Groups

Group insurers entertain a wide range of potential clients for life and AD&D coverage. Most insurers attempt to be as expansive as possible in considering groups that they deem eligible for coverage. Each group insurer's underwriting guidelines delineate groups that are eligible and ineligible to quote. A prospect may be deemed ineligible because the group:

- Is not a legally operating or legally recognized enterprise.

- Does not have a clear employer-employee relationship.

  - Examples include professional employer organizations (PEOs), multiple employer welfare arrangements (MEWAs), and seasonal and/or migratory laborers.

- Has formed solely and exclusively for the purpose of obtaining insurance.

  - Most insurers require the entity to exist for a noninsurance reason.

- May not conform to the insurer's compliance requirements.

  - Examples include non-ERISA plans and clients that have been convicted of engaging in illegal activity.

- Represents a hazard too great to underwrite.

  - Examples may include coal miners, manufacturers of cigarettes and other tobacco products, offshore oil/gas extraction, and companies with excessive employee turnover.

- Represents a financial risk too great to underwrite.

  - Examples include clients operating under Chapter 11 and clients that were cancelled by the prior carrier for nonpayment of premium.

  - Is not acceptable to the reinsurer's underwriting guidelines.

- Has contract provisions or service requirements the insurer is not equipped to handle.

  - Examples include unique premium waiver provisions requiring state filing, dedicated claims examiners, or onsite enrollment specialists.

States have various laws that regulate what can be considered an eligible group for insurance purposes as well. Insurance carriers will not quote on a "group" that is legally prohibited from purchasing insurance as a group.

Coverage Split Between Insurers

Although it is relatively rare, there can be a situation where insurer "A" provides basic life coverage for a group and insurer "B" provides the supplemental or voluntary life coverage for that group. It is usually no more challenging to assess or price each risk in this circumstance, but both underwriters are cognizant that a viable competitor exists within the overall framework of the group life plan. The risk that the client might leave to consolidate all life coverage with one carrier for ease of administration must be considered.

Such a split in coverage is not a reason to decline or not quote on the case, although both underwriters will inquire as to the reasoning behind having two different carriers. The fact that there is viable competition makes the underwriter more vigilant in meeting producer and customer expectations. The policyholder benefits since each insurer will keep the other "honest." The underwriter may ultimately view the situation as a challenge to wrest the other line of coverage away from the competition.

Foreign Exposure

Insurers vary widely in their appetite for and ability to handle foreign exposure, particularly on expatriates. An expatriate is a U.S.-based employee working for an American company abroad.

In general, group insurers prefer to cover U.S, citizens or legally documented workers from another country who are working in the United States. As the global economy grows, insurers are encountering more requests to cover citizens of different nationalities. Below is a brief overview of potential requests to expand eligibility into the group plan.

There are different exposure situations with exposure to expatriates and to foreign nationals, including:

- U.S. citizens working in a foreign country (the expatriate).

  - Most insurers are flexible enough to be able to handle nominal expatriate foreign exposure in nonhazardous environments. However, having an extraordinarily high number of expatriates to cover or having expatriates working in a hazardous environment might exceed standard underwriting guidelines and force the underwriter to decline to quote the business.

  - Some insurers might have certain countries that they have deemed too risky, and their underwriters cannot write coverage on persons residing and working there.

  - Underwriters will typically inquire as to the expected length of an expatriate's assignment abroad. Permanent assignments abroad may cause the underwriter to inquire more about the nature of the assignment.

- Foreign nationals working in the United States.

  - Most insurers can cover foreign nationals working legally in the United States, provided they have appropriate documentation (e.g., a green card) and are paying required payroll taxes.

  - Foreign Nationals working for an American company assigned to work in the United States. For example, a German citizen working for an American company in New York City.

  - Waiver of premium claims on foreign nationals can present problems. It can be very difficult for the insurer to administer waiver provisions for claimants who have returned home or who are living abroad after having worked in the United States.

- Citizens of a foreign country working for an American company in a third country [the third country national (TCN)]. For example, an Italian citizen working for an American company in Japan may be challenging in navigating through the legal and compliance regulations of the countries involved.

  - Foreign countries have insurance regulations, just as the Unites States does. Unless the U.S. insurer is licensed to do business in the foreign country, covering TCNs is generally illegal.

  - Some carriers may have arrangements with domestic insurers to cover such contingencies as TCN's or foreign nationals.

The risk for life and premium waiver claims can increase substantially if the expatriates are working in a war zone or in an area that is a prime target for terrorism or kidnapping. AD&D risk for expatriates in such dangerous situations is usually limited by the standard AD&D contractual war exclusion.

In some cases, the underwriter may arrange for expatriates in a hazardous environment to have their own separate class and possibly limit their benefits and/or increase the reinsurance level on this class. The other option is for the underwriter to arrange for separate individual coverage for the expatriates or to have the risk reinsured through a specialty insurer or reinsurer. This might be awkward administratively and may increase the case expenses, but it may be a workable solution.

Industry Risk

Insurers know that mortality rates vary by industry. Insurers vary as to how they view mortality risk from a risk management perspective. Some insurers are more willing to accept higher risk levels than others. However, there are certain high-risk industries that cause most group insurers to be very circumspect in offering life or AD&D coverage. Figure 6-1 provides a sampling of such industries.

Figure 6-1. High-Risk Industries				
Industry	**Hazardous Occupation**	**High Premium Waiver Risk**	**High Employee Turnover or Seasonal Employment**	**Many Claims in One Incident (Excessive Concentration of Risk)**
Car washing		✓	✓	
Chemical, paint manufacture	✓	✓		✓
Deep sea fishing	✓	✓		✓
Demolition	✓	✓		✓
Explosives	✓			✓
Exterminators	✓	✓		
Farming	✓	✓	✓	
Fireman	✓	✓		✓
Flight crews		✓		✓
Heavy construction	✓	✓		
Logging	✓	✓		
Mining	✓	✓		✓
Nightclubs, bars		✓	✓	
Oil and gas extraction	✓	✓		✓
Police	✓	✓		
Railroads	✓	✓		✓
Slaughterhouses	✓	✓		
Tree surgeons	✓	✓		

Does this mean that such high risk groups are not offered life or AD&D coverage from group insurers? Absolutely not. It does mean, however, that they must be underwritten with careful plan design structure and with premium rates that are likely to be considerably higher than for other groups. For insurers with greater risk tolerance, certain high risk groups may be attractive, since there is potentially less competition from other carriers.

Customer Finances

The underwriter is likely to conduct research about the nature of a prospect's business, in part, to ensure that the reported SIC or NAICS code lines up with what the business actually does. The larger the case, the more intensive will be the research. This research is likely to include an investigation of the prospect's finances. The financial research for life coverage is not as crucial as for medical or disability coverages, since unstable client finances are unlikely to have an impact on life or AD&D claims incidence.

A review of a prospect's finances also serves other important functions in the risk selection process. The review will help the underwriter to:

- gauge the prospect's ability to pay premiums;

- determine if cash flow options, such as an extended grace period, should be offered;

- determine any liens or pending lawsuits that may impact the client's ability to support the group benefits plan.

There are many good resources available to underwriters to conduct a financial analysis, such as Standard & Poors, Moody's, and D&B, not to mention the plethora of information available via the Internet on publicly traded companies.

Other Lines of Coverage

All group insurers offer multiline discounts. Most carriers consider basic life, AD&D, supplemental life, and dependent life as one line of coverage. However, when these are added to an employer's existing medical coverage, for example, the insurer might offer to reduce the rates of both lines by 5 percent. This is possible because of the administrative cost to add the life insurance to the existing medical plan is modest, since the systems and accounting are already in place.

From a risk management perspective, most underwriters would prefer to have as many lines of coverage with the client as possible. The advantages of the multiline strategy are:

- Having the ability to internally "cross apply" for projection purposes the surplus or loss from one line to another to competitively structure the rates.

- Preventing competitors from making inroads into the plan if they have a foot in the door via a line of coverage.

- Utilizing data across lines of coverage to more accurately evaluate experience data.

  - For example, an insurer could use diagnosis data from the medical plan to tie into short-term disability (STD) claim incidence and duration patterns. Or, the insurer might use long-term disability (LTD) data to help better assess premium waiver claims on life insurance.

In the past, group insurers often required the life insurance to be packaged or bundled with the medical insurance and would not offer medical coverage alone. The concept was that life coverage was generally profitable whereas medical coverage was quite volatile. Today, this practice is prohibited by statute in most states.

When quoting multiple lines of coverage, the underwriter will usually quote the lines together as a package and quote them on a self-sustaining basis. This ensures that if the policyholder selects only one or two lines, the rates will be adequate to cover the risk. Figure 6-2 provides an example.

Figure 6-2. Quoted Single and Packaged Rates of Insurance					
Life Only	*STD Only*	*Medical Only*	*Life and STD*	*Life and Medical*	*Life, STD, and Medical*
$.33 per $1,000	$.49 per $100 weekly benefit	Emp. $317.60 Deps. $446.96	Life $.31 per $1,000 STD $.47 per $100 weekly benefit	Life $.31 per $1,000 Medical Emp. $301.72 Deps. $424.61	Life $.30 per $1,000 STD $.44 per $100 weekly benefit Medical Emp. $285.84 Deps. $402.26

The factor most difficult for the underwriter to assess is the amount of individual life/AD&D coverage that employees might have through private purchase or through a mass marketer of individual life policies through their affiliation in a group. Having individual life coverage usually lessens an employee's need for group life coverage. Thus, individually covered employees will not opt for supplemental coverage through the group plan to be offered, thereby reducing profitability of the plan and increasing the participation risk.

It is impossible for an underwriter to determine how many employees have privately purchased individual life policies, much less their amounts of coverage. However, an underwriter might be able to guess at levels of individual life coverage if individual policies are mass marketed through the employee's association with the group. The following groups are routinely offered individual policies through group associations:

- Police

- Firefighters

- Teachers

- Nurses

Although individual life coverage may impact employee participation in supplemental life and AD&D, it should have minimal impact on the risk selection decision.

Managing Risk Through Plan Structure

As discussed in Chapter 5, having a plan structure that controls risk is one of the ways that an otherwise very risky group can be placed on the insurer's books. Appropriate plan design in the contract is important not only for high-risk groups but for all groups. Proper plan design is the fundamental means by which the rates for the garden variety risk are kept reasonable. Moreover, an inappropriate plan design can cause the "garden variety" group to become a high-risk client because of the overly rich plan. Finally, inappropriate plan design can cause a plan to fail the IRS's "discrimination tests" with the result that employees will not benefit from the Section 79 premium exclusion (see Chapter 10) and the employer may not be able to deduct the cost of the program as an ordinary business expense. The most common risk-managing aspects of plan design are related to the eligibility waiting period, coverage classes of employees to be covered such as part-time employees, maximum benefits, GI limits, deferred effective dates, evidence of good health, participation levels, enrollment types, step rates, and rate guarantees.

Eligibility Waiting Period

The eligibility waiting period is the length of time an employer wants a new employee to be continuously employed and at work before the employee is eligible for group coverage. It can be as short as the date of hire or as long as one or more years. It can be expressed in days, months, or years. In industries that have traditionally high turnover, a longer waiting period might make sense to avoid the administrative hassle of enrolling an employee only to have the person leave.

Although the employer establishes the eligibility waiting period for the plan, the underwriter must approve it. Generally, the underwriter accepts what the employer has established. However, in higher-risk industries, particularly those with a history of high turnover, the underwriter may require an increase in the length of waiting period, particularly if there is a history of life claimants who were recent hires.

Eligibility of Classes and Part-Time Employees

Using classes of employees to control entry into and eligibility for benefits can be an effective tool in managing risk. Benefits can vary by class. If a class of employees within a group is significantly more risky than the rest of the group, the underwriter can adjust the plan for that class.

Regardless of the line of coverage, most underwriters would prefer to cover active, full-time employees working a weekly minimum of 20 hours per week. The concern is that a part-timer might take on employment just to obtain coverage for a known condition that predisposes them for a claim. This concern is compounded by the fact that part-timers may not be physically well enough to work a full-time schedule. To mitigate the risk, the underwriter might place part-timers in a separate class and provide them with a less rich schedule than that provided for active, full-time employees.

Because there is limited choice in having a life or AD&D claim, underwriters are not as concerned with covering part-timers for life insurance as for other coverages, such as short- or long-term disability insurance. The suicide exclusion is a standard contract provision on supplemental life policies, and self-inflicted injuries are a standard AD&D exclusion. Therefore, most underwriters are more comfortable with offering life and AD&D to part-timers versus any other type of group coverage

Maximum Benefit

The underwriter is charged with ensuring that the life/AD&D maximum offered is commensurate with the insured's particular industry. For example, the underwriter might question a request for an extraordinarily high maximum in an industry in which low maximums have been historically pervasive.

Insurers apply a formula from their underwriting guidelines to determine the highest maximum benefit that can be offered to a group. The formula applies to the case characteristics and often is based on any or all of the following:

- Guaranteed issue limit

  - All carriers have limits on how much life insurance on an individual in a group they will issue on a guaranteed (GI) basis, that is, without evidence of good health.

- Industry

  - Some carriers have issue limits based on the industry in which the group works. These limits may be based on the experience of their own book of business and/ or on what is generally considered to be a high-risk industry and thus may vary from carrier to carrier.

- Overall coverage volume and/or average amount of coverage per employee or annual premium

- Number of employees

  - Risk spread through the law of large numbers may be considered in the maximum benefit formula.

- Reinsurance requirements

  - The insurer most likely will obtain reinsurance on larger face amounts or on an aggregate amount of the group as a whole. The reinsurer likely will have some risk considerations and requirements with which the underwriter must comply.

Certain high risk groups may be considered outside of the formula guidelines for determining the maximum benefit. Specific maximum guidelines would apply.

Most insurers have guidelines designed to preclude executives or high earners from having a disproportionately high maximum compared to the rank and file of the group. It runs against the principles of group coverage for executives to construct a plan that effectively amounts to individual insurance coverage. The guidelines would limit the difference in maximums to perhaps 2, 3, or 4 times that of the next highest class. Figure 6-3 provides an example.

Figure 6-3. Differences in Maximums between Classes		
Class	**Inappropriate Difference Between Classes**	**Appropriate Difference Between Classes**
Class 1 – Officers	4 × annual basic earnings, rounded to the next highest $1,000, to a maximum of $500,000	4 × annual basic earnings, rounded to the next highest $1,000, to a maximum of $500,000
Class 2 – All Other Employees	$25,000	2 × annual basic earnings, rounded to the next highest $1,000, to a maximum of $250,000

Dependent spouse maximums can be subject to certain states' statutory limitations. While a maximum of $50,000 for spouses is not uncommon, requests for significantly higher amounts will be questioned by the underwriter. Again, the underwriter is the guardian in ensuring that the group life plan is not being designed to provide what amounts to individual coverage for an executive's or high earner's spouse. Often times, such requests are the policyholder's way of providing an additional fringe benefit to the executive.

A requested maximum that is very high in relation to the industry and other risk factors can be a deal breaker, and it may cause the underwriter to walk away from a prospect. There may be reinsurance restrictions that preclude the underwriter from offering a requested maximum. However, underwriters work hard to accommodate a prospect's or existing client's plan maximum requests and endeavor to come up with creative solutions, such as helping to arrange for individual life coverage for certain employees.

Most insurers' underwriting guidelines apply a cap on the combined basic and supplemental life maximums that can be offered on a case. Some also will include AD&D as part of that cap formula.

Guaranteed Issue Limit

The *Guaranteed Issue (GI)* or "nonmedical" limit is the maximum amount of life and/or AD&D coverage an individual can obtain without having to provide evidence of good health to the insurer.

The underwriting guidelines have formulas for determining the GI level for the case. The factors typically applied in determining the case or class GI limit are:

- Schedule of benefits (earnings multiples)

- Maximum (combined) basic + supplemental benefit

- Average amount of coverage on each employee

- Number of employees and/or dependents to be covered

The GI limit is one of the most effective mechanisms the underwriter has in controlling the risk and exposure on a case. Being able to establish the appropriate GI level is a key consideration in the risk selection process.

On takeover situations, the underwriter is routinely asked to match the maximum benefit and GI levels offered by the prior carrier. Underwriters are generally comfortable in doing so, unless there is credible experience or history of abnormally high claims in excess of the GI. In some bid situations, the policyholder and/or the producer will test the market to see if a higher maximum and/or GI can be obtained. This is when the underwriter must consider all other aspects of the risk before agreeing to quote on the case.

Although it is unusual, an excessively high GI limit in relation to all of the other risk factors of a case may cause the underwriter to shy away from quoting. More than likely, the underwriting would load the rates for the additional risk.

Deferred Effective Date

The deferred effective or active, full-time requirement is a standard contractual provision that requires employees to be actively at work before coverage or increases in coverage can take effect. The deferred effective date also applies to dependents who must be able to engage in the "normal activities of their age" in order for coverage or increases in coverage to take effect. It is a prime risk-management mechanism designed to prevent those most likely to have a claim from obtaining coverage or, more frequently, increases to existing coverage.

When switching insurers, producers or policyholders sometimes ask the new carrier to waive the deferred effective date requirement out of fear that an employee may lose coverage because of the switch. Although such instances of an employee with a potentially disabling condition not being covered under either the prior carrier or new carrier are infrequent, the possibility does exist. However, waiving the deferred effective date entirely is a drastic measure to take to ease the fear. It's analogous to pulling a tooth simply to get rid of a small cavity.

Most insurers have enhanced continuation provisions that can be added to a contract to reduce the potential for this problem. Many underwriters in the quote process will request a list of potential premium waiver claimants to determine whose liability these claimants would be if a switch in carriers does occur. If the policyholder insists on having the deferred effective date waived entirely, it may cause the underwriter to decline to quote.

Evidence of Good Health (aka Evidence of Insurability, EOI, EI)

Evidence of Good Health (explained in Chapter 5) is typically required for late entrants or when an insured has exceeded the GI limit. It sometimes applies in a Section 125 plan where employees can opt for more than one level of increase in earnings multiple.

Some insurers allow "short form" or "simplified medical underwriting" as evidence of good health for situations that exceed their standard underwriting guidelines. The short-form evidence may apply when:

- minimum participation levels are not met on supplemental life;

- employees request more than one earnings level in a plan allowing a choice of earnings multiples;

- employees' coverage exceeds the GI limit on account of an increase in earnings.

A new carrier may be asked to accept the short-form evidence of good health process the prior carrier had in place. While most carriers are able to accommodate this, other carriers might not have the processes and/or systems in place to support the request. Moreover, short-form medical underwriting may run contrary to their underwriting philosophy. If an underwriter is unable to accommodate the policyholder's short-form request and it is crucial to the policyholder, it may cause the policyholder to disqualify the carrier from the bid process.

Participation Levels

To lessen the antiselection risk on supplemental life and AD&D, most underwriters require a minimum enrollment percentage or participation level of the eligible employees in the plan. The idea is to attract as many younger, healthier employees into the plan as possible. Having a minimum participation requirement is designed to protect the insurer from having only the highest risks covered, since those most in need of coverage are the most likely to enroll.

Many insurers establish a minimum participation of 20–25 percent of the eligible employees. If the current or projected participation level is below minimum underwriting guidelines, it may be a reason to not quote on the supplemental life and AD&D.

Determining the projected participation level with a change in carriers is tricky. The underwriter will typically assume that the most current level of participation will continue after the changeover. The tricky part is projecting how successful the new insurer's enrollment tactics might be in increasing enrollment. The questions the underwriter will try to answer are:

- How will the underlying basic life plan affect participation in supplemental life and AD&D?

  - Does a rich basic life plan discourage employees from enrolling in supplemental?

- How much can the average employee afford to spend on supplemental life and AD&D?

- How will the enrollment process be different than that of the past?

  - Will there be a new or different communication campaign to the employees?

  - Will the policyholder actively endorse and communicate the value of the plan?

  - Will the policyholder allow and encourage the insurer's enrollment specialists access to the employees?

  - How can technology be used to make enrollment easier?

The underwriter usually has confidence in the insurance company's ability to increase participation in the supplemental life/AD&D plan over the prior carrier's participation level. If the underwriter is not confident that projected participation minimums can be met after the sale, the underwriter may abstain from quoting.

The underwriter is likely to adjust the formula rates based on projected employee participation in the plan. The trickiest element is what to do if, after accepting the risk, the minimum participation levels are not met at enrollment? Readjusting the rates upward to account for the increased risk is likely to drive participation downward as those who need the coverage least will be driven out by the increased cost. Rejecting the case and refusing to accept the policyholder on the books after all the change processes are underway is impractical. Thus, trying to project anticipated participation is integral in the risk selection process and looms large in the decision of whether or not to quote on a case.

Enrollment Type

To protect against anti-selection, most life and AD&D policies require a late entrant to submit evidence of good health. A "late entrant" is an eligible employee who previously declined coverage but is now seeking it outside of the normal initial enrollment period. The risk is that such persons change their minds because they have contracted a potentially life-threatening or potentially disabling condition.

In a traditional life plan, the underwriter will want to establish:

- limits to the amount of coverage for which a late entrant can apply;

- if the late entrant's evidence of good health application is denied, whether the applicant can reapply at a later date.

In a Section 125 or flexible benefits plan, the underwriter needs to consider the ways in which a late entrant can enroll:

- Will there be an "open enrollment" at change in carriers?

    - An open enrollment allows a late entrant to enroll during the annual enrollment period up to the GI limit without evidence of good health.

- Will open enrollments be allowed each year?

    - Many underwriters are uncomfortable with allowing an open enrollment each year, as it dilutes one of the most effective risk management provisions in the contract.

- At annual enrollment, can an employee increase the amount of coverage one or more levels without evidence of good health?

If standard anti-selection provisions relating to enrollment are not in the life contract and if the policyholder refuses to accept them, it may be cause for the underwriter to refrain from quoting. Further, if the administrative process on the part of the employer for allowing late entrants to enroll is unclear, this may cause hesitancy on the part of the underwriter to place the business on the books.

Step Rates versus Composite Rates

Basic life is typically noncontributory. Since all employees are enrolled, there is a good spread of risk between younger and older employees, so a single, composite rate usually applies.

Because of the elective nature of supplemental life and AD&D where employees usually pay the full cost, underwriters routinely require the rates to be structured on a step-rated or age-bracketed basis. This is done to ensure the rates are fairly distributed based on age and in order to ensure maximum participation in the plan.

Some clients are resistant to step rates because of the increased complexity required to report on the monthly billing calculation. It's not necessarily a deal breaker in terms of risk selection and is understandable with smaller policyholders. The underwriter may load the composite rate to account for the fact that the younger employees are less likely to enroll at the higher rate that is being driven by the older employees.

Reinsurance

Most group insurers will have some form of reinsurance on the life and AD&D blocks of business. The types of reinsurance arrangements vary widely among insurers based on an insurer's:

- total assets and balance sheet;

- risk tolerance;

- objectives and targets for the life business.

Since the reinsurer is a business partner of the insurer and has a vested interest in the financial performance of the programs that are being reinsured, the reinsurer will ensure that its underwriting guidelines are applied on top of the insurer's own standard underwriting guidelines.

When a reinsurer's underwriting limits are exceeded on a particular case, the reinsurer will generally refuse to reinsure the risk or will suggest a load to the rate. It would be unusual for an insurer to select and cover an insurance program on which the reinsurer has refused to extend an offer of reinsurance coverage.

Concentration of Risk

In a post 9/11 world, most carriers evaluate the terrorism or catastrophic event risk they face if a prospect's worksite were to be attacked, resulting in numerous employee deaths and disabilities. This consideration is extended to other situations in which a catastrophic loss of life or disability might occur, such as a construction site, a mine, or an offshore drilling derrick.

The underwriter is charged with determining how many employees are in a particular location as well as the amount of life coverage those employees have. If the number of employees in a certain work location exceeds underwriting guidelines, it is likely the underwriter will need to submit the details of the exposure to the reinsurer.

In most situations, concentration of risk has a minimal impact on the risk selection process because of the random nature of such catastrophic events. However, the initial rates developed by the underwriter may have to be adjusted to account for the additional charge that a reinsurer might have on an excessively high exposure. The reinsurer's additional costs would typically be passed on to the policyholder's rates in the form of a load.

Rate Guarantee

As a low-frequency claim event with limited credibility in experience results, a policyholder's life claims can vary widely from year-to-year. The underwriter often doesn't have a great deal more credible data than the manual rate in evaluating the need for a rate change. So an annual renewal is generally not necessary. Life rate guarantees of two years are common. Three-year rate guarantees and longer are now becoming a common expectation in the group life industry.

A request for an extraordinarily long rate guarantee (longer than 3 years) might cause the underwriter to be concerned about the risk. Yet the rate guarantee is quite negotiable. Depending on how comfortable the underwriter is with the risk factors and the adequacy of the pricing, the request for an extended rate guarantee is rarely a reason to refuse to quote on a case.

Administrative Capabilities

It is generally not at the top of the underwriter's mind whether or not his/her company has the appropriate administrative support to meet a policyholder's service requirements, particularly with life coverage. Life insurance claims have a low frequency, and the need for client-specific claim processes is rare. Having alignment between the insurer's administrative capabilities and the policyholder's requirements are a part of the risk selection process. Inability to meet a client's expectations jeopardizes the long-term relationship with the client.

While most service requirements that are outside of the insurer's standard life plan processes can be accommodated with workarounds, there may arise situations where the underwriter must make a decision about a service requirement that the insurer is ill-equipped to handle.

The underwriter may need to load the rate to accommodate a nonstandard service requirement to account for the manual intervention and man-hour costs caused by the disruption to standard processes. However, there may come a point where the service requirement is so far out of the insurer's bailiwick that the underwriter may be faced with a decision of whether or not to quote on the case. Most unusual service demands come from larger policyholders, but that is not always the case. They are often driven by the policyholder's desire to replicate the service provided by the prior carrier.

The following might cause an underwriter to consider the efficacy of the insurance company to deliver the requested service at a reasonable rate:

- Refiling of contract language

  - Most group insurers are well-equipped to re-file contract language with the state's Department of Insurance to accommodate a policyholder's request for a unique benefit provision or to duplicate a prior carrier's policy language. However, it can be cost-prohibitive based on the policyholder's size. Most insurers have administrative guidelines establishing a minimum of lives and/or standard premium before a case-specific filing can be done.

- Electronic filing of premium waiver claims or online status of life/AD&D claims

  - Carriers vary in their level of technological sophistication. While this requested service may be a standard process for some insurers, it cannot necessarily be supported by the systems or processes of others. Some carriers may not want to invest in the systems required to match another insurer's process.

- Beneficiary administration service

  - For policyholders who want to reduce the administrative burden of their group plan, this is a popular service. The insurer takes on the responsibility of maintaining the beneficiary cards.

  - Again, this requested service may be a standard process for some insurers but cannot be supported by the systems or processes of others. Some carriers may not want to make the investment in developing such a process. In such cases, some insurers will engage a third-party vendor to administer it on their behalf, and it will appear seamless to the policyholder.

Key Takeaways

- Risk selection encompasses all aspects of a case. All risk factors must be weighed together before deciding to quote or to renew.

- Insurers vary widely in their tolerance for risk. Some insurers routinely quote on business from which others shy away.

- Underwriters use plan design and plan structure as a means of controlling risk.

- The plan offered to a group of employees must be commensurate with the risk. Offering excessively high amounts of coverage to a low-earning group, for example, might not make sense.

- A reinsurer's underwriting guidelines are in addition to the insurer's underwriting guidelines. They may have restrictions that the insurer's guidelines do not.

- The policyholder's SIC or NAICS code is a key element in seeking preferred risks, but it is by no means the only factor making a risk preferred or not.

- Insurers vary in their administrative and service capabilities, although most insurers seek ways to accommodate a life policyholder's unique service requirements.

- Gauging employee participation in supplemental/voluntary life and AD&D is a key factor in the risk selection process. If minimum participation is not expected, the anti-selection risk may be too great to underwrite.

- Having alignment between the insurer's administrative capabilities and the policyholder's requirements are a part of the risk selection process. Inability to meet a client's expectations jeopardizes the long-term relationship with the client.

Chapter 7

Life Manual Rates

Manual rates are used by insurers to price the majority of Group Life and Accidental Death & Dismemberment (AD&D) cases. Because manual rates are crucial for pricing most group life and AD&D cases, insurance professionals should find this chapter particularly informative. This chapter will explain how manual rates are developed by the insurer and how the rates are used to develop the price on a particular case. The information in this chapter may provide insight as to the factors that drive the rates policyholders see at renewal or in Request For Proposal (RFP) responses.

Manual Rates Defined

Manual rates are premium rates that are used by group insurers to calculate the theoretically "correct" rate to charge for a particular group. They are "manual" rates because the factors used to derive the "correct" rate were historically documented in manuals, frequently as a series of tables. Manual rates are also sometimes referred to as "book rates" as the rate factors were in manuals or "books". In the days before hand-held calculators and computers, they were also referred to as "manual" because the calculations were done by hand. Insurers and producers may also refer to the manual rates as "book rates," "table rates," or "actuarial rates," but the concept is identical. They are the rates that the insurer believes should be charged to a group at a point in time in order to collect enough premium from the policyholder to cover projected claims, reserves, and expenses (including profit) for the rate guarantee period.

From an actuarial perspective, the perfect manual rate would be one in which the premium collected matched exactly the amount for claims, reserve, and expense liabilities actually incurred. Manual rates are not designed to include extra profit *or margins*. Rather, they are designed to most accurately reflect the best guess as to the upcoming financial liability for a particular risk.

Manual rates are developed by the actuarial staff within each group insurer. They are applied by the underwriters and other staff to cases being renewed and on new business being quoted.

Importance of Life Manual Rates

Life manual rates are of the utmost importance in helping the underwriters to figure out the correct rates to charge a policyholder. They are the cornerstone of group life pricing. Moreover, manual rates are used almost exclusively in determining needed AD&D rates.

Manual rates are routinely studied and evaluated by an insurer's actuarial staff to ensure rate adequacy and for competitiveness. Besides helping the underwriter to determine appropriate pricing, life manual rates are also useful to the insurer in:

- Managing the block of business for profitability.

    - Insurers routinely evaluate the factors they use in their manual rates by comparing them to the claims results that actually emerge, and they adjust the factors to ensure overall block-of-business profitability.

- Recognizing sales patterns.

    - Insurers routinely evaluate the competitiveness of the manual rates based on the close ratio of the manually rated cases. Adjustments to the factors are made based on the insurer's appetite for risk, growth plans, and the actual results that emerge. For example, are we selling far greater or lesser business in a certain area of the country than we expected?

- Benchmarking against sales and/or profit targets during the year.

    - Insurers can use the manual rates during the year to project how final sales and profit results should emerge based on what has emerged so far. If it appears sales and/or profit results will fall short of targets, it can serve as an early warning signal to evaluate the manual rates and make necessary adjustments.

To manage a book of business or block of business, the actuary may compare the premiums collected for all cases to the manual rate premiums. The actuary can also evaluate segments of business based on common characteristics, such as industry, plan design, location (state or zip code), number of employees, and so on. Manual rates can be compared to actual premiums to determine if the segment is performing according to expectations. The actuary can then adjust factors to achieve the targeted premium for the segment.

When developing the manual rates, the actuaries project an expected "close ratio" on the block of business and by industry. The close ratio is the proportion of cases sold compared to all cases quoted. Depending on appetite for risk and the insurer's financial goals, the projected close ratio usually ranges from 5 percent to 15 percent. If the close ratio for a particular industry or geographic market is unusually high or low, the actuaries will investigate the conditions impacting sales patterns to determine if there is some inherent flaw in the manual rates or the rating methodology. The close ratio may also be indicative of other problems, such as inadequately trained sales or other staff, antiquated or inappropriate plan provisions, or services not meeting market demand.

Theory of Manual Rates

Like all other manual rates, group life and AD&D manual rates are developed using the Law of Large Numbers (LLN). By studying huge sources of data, group actuaries are able to discern many factors that affect claim life patterns. The idea is that the larger the data base, the greater the predictive value of the data. The actuaries often use many different sources of data in their manual rate evaluations, including:

- Actuarial Life Industry studies (such as the Society of Actuaries Group Life Mortality and Morbidity Study);

- U.S. Census Bureau data;

- U.S. Bureau of Labor Statistics;

- National Vital Statistics reports;

- their company's own in-force data (also known as block-of-business or book-of-business data).

The actuaries then must determine how the factors they have developed from this data can be applied to a group of covered workers and their dependents, if applicable. They need to account for both rates of death and rates of disability to account for premium waiver claims. For example, they may lump certain similar risks together in conducting an evaluation of claim patterns as a means of leveraging the law of large numbers. Most importantly, the actuaries develop the manual rates within the framework of the appetite for risk that the insurer's management has established.

Excepting suicide, actuaries studying the data for life and AD&D manual rates aren't faced with accounting for some level of choice in submitting a claim that may be inherent in medical or disability coverage. However, evaluating the data on disability claims to determine potential premium waiver liability can be challenging because of the low frequency of waiver claims and because of the numerous plan options for waiver that most carriers offer. Obtaining enough observable events for waiver claims by waiver option makes the task challenging for actuaries.

Predicting how many life claims and their benefit amounts on a particular case is impossible using manual rates, as most cases are simply too small for the law of large numbers to apply. While actual experience results at the case level rarely equals the manual premium collected, in aggregate across the entire block of business, the premium collected should be enough to cover the liability incurred by all cases' claims, reserves, and expenses. The manual rate is the best guess at what the theoretical case rate should be when applying the manual factors to the unique characteristics of the plan and the associated insured population.

Claims Incidence

Group life claims are a low-frequency event with moderate to high severity. Because of such low claim frequency, the use of historical life claims results for predicting the future of a particular plan's performance is limited. Hence, manual rates are of utmost importance and are the cornerstone of life and AD&D pricing. Figure 7-1 provides a chart for estimating claims incidence in a "garden variety" plan.

Figure 7-1. Estimating Claims Incidence	
Group Coverage Type	Expected Claims per 1,000 Employees per Year*
Basic and supplemental life	2 – 3
Life premium waiver	1 – 2
Dependent spouse	3 – 5
Dependent child	1 – 2
Retirees	15 – 20**
Accidental death & dismemberment	0.1 – 0.5 (1 – 5 per 10,000 employees)

*Assumes an average age of 40 in a nonhazardous industry
**Assumes an average age of 70

Of all group coverages offered (excepting AD&D), group life has the lowest claim frequency, as shown in Figure 7-2. Underwriters therefore typically rely on life manual rates heavily.

Figure 7-2. Claims Frequency by Type of Insurance				
	Type of Group Coverage*			
	Life	Short-Term Disability STD**	Long-Term Disability LTD***	Medical/ Prescription****
Expected claims per 1,000 employees per year	2 – 3	60 – 80	4 – 6	800 – 900

*Assumes an average age of 40 in a nonhazardous industry
**8-8-26 plan with 40% females
***6-month elimination period, 2-year own occupation/any thereafter
****Number of employees/family units utilizing the plan

Life Credibility

Credibility is the term used to describe the believability or reliability of experience data as a predictor of future experience results.[1]

"Life years" are used in the credibility formula of an underwriting analysis. It is the average number of lives covered in the plan for a year or a portion of a year. If multiple years of experience are used, the underwriter will add up the average lives for each year being considered. The more life years used in the analysis, the higher the group's experience credibility.[2]

The more observable events that have occurred, the greater the predictive value. The belief is that claim events will repeat themselves if other factors remain relatively constant. However, group life and AD&D claims are low-frequency events, and being able to observe them over time on a particular case and to derive patterns from such a sampling is extremely limited. As such, manual rates are of vital importance in helping the underwriter to establish accurate pricing at the case level.

Each group insurer has its own proprietary life credibility formula, which is typically based on life years. The credibility formula comes into play when the case underwriter is able to use historical experience data as a predictor of future plan performance and then blend or meld that analysis with the manual rate. A generally accepted rule of thumb for a group life case to be fully credible is a minimum of 25,000–30,000 life years. There are simply not a lot of 15,000-life cases that an underwriter can observe over a two- or three-year period to have full credibility in the experience data. AD&D has so little credibility at the case level that most insurers have not developed underwriting formula tables for this line of coverage.

Manual Rate Factors

To put the data the actuaries have studied into action, the actuaries develop factors that can be programmed and applied to a specific case. The factors are structured so that they can be applied to the unique risk characteristics of a particular policyholder using the following formula:

Manual Rate Factors × Case Characteristics = Manual Rates

Insurers will vary in the types of factors they utilize in their rate manual. In addition, how the factors are applied and programmed at the case level vary significantly. Regardless, most carriers apply the factors at the individual insured level and then tally up and compute an aggregate of all the individual results to generate one rate for all.

The manual rate factors most commonly used by group life insurers are age distribution, gender distribution, industry, geographic area, plan design, expenses, and participation level. We'll examine each of these.

Age Distribution

The most important factor in driving manual rates is the ages of the individuals who are covered in the group. Clearly, the older employees will drive the rates up since they are at higher risk of dying or becoming disabled.

The age distribution factor by itself generally contemplates the potential incidence risk, but not necessarily the severity risk. For example, two 59-year-old female employees have essentially the same risk of dying or becoming disabled. However, one employee having $10,000 in life coverage versus the other having $150,000 in life coverage represents a considerably different outcome if one of them were to die or become disabled. To account for the severity risk, it is essential for the insurer to determine the amount of coverage or exposure each insured has at his or her given age as part of the manual rating process.

A widely accepted group insurance industry standard for the "average" age of a group of covered employees in a group life plan is 40. A policyholder having a group with an average age under 40 might reasonably expect lower manual rates than an identical policyholder with an average age above 40.

Gender Distribution

It is widely known that females in the United States live longer than males. Aside from retiree coverage, the group actuary must determine factors based on gender for covered employees during their working ages. The survivability of females is also significantly greater than males in the working population, ages 20–70, as illustrated in Figure 7-3.

Figure 7-3. Average Remaining Life Expectancy for Ages 20–70		
	Remaining Life Expectancy	
Current Age	**Male**	**Female**
20	56.4	61.2
25	51.8	56.3
30	47.1	51.5
35	42.5	46.7
40	37.8	41.9
45	33.3	37.2
50	29.0	32.7
55	24.9	28.2
60	20.9	23.9
65	17.2	19.9
70	13.7	16.0

Source: "Table 7. Life Expectancy at Selected Ages, by Race and Sex: United States, 2007," *National Vital Statistics Report*, Vol. 58, No. 19, May 2010 (Hyattsville, MD: U.S. Department of Health and Human Services), p. 26.

The differences in mortality between men and women increased slightly in 2007 from 2006. The age-adjusted death rate for men was 40.8 percent greater than that for women, up from 40.6 percent in 2006; while the difference between male and female life expectancy was 5.0 years in 2007, a slight decrease from the 2006 gap of 5.1.[3]

Although the gap between the genders is closing, American males are more likely to engage in high-risk behaviors than their female counterparts. For example, 19.1 percent of males smoke cigarettes, compared to 15.1 percent of females.[4] Further, males are more likely to have habits that lead to obesity (71.2 percent versus 57.0 percent),[5] are more likely to commit suicide (17.7 percent versus 4.1 percent),[6] and are less likely to have regular health checkups with their doctor (48.3 percent versus 51.7 percent).[7] Despite having significantly better mortality rates during working ages, females have higher rates of disability at all ages.[8]

Industry Factors

One of the most effective ways of developing manual rates for groups is to categorize them by Standard Industrial Classification (SIC) or North American Industry Classification System (NAICS) codes. Using the SIC or NAICS codes allows actuaries to study the mortality patterns of these groups. Certain industries have greater risk for employee death due to the very nature of the work performed. Moreover, these high-risk industries tend to have workforces that are predominantly male. Most insurers have higher industry factors for workers in the following categories:

- Commercial fishing

- Logging

- Heavy construction

- Fire and police

- Mining

- Oil and gas extraction

The beauty of the SIC and NAICS codes is that they allow the actuaries to assign industry factors to the precise nature of the business. For example, the codes distinguish between Fish Hatcheries and Preserves versus Catching Shellfish. The on-the-job risk for a hatchery employee is significantly less than that of fishers catching crabs on the open sea (think *Deadliest Catch*).

Insurers may adjust their industry factors on particular industries to control the composition of their book of business. For example, many insurers might find the banking industry to be an attractive risk due to the low physical and/or moral hazard and the relatively high female content of those groups. One could expect a favorable industry factor compared to other industries. However, an insurer may decide to increase the industry factor on banking because they feel they already have enough banks on the book of business or they may have detected a trend in that industry's life claim incidence. By increasing the industry factor, the resulting end manual rate will likely be higher and less competitive and thereby fewer bank policyholders will buy at that price.

Geographic Area Factors

Many insurers include an area factor in the manual rates, which is usually based on where the employees work. Getting the information on where they live might be problematic, but in most cases, employees live near to where they work. The purpose of the area factor is to further enhance the gender and industry factors to account for overall mortality rates in certain areas of the country. Life expectancy does vary by state, and some insurers apply factors that may vary between areas within a state as well. Some insurers use zip codes in their programming to refine the area factor. Figure 7-4 shows the top and bottom five states and territories by average life expectancy.

Figure 7-4. Top and Bottom Ranking States and Territories for Life Expectancy	
Top Five States & Territories for Life Expectancy	
1. Hawaii	81.5
2. Minnesota	80.9
3. New York	80.4
4. California	80.4
5. Connecticut	80.2
Bottom Five States & Territories for Life Expectancy	
47. District of Columbia	75.6
48. Louisiana	75.4
49. West Virginia	75.2
50. Alabama	75.2
51. Mississippi	74.8

Source: "Life Expectancy at Birth (in years), 2007," statehealthfacts.org, http://www.statehealthfacts.org/comparemaptable.jsp?ind=784&cat=2&sort=a&gsa=2 (accessed July 5, 2012). Data from The Centers for Disease Control and Prevention, National Center for Health Statistics mortality data and US Census Bureau population data, 2007; calculations from the American Human Development Index.

Plan Design

The plan design itself reveals the amount of potential claim of each insured. The volume for which each insured is covered is reported each month to the insurer for billing purposes.

It is not uncommon for older employees to have substantially higher amounts of life coverage than younger employees. They are likely to have dependents, to have more disposable income with which to buy coverage, and to recognize the age-related risk of death. However, when there is an abnormal distribution of coverage amounts by age or class, the rating system and process needs to account for this aberration in the spread of risk.

Insurers often have approval authority required as part of their underwriting guidelines, particularly when high amounts of coverage are offered to older employees. For example, an insurer might require manager approval if 25 percent or more of the entire volume of a case is on employees age 55 or older. This would be programmed into the manual rating system as a flag. Other responses to this manual rating flag might be to:

- adjust the rate to account for the excessively high exposure, according to the underwriting guidelines;

- reduce the schedule of benefits being offered;

- obtain reinsurance for the exposure.

Manual rating programs will typically include factors for options the policyholder may want to add to the life contract. Most insurers offer several choices for policyholders within each option.

Some insurers offer different rates for smokers and nonsmokers because of the inherently higher risk of death and disability for smokers. At enrollment time, employees are asked whether or not they have used tobacco products in the past 6, 12, or 24 months. If an employee answers "yes," the employee is considered a smoker. The manual rates will include a factor that distinguishes smokers from nonsmokers.

Examples of life options likely to have a separate rating factor include:

- accelerated death benefit or enhanced options;

- portability;

- beneficiary assistance services;

- other than standard elimination period for premium waiver (such as 3 or 6 months);

- education benefit;

- repatriation benefit.

Examples of AD&D options likely to have a separate rating factor include:

- seatbelt and airbag benefit;

- education benefit;

- repatriation benefit;

- common carrier benefit;

- coma benefit;

- travel assistance benefit.

Examples of dependent life options likely to have a separate rating factor include:

- coverage of dependent students to age 25 or 27;

- survivor portability.

Expense Factor

While the age, gender, industry, and area factors apply to the unique census and volume characteristics of the group, the expense factor built into the manual rates covers the costs for administering the plan in the current year and for any required administration after the case cancels coverage. The expense factor is applied at the case (not individual insured) level. Typical items covered by this expense factor include:

- claim handling, including premium waiver claims;

- case set-up, maintenance, and overall administration;

- insurer overhead;

- state premium tax;

- commissions to producer;

- risk charge;

- profit.

State Premium Tax

It is the responsibility of the group insurer to pay the appropriate state premium tax to each state in which it conducts group life and AD&D business. The insurer collects the tax as part of the premiums and remits it to the state. The tax is based on a percentage of premiums collected and range from 1.75 percent to 3.00 percent.

The underwriter needs to account for the amount that must be included for the state premium tax as an expense when establishing the premium rates. Each state's premium tax is built into the expense component of the manual rating system.

Extraordinary Expenses

Most manual rating systems would not include the cost of extraordinary items that a policyholder might request, such as:

- english translation printing and/or services;

- dedicated claims examiners;

- customized booklet/certificate printing or distribution;

- covering a significant number of employees working outside of the United States.

Standard Expenses

The expense factor applied is usually related to the annual premium that the case is expected to generate. Because some of the expense costs are fixed, cases with larger projected premiums will have lower expense factors. A fixed cost of $10,000 is significantly higher as a percentage on a case generating $35,000 in annual premiums than a case that generates $100,000 in annual premiums.

A lower expense factor means fewer cents out of every premium dollar are allocated for expenses while more is allocated to claims and reserves. Most carriers apply a desired, permissible, or target loss ratio as a divisor to the projected annual premium. The loss ratio is usually expressed as the inverse of the expense factor. So, a case with a higher permissible loss ratio is assumed to have fewer dollars allocated towards expenses than a case with a lower permissible loss ratio. An insurer's expense factor in the manual rating system might look as shown in Figure 7-5

Figure 7-5. Incurred Constant Loss Ratios and Expense Percentages		
Annual Projected Premium	*Permissible Loss Ratio*	*Expense Percentage (inverse of loss ratio)*
$0–$24,999	.65	35%
$25,000–$74,999	.70	30%
$75,000–$124,999	.75	25%
$125,000–$174,999	.80	20%
$175,000–$249,999	.85	15%
$250,000 and over	.90	10%

Participation Factor

Supplemental or voluntary life coverage is typically 100 percent contributory by the employee. Since there is a choice of whether or not to enroll and since there is often a choice in the amount of coverage to elect, there is an element of antiselection in such plans. Clearly, those employees who feel that they are at highest risk for dying are going to enroll for as much coverage as they can. In other words, the older, less healthy employees are more likely to enroll and for higher amounts than the younger, healthier employees.

An antiselection or participation factor is often applied to the voluntary manual rates after the initial manual rate has been calculated. It accounts for the potential for there being a limited spread of risk that is essential in a sound group plan. The participation factor is usually based on a percentage of employees who are eligible to enroll compared to those who have actually enrolled in the past or the percentage of those who are expected to enroll when the plan takes effect.

Most group voluntary life and AD&D insurance contracts have a suicide exclusion. This ameliorates the suicide risk. But an antiselection load is typically applied on voluntary life to account for the lesser spread of risk that might be seen comparatively on noncontributory basic life. An insurer's participation factor in the manual rating system might look as shown in Figure 7-6

Figure 7-6. Participation Factor	
Participation Percentage	*Load Factor to Manual Rates**
Less than 15%	Exception required
15% – 25%	1.25
26% – 50%	1.20
51% – 74%	1.10
75% – 99%	1.05

* Manual rate systems tend to use multiplication to apply loads and discounts. Thus, a cost loaded 25% has its rate multiplied by 1.25. A case discounted 25% would have its rate multiplied by .75.

Application of Manual Rates

The manual rates are designed to apply to the unique risk characteristics of the group being rated. Most insurers apply the manual rating factors to each individual insured, and then sum the rates to generate the group rate. Individually rating each insured allows the rating factors to be most accurately applied, and with computer technology and programming, it can be done quickly.

Each insurer has its own unique and proprietary set of manual rating factors. Some have more sophisticated calculation methods and programs than others. Regardless, because of the wealth of data available on life coverage, policyholders should feel confident that their insurer's manual rates are derived in sound fashion.

Many insurers have life and AD&D manual rating factors that are not addressed in this writing, but most of the preeminent ones have been mentioned. Figure 7-7 is an illustrative example of how manual rates would apply at the case level. The factors are fictitious, but the structure demonstrates how factors appear as if done by hand.

Assume:

- Basic life, noncontributory

- A low-risk industry

- Location in suburban Alabama

Figure 7-7. Example of Manual Rates Applied Individually and Summed for Total Case Premium

Employee	Sex	Age	Start Rate [based on age & sex] (A)	Industry Factor (B)	Geography Factor (C)	Amount of Insurance (D)	Monthly Premium [A × B × C × (D ÷ $1,000)]
Smith	M	55	.94	.92	1.03	$ 10,000	$ 8.91
Jones	F	55	.47	.92	1.03	10,000	4.45
Henry	M	47	.41	.92	1.03	25,000	9.71
Peale	M	33	.14	.92	1.03	20,000	2.65
Robinson	F	33	.09	.92	1.03	15,000	1.28
Velez	F	27	.06	.92	1.03	15,000	0.85
Rooney	F	38	.11	.92	1.03	10.000	1.04
O'Leary	M	62	1.31	.92	1.03	25,000	31.03
Kendrick	F	26	.06	.92	1.03	20,000	1.14
D'Onofrio	M	44	.32	.92	1.03	15,000	4.55
Total						$165,000	$65.61

In this very small sample, the projected annual premium would be $787.32 ($65.61 × 12 months).

Because the annual projected premium is so small, the expense percentage would be very high. In fact, some insurers may require a minimum annual premium of $1,000 regardless of how the manual rating calculation ends up to ensure their expenses are covered. Assuming an expense factor of 35 percent, the total needed monthly premium would be $100.94 ($65.61 ÷ .65).

Assuming a single composite rate would be charged to all employees, the monthly rate per $1,000 of coverage for each employee would be $.612 ($100.94 ÷ $165,000 monthly volume × 1,000).

Insurers vary in how and where in the calculation process they would apply adjustments such as smoker versus nonsmoker or to apply a charge for an optional benefit such as portability.

It is important to note that the Department of Insurance in many states requires group insurers to file their manual rates. This provides a consumer protection mechanism that ensures that the rates are reasonable and that the insurers are not purposely trying to omit certain groups from the possibility of obtaining life and AD&D coverage.

Policyholders and employees have benefitted from the long history the insurance industry has had in studying life mortality and morbidity data on individual and group coverage. Insurers continue to perfect their techniques for generating the most accurate manual rates possible to remain competitive and to provide buyers the best products at the best prices possible.

Census Data Collection

The rubber meets the road when it comes time for collecting the data needed to calculate the manual rates. If the census data is missing, inconsistent, unclear, or outright incorrect, it will jeopardize the accuracy of the manual rate, if not make it impossible altogether. Fortunately, most payroll vendors in today's world are easily able to provide the insurers the needed information in order to conduct an accurate manual rate analysis. Most insurers require the following information in order to generate a manual rate:

- Effective date of policy

- Employee date of birth or current age

- Employee gender

- Description of business to determine SIC or NAICS

- Amount of coverage on each insured

- Locations of employees by zip code

- Requested rate guarantee

- Proposed plan design

Obtaining census information on dependents can be difficult. Many insurers use some type of formula to determine estimated dependent life exposure and then apply dependent life manual rating factors. For example, the formula may assume that the spouse is the same age as the employee.

Since extended rate guarantees of two years or more are commonplace, obtaining updated census data for renewing customers is vital for insurers, regardless of case size. Significant demographic changes can and do occur during a rate guarantee period. Considering the mobility of today's workforce coupled with employment uncertainty, it is essential for insurer's to obtain updated census information from their existing customers to ensure the most accurate pricing possible.

Key Takeaways

- The data collected by the insurer from the RFP is critical in developing a manual rate. Incorrect or missing data may well mean an incorrect manual rate.

- Because insurers use their own book-of-business data in developing and modifying manual rates, it is not unusual for a case RFP to generate different rates from different insurers.

- Generally speaking, the older the group's average age, the higher the rate. But, even on a younger group, high face amounts on older employees will tend to drive up the rate.

- The insurer's expense factors anticipate the insurer's normal administrative methods. Exceptions to these incur additional costs for which the underwriter should load the rates.

- Not all insurers have the same appetite for risk. A conservative insurer may seek reinsurance at lower levels of coverage, which incurs additional expense on the case. Some insurers will be more comfortable with accepting high-risk industry cases than others.

Endnotes

1. Kirner, Tom and Pete Silkowski, *Group Benefits Disability Specialist Course Handbook* (Erlanger, KY: The National Underwriter Company), p. 17-2.

2. Ibid.

3. *National Vital Statistics Report*, Vol. 58, No. 19, May 2010 (Hyattsville, MD: U.S. Department of Health and Human Services), p. 2.

4. "Percent of Adults Who Smoke by Gender, 2010," *statehealthfacts.org, http://www.statehealthfacts.org/comparetable.jsp?ind=81&cat=2&sort=a&gsa=2* (accessed July 5, 2012).

5. "Overweight and Obesity Rates for Adults by Gender, 2010," *statehealthfacts.org, http://www.statehealthfacts.org/comparemaptable.jsp?ind=90&cat=2&sort=a&gsa=2* (accessed July 5, 2012).

6. "U.S. Suicide Statistics (2001): Breakdown by Gender / Ethnicity / Young, Old Age Groups," *Suicide.org, http://www. suicide.org/suicide-statistics.html* (accessed July 5, 2012).

7. "Summary Health Statistics for U.S. Adults: National Health Interview Survey, 2009". *http://www.cdc.gov/nchs/data/series/sr_10/sr10_249.pdf* (accessed July 5, 2012).

8. "Table D-1. Prevalence of Disability by Sex and Age—All Races," *Americans with Disabilities: 2005, United States Census Bureau website, http://www.census.gov/hhes/www/disability/sipp/disable05.html* (accessed July 5, 2012).

Chapter 8

Underwriting and Risk Management

This chapter explains the process by which a group life Request For Proposal (RFP) is evaluated for benefit plan design, services to be delivered, and pricing. The information can help the producer and other insurance professionals understand why a rate and associated benefits plan are offered in response to an RFP. Most importantly, it will help the producer understand the insurer's information needs so that he or she can gather good information from the client for an RFP that will result in the most accurate rate and proposal to meet the client's needs.

After going through the risk selection process, it is up to the underwriter to develop a proposal to offer in response to the RFP. The proposal is the culmination of a thorough risk evaluation and pricing process. It is common for the underwriter to deliver the offer to the insurer's sales representative who customizes and refines the proposal for delivery to the producer. Some carriers allow the sales representative underwriting authority and the representative deals directly with the producer, based on case size, case characteristics, and/or distribution model.

Regardless of who for the insurer makes the offer in response to the RFP, the offer comes as a letter to the producer that documents the quote essentials and customarily encompasses:

- The benefit plan of the offer

- Service considerations

- Grandfathered employees, if applicable

- Premium rates and rate guarantee

- Any assumptions and contingencies

The producer evaluates the RFP responses from each insurer and makes recommendations to the client as to which are the best offers. The client ultimately decides carrier selection based on producer input and guidance.

Benefit Plan

One of the most effective techniques in managing risk is through plan design.[1] The underwriter will review the current plan and compare it to the RFP proposed plan. When evaluating the benefits plan, the underwriter will assess how the plan design might impact claim incidence, claim severity, and pricing structure. The underwriter may propose a plan design that will reduce risk, especially for a proposed low rate. Conversely, the underwriter may also propose a richer plan based on case experience and/or census characteristics of the group, if warranted.

How Can the Plan Impact Claims Incidence?

Outside of suicide risk, the life and AD&D benefits plan generally has little impact on life/AD&D claims incidence. Insureds generally want to live as long as possible. Life/AD&D claims have two underwriting components: incidence and severity, both of which impact risk management and pricing.

However, the type of waiver of premium provision may have an impact on waiver claim frequency, as there may be some level of choice in remaining disabled and out on claim. If credible experience information is available, the underwriter will evaluate if the waiver claims emerged at a higher or lower level than expected based on the type of waiver of premium provision. The underwriter will also note the level at which the current carrier reserved for the waiver claimant.

Figure 8-1 illustrates how the type of waiver provision can potentially impact incidence and pricing.

Figure 8-1. Examples of Waiver Provision Impacts on Pricing		
Provision	*More Expensive Premium Waiver*	*Less Expensive Premium Waiver*
Elimination period	3 or 6 month	9 month
Occupation definition	24 month own occupation	Any occupation
Reserved percentage	65% or 50% of face value	75% of face value
Maximum Waiver Qualifying Age	No limitation or Normal Retirement Age	Age 60

If experience data is available on the group Long-Term Disability (LTD) plan, the underwriter may review the LTD experience claims incidence to see if it was lower or higher than expected. While there is not a direct connection, there is often a correlation between higher or lower than expected incidence between life and LTD.

Retiree incidence will be significantly higher than that of active employees, regardless of plan design. However, most retiree plans have limited benefits. It is worth noting that retiree claims incidence is usually easier to predict than that of active employees. The more an event occurs, the greater it's predictive value.

How Can the Plan Impact Claims Severity?

The underwriter's greatest challenge lies in ensuring that an attractive plan is offered, balanced against having an inappropriately rich benefit. It is essential to make a contributory supplemental life plan attractive to achieve maximum employee participation and thereby lessen the *antiselection* risk.

The underwriter will consider the combination of basic and supplemental life as a potential claim since it is likely a claimant will have both with the same carrier. The underwriting guidelines usually provide the underwriters with formulas for determining the overall plan maximum that can be offered, but it makes sense to ensure that one class's benefits are not inordinately different than another. Usually, the guidelines limit the difference in class maximums to not more than 2 or 3 times higher than the next lowest class. Section 79 antidiscrimination rules (discussed in Chapter 10) also come into play.

Earnings multiples are considered in the overall construction of a plan. For example, if the basic life plan has a two-times-annual-basic-earnings schedule, the underwriter may limit the supplemental multiple to two or three so that the combined multiples of basic and supplemental do not exceed five.

Establishing an appropriate Guaranteed Issue (GI) limit is of the utmost importance. Based on underwriting guidelines, the underwriter may ask of himself/herself:

- Does the current GI limit still protect the financial integrity of the plan?

- Can the GI limit be increased to make the plan more attractive?

- How many claims in the past exceeded the GI limit?

Ensuring that the plan's age reduction schedule is compliant with the Age Discrimination in Employment Act (ADEA) of 1974 is also a key element in managing risk through plan design. Recall that mortality increases dramatically with age. If there are high amounts of coverage on older employees, the underwriter will take note and evaluate if the current ADEA schedule is adequate to keep those amounts within reasonable tolerances. If the underwriter decides to introduce a new ADEA reduction schedule, the schedule will typically be run by the sales representative beforehand, as such a change may impact some of the senior employees or executives in charge of the business.

How Can the Plan Impact Overall Risk and Pricing?

Several plan provisions may require thorough examination. The underwriter will theorize how each one could potentially impact claim incidence and/or severity. Provisions to be analyzed include minimum benefit, maximum benefit, continuation of coverage, portability, any unique provisions, and the balance of richness of benefits.

Minimum Benefit

While it may not appear in the schedule of benefits, insurers sometimes require a minimum amount of coverage. If not enough coverage is sold, the insurer might incur more in administrative charges than the value of the premiums collected.

A minimum benefit is most likely to be part of a plan where employees have had historically low levels of coverage or where the employer wants to provide only the leanest amount of coverage. Conversely, an employer may request a minimum benefit to prevent the ADEA age reduction from causing too little coverage on older employees. Typical minimums are $5,000 or $10,000.

Maximum Benefit and Reinsurance

If a very high maximum is being requested or if an unusually high risk plan or group is presented, it may involve reinsurance. If reinsurance does apply, the underwriter will have to ensure the risk is approved by the reinsurer before a quote can be issued. In addition, the reinsurer's charges for accepting the risk must be factored into the final rate the underwriter quotes.

Continuation of Coverage

The underwriter will assess the nature of the risk, based on the group being evaluated. The decision to offer a nonstandard or an extensive continuation provision rests largely on how the group is likely to use the extension. For example, if considering a continuation of coverage due to sabbatical when evaluating a university, the underwriter will try to determine the nature of the sabbaticals that are taken. Will the sabbaticals take place stateside or will the sabbaticals take place overseas in a high-risk location? The risk for an archeology professor who goes on sabbatical domestically is substantially different than the one who goes to Iraq. If such a continuation is offered, the underwriter must decide the pricing impact, if any, for it.

Portability

As a risk management tool, portability can cut both ways. On one hand, it encourages employee participation in the contributory basic or supplemental life plan at little cost to the employer. On the other hand, the insurer is now taking on risks that would otherwise not have been on the life block of business. In the final analysis, if portability already exists in the contract, the underwriter will most likely continue it under the proposed contract. Or, if the policyholder wants to add it, the underwriter is likely to agree in order to meet the competition's likely response to the request.

Portability claims typically are not used when evaluating plan experience, but the underwriter will check the experience information to ensure any portability claims are identified separately. If portability claims appear in the experience, the underwriter will evaluate if there is a higher or lower than expected incidence and severity. If higher than expected, the underwriter may have to adjust for the increased risk exposure.

Duplicating Benefits

Some policyholders may insist on maintaining the policy language of their plan with the previous carrier. In which case, the underwriter must ask: Are any of the benefits or provisions being requested unique to the prior insurer? Even if not unique, would the contract language require filing with the state's Department of Insurance? If so, the expense to file the language must be considered and built into the premium rates. Some carriers apply minimum case size guidelines before case-specific language filing can be considered.

Balancing Richness of Benefits

When contributory supplemental life is offered in conjunction with noncontributory basic life, it is essential that a balance between the richness of both plans be established. A basic life plan that is too rich can serve to discourage employees from participating in the supplemental life plan. Employees who get free coverage under basic life may feel they have adequate protection or that basic life coverage is "good enough" without the need to purchase more group coverage. Since the underwriter wants to maximize enrollment in the supplemental life plan to spread the risk, the underwriter will scrutinize how the plans would work in tandem. Figure 8-2 provides an illustrative chart of a reasonable richness-of-benefits balance between basic and supplemental life.

Figure 8-2. Example of Balanced Richness of Benefits		
Assume average annual salary is $38,000	Basic Life	Supplemental Life
Earnings multiple	1 times	2, 3, 4, or 5 times
Maximum	$50,000	$150,000–$500,000

Figure 8-3 provides an illustrative chart where the underwriter would likely be uncomfortable with the richness-of-benefits balance between basic and supplemental life.

Figure 8-3. Example of Unbalanced Richness of Benefits		
Assume average annual salary is $38,000	Basic Life	Supplemental Life
Earnings multiple	3 times	4 or 5 times
Maximum	$500,000	$750,000

Considering the average annual salary of employees in Figure 8-3, most of the employees would probably feel they have adequate coverage under basic life at 3 times annual earnings and would not be inclined to enroll in the supplemental life program.

Another technique that can be applied to increase supplemental life participation is to request that the policyholder make the basic life plan partially contributory and apply that portion of employer contributions to the supplemental life plan, thus reducing the supplemental life rate for employees. If the basic life premium is only modestly contributory, most employees are likely to remain in the plan. And with the supplemental rate now reduced for employees, they will be more likely to enroll in supplemental life. Although this is unusual, it can help provide balance between basic and supplemental life enrollments. Figure 8-4 provides an example of how a modest change to the contribution structure would work.

Figure 8-4. Example of Obtaining Balance through Contribution Structure		
	Basic Life Employer Contribution	Supplemental Life Employer Contribution
Old plan	100%	0%
New plan	90%	10%

Service Considerations

The underwriter will scan the RFP for any service requirements that might be challenging to the insurer or have a pricing impact. Carriers vary in their array of optional services on life insurance, and many of these service options are available only to policyholders who meet certain size requirements. Optional services that typically have a pricing impact include:

- beneficiary card management service;

- customized enrollment packages, including online enrollment;

- direct mailing of insurance materials to employees;

- onsite enrollment specialists;

- special printing arrangements for the booklet/certificate;

- unusually high number of billing and/or reporting locations.

Grandfathered Employees

It is not uncommon for the policyholder to request coverage for "grandfathered employees." Grandfathering usually means that the insurer is being asked to take on special benefit levels on a small group of employees that are outside of the current or proposed policy. The most common exceptions usually involve maximum benefits and/or GI limits set higher for this special group than normal policy limits allow. Sometimes a separate ADEA age reduction (or no reduction) might apply to their benefits.

The underwriter must evaluate the feasibility and pricing implications of handling such exceptions. Of vital importance is the assurance that claims can be processed appropriately and on a timely basis if grandfathered risks are accepted.

It is usually considered uncompetitive to refuse to consider grandfathered employees, even though they may represent a difficult-to-measure risk and an increased administrative cost to the insurer. Most underwriters try to find a way to work the grandfathered employees into the plan.

When employees are to be grandfathered for any reason, a clearly written document must outline who the grandfathered employees are and for what they are being grandfathered. This should become part of the formally documented agreement (contract) between the insurer and policyholder.

Rates/Premium

Employee life and AD&D rates are almost always charged as a rate per $1,000 of coverage. On plans where each employee has the same flat benefit, such as $10,000, a charge "per employee" can be accommodated since each employee's individual amount of premium is the same.

Dependent life rates can be billed by family unit or for spousal coverage at a rate per $1,000 of coverage. When charged as a family unit, a rate per employee is charged, regardless of the number of family members. When there is a substantial spousal schedule, many underwriters prefer to have the rates based on $1,000 of coverage basis.

A composite or single rate for all is standard for most basic life and basic AD&D plans. Composite rates can apply to supplemental life and AD&D, but age-bracketed or step rates are preferable. Since most supplemental life/AD&D plans are contributory, the underwriter wants to encourage maximum participation in the plan to spread the risk. Charging rates based on age distributes the premium burden to those who are the highest risks. Charging higher rates to older employees who are at higher risk of dying and who are likely in greater need of coverage maintains plan integrity and makes the plan more attractive for younger employees to participate.

When setting up the age brackets for step rates, the underwriter will calculate the overall premium need for the case and then work backward in figuring out who is likely to participate at given rate levels. They will also gauge the policyholder's ability to calculate the monthly bill correctly, because step-rate calculations are considerably more complex than composite rates. Underwriters can offer an array of age-bracketed rate structures that can be tailored to the situation. Examples of age-brackets are shown in Figure 8-5. Each bracket has its own rate, with the youngest age bracket having the lowest rate.

Figure 8-5. Age Bracket Examples		
Age	*Age*	*Age*
Under 30	Under 25	Under 25
30 – 49	25 – 34	25 – 29
50 – 69	35 – 44	30 – 34
70 and over	45 – 54	35 – 39
	55 – 64	40 – 44
	65 – 74	45 – 49
	75 and over	50 – 54
		55 – 59
		60 – 64
		65 – 69
		70 – 74
		75 and over

The period for which the insurer agrees to maintain the quoted rates (barring "changes" specified in the life/AD&D contract) is referred to as the rate guarantee. Most insurers offer a two year rate guarantee as a standard part of a quote. RFP requests for longer rate guarantees are common and may be considered by the underwriter depending on all of the risk elements associated with the case and/or underwriting guidelines.

Experience Rating Process

Based on the number of employees in the plan, the underwriter must first decide whether the case will be priced using only manual rates or if there are enough employees and data available to warrant an experience evaluation. With an experience evaluation, the underwriter assesses the risk based on historical data (experience) and develops a premium rate to support the plan. The rate derived from the experience evaluation is usually blended or melded with the manual rate to produce one "formula rate" or "needed rate". Carriers vary in their definition of "formula" and "needed" rate.

The items to be evaluated include the plan design and the components that drive pricing, such as paid claims, claim incidence, services provided to the client, case expenses, and reserves.[2] The underwriter will carefully analyze the plan design to balance risk while providing adequate and attractive coverage to the insureds.

As a baseline, the underwriter will have a manual rate for each line of coverage being quoted. If an experience evaluation is to be conducted, the underwriter will frequently separate out the lines of coverage and evaluate the experience for each line separately. Depending on case size and available experience information, the most common separation of the experience data is:

- Basic life

- Supplemental life

  - Noncontributory basic life should theoretically be evaluated separately from supplemental life, since the employees typically pay the full cost of the premiums on supplemental life. The argument is that good experience results on supplemental should not be used to offset poorer experience results on basic, because employee contributions could effectively be used to support the employer's premium on the noncontributory plan. Conversely, combining poor experience results from supplemental life with a better-running, noncontributory basic life plan would not be fair to the employer, since a combined increase to the rates effectively "subsidizes" the employee-paid premium in the supplemental life plan.

- Dependent life (whether basic or supplemental)

  - Spouse and child experience is rarely examined separately. If there is not credible dependent experience data or if the experience is missing altogether, the underwriter may simply quote the manual dependent life rate.

- Accidental death & dismemberment (AD&D) (whether basic or supplemental)

  - An underwriter will look at AD&D experience data but will rarely stray from the manual rate unless underwriting a jumbo case.

Checking the Manual Rate

As discussed in Chapter 7, the manual rates are the cornerstone of pricing most cases, but the underwriter will ensure the accuracy of the manual so that a solid foundation for pricing can be established. With the explosion of technology, new products, and the global economy, the SIC code system may not adequately reflect the true nature of a company's business.[3] The underwriter will ensure that the correct SIC or NAICS code has been used in the manual rating system. In certain situations, the underwriter may have different SIC/NAICS codes applied by class to more accurately capture the nature of the risk, particularly in industries where blue collar and white collar employees receive substantially different life benefits.

All other elements of the manual rating will be checked for accuracy. The underwriter will run calculations to see if the volume reported in the manual rating equates to the volume reported on the billing statement or what the estimated volume should be based on rate and reported premium. The correct plan design being quoted will be checked as well. Corrections and adjustments will be made to the manual rating as appropriate.

The AD&D rate quoted is almost always derived from the manual rate. Therefore, the manual AD&D rate is almost always also the "needed rate." Any adjustments to the AD&D manual rate would be based on multiline discounts or business decisions, as described in Chapter 6.

Aside from generating a rate for the proposed plan, the manual rating provides essential background information about the demographics and benefit spread in the census. The manual rating indicates the:

- number of employees by class and age bracket;

- volume of coverage by class and age bracket;

- male/female split;

- average amount of coverage per employee (or average certificate).

With this information, the underwriter can determine the spread of risk—if there are abnormally high amounts of coverage on older employees or on younger employees, or if there is a normal distribution of coverage.

Life Credibility

The credibility of the data in a group life experience analysis is limited in most cases. Each insurer has its own proprietary credibility formula that underwriters apply in their pricing evaluations.

Credibility is a crucial factor in the rate formula. In effect, the credibility of the experience directly affects how the manual rate will be influenced in the blending process. The higher the credibility percentage, the greater will be the experience's impact.

"Life years" are used in the credibility formula of an underwriting analysis. It is the average number of lives covered in the plan in a year or portions of a year. If multiple years of experience are used, the underwriter will add up the average lives for each year being considered. The more life years used in the analysis, the higher the group's credibility.[4]

The life years are calculated by taking the average number of employees insured over a 12-month period by the number of periods used in the experience. Partial years are routinely considered in the experience base, so the proportion of the months in the year is multiplied by the average number of lives. Figure 8-6 provides an example of determining life years.

Figure 8-6. Life Years Determination		
Time Frame	*Average Number of Employees*	*Life Years*
12/1/09 – 12/1/10	412	412
12/1/10 – 12/1/11	417	417
12/1/11 – 10/1/12	422	352 (10/12 of 422 = 352)
12/1/09 – 10/1/12		1,181 (412 + 417 + 352)

If the underwriter decided to use only two years of experience from 12/1/10 to 10/1/12, then 769 life years (417 + 352) would be used to determine credibility.

Figure 8-7 provides an illustrative example of the credibility percentages assigned to life years. You will note that as more life years of data are available, higher credibility percentages are assigned.

Figure 8-7. Credibility Percentages Assigned to Life Years	
Life Years	*Credibility %*
Below 500	N/A—Manual rates only
500—2,499	25%
2,500—4,999	40%
5,000—11,999	50%
12,000—19,999	70%
20,000—27,999	85%
28,000 and greater	100%

Data Needed for Evaluating Experience

The results of the experience analysis are ultimately blended or melded with the manual rate, with the blend being driven by the credibility of the experience data. If the case size warrants, the underwriter will conduct an evaluation on the experience as if the experience alone were 100 percent credible.

Underwriters prefer to have three to five years of the most recent experience data. If the data isn't available for three years or more, underwriters are able to work with one or two years of data. However, using only one or two years of data will generate lower life years and thereby lower credibility. Underwriters generally won't use more than five years of the most recent experience information because the demographics of the census would have likely been different five years ago or more.

In order to conduct a thorough life experience analysis, the underwriters typically require the following:

- Benefit plan that generated the experience

  - Copy of the booklet/certificate or group life policy is preferable. The underwriter will check to ensure that the plan described in the booklet matches to the RFP description. The booklet is very valuable in revealing any unusual or unique provisions that:

    - the insurer's systems or processes are unprepared to handle;

    - would require filing of the policy language with state's Department of Insurance;

    - may have a pricing impact on the benefits or services;

    - would influence the manner in which the underwriter evaluates the experience information.

- Current rate and rate history

  - A copy of the current bill is preferable, particularly if there are multiple classes with different rates. Many policyholders and producers believe that providing the rate in the RFP discourages insurers from quoting their most competitive rate. They contend that "blind bids" produce the most competitive pricing. While that may be true in some situations, it can have the opposite effect in others. Underwriters may quote conservatively without knowing the current rate, as it is a vital data point in the experience evaluation process.

- Paid claims

  - A listing on current carrier stationery or on producer letterhead is preferred. This ensures accuracy of the claims recorded and limits the possibility of typographical errors in the RFP. The paid claim amounts the underwriter expects to see by date of occurrence are:

- Deaths claims, including interest paid and dependent death claims.

- Waiver of premium claims with the claimant's face amount of life coverage. Because waiver claimants are at a significantly higher risk of dying, insurers set up a reserve for such claimants on the date they are approved for waiver. It is considered a "claim" in the experience rating process. Carriers reserve from 50 percent to 75 percent of a waiver claimant's face amount of coverage at the time of approval.

- Accelerated death benefit payments.

- The amount (in 1,000's) of coverage converted under the conversion privilege. Some insurers account for conversion charges among paid claims. Others account for them in expenses.

- Premiums

  - A listing of premiums paid by month is preferred, but premiums are often reported in an aggregated amount by policy year. Underwriters will compare claims and reserves to collected premiums to develop a loss ratio.

- Plan changes during the experience

  - The underwriter can apply adjustment factors to the experience analysis by estimating how the claims would have emerged under the plan had the change been in effect during the entire experience base.

Data Integrity

One of the first steps the underwriter takes in a pricing and risk evaluation is to assess the quality of information provided in the RFP. It is vital for the information to be as accurate and complete as possible. The underwriter is looking for:

- Gaps in the information or missing data.

  - The underwriter is concerned that poor experience data may be purposely suppressed or that a mistake has been made in the compilation of the RFP.

- Inconsistent data.

  - If a claim appears as $25,000 in one experience report, but appears as $25,412 in another, the underwriter is going to question why.

The underwriter will also run tests on the numbers to ensure their accuracy and that they "hang together." Do rates times reported volume approximate the premium reported in the experience? Does the reported number of employees participating in the life plan in the RFP align with the number appearing on the billing statement? Do the numbers from the various reports add up?

In most cases, questions about the data provided are readily answered during the underwriting evaluation process. However, there are situations in which the information is simply not available or the underwriter's questions can't be answered. In such cases, the underwriter will generate theoretical numbers or "guesstimate" the missing numbers.

Benchmarking

After being assured of the experience information's accuracy, the underwriter may set a few high-level mental benchmarks in order to start to get a "feel" for how the experience has emerged relative to general expectations.

To benchmark incidence, the underwriter might assume 3 claims per 1,000 covered lives per year and calculate the expected number of claims. Assuming on the supplemental life there were 1,397 life years over a 3-year period, the underwriter would expect about 4.2 (1,397 ÷ 1,000 × 3 = 4.191) life claims in the experience base. Applying the same logic to waiver frequency of 1 claim per 1,000, the underwriter could expect roughly 1.4 (1,397 ÷ 1,000 × 1 = 1.397) claims in the 3-year experience base.

To benchmark severity, the underwriter would first determine the average face amount per employee or "average certificate." Assuming the most current reported monthly volume of $41,500,000 is representative of the previous volume on 488 employees, then the average amount of coverage on supplemental life is $85,041 (41,500,000 ÷ 488).

Putting these two very rough benchmarks together, the underwriter would expect 4.2 life claims averaging $85,041 amounting to $357,172. The expectation for waiver claims, reserved at 75 percent of face value would be 1.4 waiver claims at $63,781 (75% × $85,041). The total estimated waiver claims for the 3-year experience period would be $89,293 (1.4 × $63,781).

Figure 8-8 provides an illustrative experience report. The manner in which experience is shown varies extensively by carrier. Note that claimant names often do not appear on RFP experience reports due to privacy concerns. This is a routine practice that underwriters fully understand. Names typically appear on claim experience reports from the current carrier that go directly to the policyholder.

Figure 8-8. Experience Report

Experience for: ABC Company

Employee Life Claims

Date of Claim	Claimant	Basic	AD&D	Supplemental
11/14/09	Jones, R	$25,000	$0	$ 34,000
04/07/10	Smith, P	25,000	0	0
09/18/10	Johnson, L	25,000	0	202,000
02/26/11	Richards, B	25,000	0	58,000
12/04/11	Kowalski, T	10,000	0	26,000
03/22/12	Elliott, S	25,000	0	0

Waiver Claims (Reserved at 75% of face value)

Date of Claim	Claimant	Basic	AD&D	Supplemental
06/06/10	Dunbar, O	$18,750	N/A	$ 20,250
08/13/11	Martinez, T	18,750	N/A	56,250
07/18/12	Wells, R	18,750	N/A	63,000

Accelerated Death Benefit Advance Payments

Date of Claim	Claimant	Basic	AD&D	Supplemental
10/27/10	Kowalski, T	$15,000	N/A	$40,000

Dependent Life Claims

Date of Claim	Claimant	Basic	AD&D	Supplemental
09/10/11	Pope, M	$2,000	N/A	N/A

Conversions (Face amounts converted)

Date of Claim	Claimant	Basic	AD&D	Supplemental
12/28/11	Ley, K	$25,000	N/A	$ 71,000
05/20/12	Triss, T	25,000	N/A	107,000

Premiums

Date	Basic	AD&D	Supplemental	Dependent Life
10/1/09 – 10/1/10	$27,308	$ 8,775	$198,065	$11,087
10/1/10 – 10/1/11	28,007	8,965	204,686	11,987
10/1/11 – 10/1/12	28,998	9,238	213,907	12,654
Total	84,313	26,978	616,658	35,728

An example of a supplemental life experience evaluation based on the experience provided for ABC Company in Figure 8-8 follows.

Assume:

- Rate is $.43 composite

- Rate prior to 10/1/10 was $.37

- Most current volume is $41,500,000

- Insurer will charge $125 per $1,000 of converted coverage

The underwriter will create a one- or two page experience exhibit that will serve as a "snapshot in time," telling a story with numbers. The underwriter can use this snapshot as a basis for projecting the needed rate. Figure 8-9 provides such an experience exhibit based on ABC Company's experience. We'll examine each line to learn the story.

Figure 8-9. Experience Exhibit				
Supplemental Life Rate Projection	**10/1/09-10/1/10**	**10/1/10-10/1/11**	**10/1/11-10/1/12**	**10/1/09-10/1/112 3 Year Total**
A) Premium paid	$198,065	$204,686	$213,907	$616,658
B) Constant premium	230,183	204,686	213,907	648,776
C) Life claims	236,000	58,000	66,000	360,000
D) Premium waiver amounts	20,250	56,250	63,000	139,500
E) Conversion charges	0	0	22,250	22,250
F) Total paid claims (C + D + E)	256,250	114,250	151,250	521,750
G) Change in IBNR reserves	0	(12,780)	3,330	(9,450)
H) Incurred claims (F + G)	256,250	101,470	154,580	512,300
I) Incurred loss ratio (H ÷ A)	129.4%	49.6%	72.3%	83.1%
J) Incurred constant loss ratio (H ÷ B)	111.3%	49.6%	72.3%	79.0%
K) Average number of employees	457	469	488	1,414 life years

The accumulated incurred constant loss ratio is 79.0%.

The accumulated incurred constant loss ratio for all the periods in the experience base is used for determining the "experience rate." This ratio represents the claim and reserve liability that surfaced in the experience compared to the premium that would have been collected had the current rate been in effect throughout the experience base.

The next step is to adjust the ratio for case expenses. This is done by applying a permissible loss ratio. The case expense percentage is the inverse of the permissible loss ratio percentage. Assume the permissible or desired loss ratio is 81.0%. This leaves 19% or $.19 of every premium dollar allocated for expenses.

Incurred Constant Loss Ratio	$= \dfrac{79.0}{81.0} = .975$
Permissible Loss Ratio	

In the calculation above, the actual experience loss ratio (79.0 percent) performed better than the expected or permissible loss ratio (81.0 percent). This means only $.975 of every premium dollar was needed to fund all aspects of the cases, including expenses. To get the case to breakeven, the current rate could be reduced 2.5% (1.00 – .975). A reduction factor of .975 can be applied to the current rate.

Current rate $.43 × .975 reduction factor = $.419 needed or formula or experience rate.

In the above experience analysis, if experience were 100 percent credible, the current rate of $.43 is adequate to support the case. In fact, the rate could be reduced 2.5 percent, down to $.419.

Had the incurred constant loss ratio been 85.5 percent, then the calculation would have called for an increase to the current $.43 rate.

Incurred Constant Loss Ratio	$= \dfrac{85.5}{81.0} = 1.056$
Permissible Loss Ratio	

Current rates would have to increase 5.6 percent.
Current rate $.43 × 1.056 increase factor = $.454 needed or formula or experience rate.

Experience Exhibit Summary

Below is a detailed explanation of each line of the life experience exhibit in Figure 8-9.

A. *Paid premium* – These are the reported premiums paid or payable to the insurer for supplemental life coverage for each 12-month period. If premiums are due but yet unpaid, they are generally presumed to have been paid for rate projection purposes. As a cross-check of the data integrity, the underwriter will multiply the reported volume times the reported rate, then annualize it. The underwriter would expect that calculation to be within roughly 10 percent of the reported premium of the most current 12-month period. In our example, this checks out [($41,500,000 volume ÷ 1,000) × $.43 rate × 12 = $214,140]. The $213,907 actually reported is well within 10% of the calculated estimate of $214,140.

B. *Constant or common premium* – This is the paid premium that has been adjusted to reflect what the paid premium would have been historically had the current rate been in place during the entire experience base. In this example, the rate for the period 10/1/09 – 10/1/10 was $.37. The difference between the current rate and previous rate is proportionally applied to the paid premium for the period [($.43 ÷ $.37) × $198,065 = $230,183]. Since the current rate is used in evaluating historic rate adequacy, the constant premium is used to generate a loss ratio for projection purposes.

C. *Life claims* – These are amounts paid out in death benefits. Some insurers include interest paid to the beneficiary in the claim amounts, which may give rise to questions if the underwriter is expecting only an even number based on a rounding schedule. Inclusion of interest is routine. It simply will cause the underwriter to question whether interest is included in the claim figure or not.

Occasionally, the underwriter may adjust for a "shock claim." A shock claim is one of such high severity that it is considered aberrant and is very unlikely to occur in such magnitude again during the rate projection period. Underwriting guidelines often define a shock claim as well as the formula for adjusting for the claim. For example, the guideline might state that to be considered a shock claim, the claim must be 3 or 4 times greater than the average certificate amount or 3 or 4 times greater than the average claim over the past 3, 4, or 5 years. If a claim is considered a shock claim, the guidelines might suggest reducing the total claim by 20 percent to 40 percent for the purposes of rate-projection modeling (it would in no way diminish the amount payable to the beneficiary or the liability the insurer has on the claim).

In Figure 8-8, the Johnson claim of $202,000 appears significantly higher than all of the others in the experience base. So much so, that the underwriter may wish to check if it qualifies as a shock claim. Assume the average certificate is $85,041 and the guidelines suggest a factor of 3 to establish a potential shock claim. The Johnson claim is below $255,123 (3 × $85,041) and would therefore not be considered for reduction as a shock claim.

D. *Premium waiver amounts* – Most insurers account for waiver of premium approvals as a claim since the risk of death is so much higher. Carriers report this number differently and have various reserving methods as well. The underwriter will clarify whether the reported waiver claims are at full face value of the claim or if they have already been reduced. The underwriter will determine the full face amount and then apply the company's reserving method to it. In the ABC Company example, we continued to assume the waiver claim to be 75 percent of face value.

E. *Conversion charges* – The policyholder's experience may be used as the basis for accounting for the additional administrative costs to the insurer to process the conversion applications. Most carriers charge at a rate per $1,000 of converted amounts. Some carriers account for the charge among the paid claims while other carriers account for the conversion charges as part of the case expenses. In the ABC Company example, we assumed a charge of $125 for every $1,000 of coverage converted. The two individuals who coverted (Ley and Triss) did so in amounts totaling $178,000. ($125 × $178,000 ÷ 1,000 = $22,250).

Conversion charges vary widely by carrier and may range from $100 to $350 per every $1,000 of coverage converted by an insured individual.

F. *Total paid claims* – This is the sum of life claims, premium waiver amounts, and conversion charges.

G. *Changes in IBNR reserves* – Carriers vary in accounting for incurred but not reported (IBNR) claim liabilities in their rate projection model. Reserves are an essential element that must be built into the premium to account for potentially unreported claims that surface after case termination.

Each carrier has its own proprietary set of factors and formulas to calculate needed reserves and changes to the IBNR reserves. Some carriers do not account for IBNR changes for rate projection purposes. Those who do account for IBNR are attempting to capture unrevealed claim liability that might have occurred but has not yet been revealed in the numbers. The concept is to capture the *change* in unreported liability with the idea that if reported claims increase, unreported claims will also. The reverse is true when claims go down from year to year and may result in a release of reserves or a negative number. Reserves of $12,780 were released during the 10/1/10–10/1/11 period for ABC Company. When the negative number is added to total paid claims for the 10/1/10–10/1/11 period, it acts to reduce the total paid claims.

H. *Incurred claims* – This is the sum of total paid claims plus changes in IBNR reserves. This number represents the full claim liability, reported and unreported, that the carrier would have had at that snapshot in time. It does not account for case expenses.

I. *Incurred loss ratio* – This ratio tells the underwriter how experience has performed from a profit/loss perspective. It is determined by dividing the incurred claims by the paid premiums.

In the ABC Company example, the permissible loss Ratio is 81.0 percent. Another way of stating the permissible loss ratio is to say that $.81 of every premium dollar is allocated for all claims and reserves. The remaining $.19 is allocated for case expenses. The actual incurred loss ratio over the 3-year experience base was 83.1 percent. This means the case was underfunded for incurred claims during the 3 years of experience by a little over $.02 for every premium dollar collected.

J.   *Incurred constant loss ratio* – This is the ratio upon which the rate projection is based. It is determined by dividing the incurred claims by the constant premium. Had the current rate been in place throughout the experience base, the paid premium (A) and constant premium (B) would have been the same, and the same ratio would have resulted as for (I) incurred/loss ratio.

In the ABC Company example, the incurred constant loss ratio was 79.0, which is a bit lower than the permissible loss ratio of 81.0. This means only $.79 of every premium dollar collected would need to be allocated for all claims and reserves.

Permissible Loss Ratio or Case Expenses

Expenses to administer the case during the projection period and after case termination need to be included in the premium charged. The projected rate must capture the insurer's cost of doing business as well as profit. The permissible loss ratio is also known by many other names, including acceptable loss ratio, desired loss ratio, or target loss ratio.

Most carriers apply the permissible loss ratio as a divisor to the incurred constant loss ratio. The loss ratio is usually expressed as the inverse of the expense factor. So a case with a higher permissible loss ratio is assumed to have fewer cents per premium dollar allocated towards expenses than a case with a lower permissible loss ratio, as discussed in Chapter 7.

In the ABC Company example, we've applied a permissible loss ratio only to supplemental life. In an actual case, all the incurred claims from basic, supplemental, and dependent life coverage would be combined together, and a single permissible loss ratio would be applied. An insurer's expense factor in the manual rating system or in its underwriting guidelines might look as shown in Figure 8-10.

Figure 8-10. Incurred Constant Loss Ratios and Expense Percentages		
Annual Projected Premium	*Incurred Constant Loss Ratio*	*Expense Percentage (inverse of incurred constant loss ratio)*
$0–$24,999	.65	35%
$25,000–$74,999	.70	30%
$75,000–$124,999	.75	25%
$125,000–$174,999	.80	20%
$175,000–$249,999	.85	15%
$250,000 and over	.90	10%

Most insurers' systems are able to calculate state premium tax, which varies by state. Taxes are included in the expenses that must be covered by the expense percentage.

When applying a permissible loss ratio, the underwriter must account for any extraordinary case expenses that the standard permissible loss ratio does not accommodate. For example, specialized services such as beneficiary card administration may require the underwriter to adjust the permissible loss ratio to account for more of the premium dollar needing to be allocated for case expenses.

Instead of applying a permissible loss ratio to the incurred constant loss ratio, some insurers may have a formula that calculates the projected expenses for the case. The incurred claims are added together with case expenses for an overall projected needed premium. This overall projected needed premium is divided by 12 to get a monthly needed premium and then divided by the reported monthly volume and multiplied by 1,000 to obtain a rate per 1,000 of coverage.

Carriers who normally use a permissible loss ratio approach may calculate actual case expenses in a jumbo account with a formula to give a more accurate depiction of the projected expenses. Using case-specific expenses, an illustrative breakdown might look like Figure 8-11.

Figure 8-11. Breakdown of Case-Specific Expenses	
Claim handling, including premium waiver claims	$ 2,250
State premium tax	4,190
Case setup, maintenance, and overall administration and overhead	17,301
Commissions to producer	5,237
Profit & risk	5,761
Extraordinary charges	1,175
Total expense charge	$ 35,914

The total expenses from Figure 8-11 would be used to calculate the premium rate per $1,000 of coverage as follows:

Projected incurred claims	$173,885
Total expense charge (Figure 8-11)	+ 35,914
Projected needed premium	$209,799
Divided by 12 months	÷ 12
Monthly needed premium	$ 17,483
Rate = Monthly Needed Premium ÷ Volume × 1,000	
= $17,483 ÷ $41,500,000 × 1,000	
= $.421	

Comparing Benchmarks to Experience

After completing the experience analysis, the underwriter will benchmark the needed experience rate to the manual rate. If there is a significant difference between the needed experience rate and the manual rate, the underwriter will likely go back through the evaluation to check the data used and assumptions applied.

If enough credible data exists, the underwriter may compare the claims that actually emerged in the experience to those estimated using the very rough industry benchmarks and average coverage per employee. The rough benchmarks are used with a large grain of salt; they merely gauge whether the experience is extraordinarily higher or lower than "normal." Figure 8-12 shows a comparison of ABC Company's actual experience to the rough benchmarks that were outlined.

Figure 8-12. Comparing ABC Company's Experience to the Benchmarks		
	ABC Company Experience 10/1/09–10/1/12	Rough Benchmarks
Supplemental life claims	$360,000	$357,202
Supplement life waiver claims	139,500	89,293

It so happens that ABC Company's three-year claims experience tracks remarkably close to the rough benchmarks. This is the exception rather than the rule, as most life experience with limited credibility comes nowhere near the benchmarks.

Blending or Melding

Believing the retrospective review to hold true into the future, underwriters project a needed rate for the period of coverage. Based on credibility, the underwriter will meld this rate with the manual rate. This blending process allows the manual rate to be adjusted according to how the case's experience actually emerged.[5]

In our ABC Company example, three full years of experience was used with 1,414 life years. We'll assume the insurer's credibility formula determined the experience to be 25 percent credible.

The underwriter might choose to use only the most recent two years of experience as a projection model. While the Incurred Constant loss ratio would be considerably lower for the two-year model versus the three-year model, the number of life years would also be lower, thereby reducing the credibility of the experience to 15 percent to 20 percent.

The blending formula is:

Blended Rate = (Experience Rate × Credibility %) + [Manual Rate × (1 − Credibility %)]

Using the ABC Company example, assume:

- ABC Company's case experience rate is 25% credible (3 full years of experience was used)

- Manual rate is $.46

- Experience rate is $.419

With this information, the blended rate would be calculated as follows:

Blended Rate = (Experience Rate × Credibility %) + [Manual Rate × (1 − Credibility %)]

$$= (\$.419 \times 25\%) + [\$.46 \times (1 - 25\%)]$$

$$= \$.105 + \$.345$$

$$= \$.45$$

In this example, the favorable experience rate influenced the manual downward slightly. Despite the favorable experience, the limited credibility of the experience had only a modest impact on the final needed rate. If no other factors are considered, this formula blended rate is the "needed rate" the underwriter would quote on the supplemental life.

Participation Adjustment

After the initial needed rate has been established, the underwriter may need to adjust it for projected or potential changes in the participation level of the contributory supplemental life plan.

The experience generated by the insured population reflects the spread of risk in that population. A participation level of 25 percent of the eligible employees is likely to produce a worse loss ratio than a participation level of 55 percent. The underwriter will examine the participation level that occurred during the experience base. The underwriter will then project whether the participation level will remain constant, increase, or decrease.

Participation levels in a supplemental life plan could change for any number of reasons. The underwriter will likely have evaluated those reasons during the risk selection process. The most common factors impacting employee participation in a voluntary plan are changes:

- to the rate;

- to the plan;

- in access to the plan, especially based on eligibility and enrollment processes;

- in employer level of premium contribution;

- in employer communications about the plan.

In the event that projected participation is different than that during the experience base, the underwriter may adjust the needed rate up or down. This holds true for both the manual rate and the experience rate. So, if contributory rates are to increase, the underwriter will have to factor into the projected rate what impact the rate increase itself will have on plan participation.

Assumptions and Contingencies

It is rare for the underwriter to have all the information he or she deems necessary to make an accurate proposal, so underwriters routinely quote with stated assumptions and contingencies to lessen areas of uncertainty.

If the assumptions are flawed or incorrect, the underwriter usually reserves the right to reevaluate the risk in total. It is incumbent upon the producer to identify any situation where the underwriter's assumptions are invalid. For example, the underwriter may assume that a minimum participation percentage will be achieved on the supplemental life plan at the enrollment. The underwriter may even make the quoted supplemental life rate contingent upon achieving a minimum participation level. If there are reasons assumed participation levels may be impaired, the underwriter needs to know.

An underwriter may offer a quote that is contingent on certain things happening. If these events do not occur, the underwriter reserves the right to reevaluate the risk and, if necessary, to pull the quote entirely. For example, an underwriter might quote contingent upon receiving certain experience data that was missing from the RFP but which was told to him or her verbally. If the hardcopy experience isn't received, the underwriter can invoke the contingency.

Most quote letters indicate the proposed effective date of coverage as well as a stated time limit for how long the offer is valid. The letter will also indicate the rate guarantee. The letter will state the benefit plan for which the rates are being offered. Any concerns related to the RFP will also be addressed in the quote letter.

The assumptions and contingencies stated in the quote letter are an essential risk management component of the quote. They empower the underwriter to reevaluate and/or renegotiate the terms of the offer if the assumptions and contingencies are not valid. This includes the insurer subsequently rejecting the case if material differences surface that would significantly affect the risk level.

Key Takeaways

- Life rates are heavily reliant on the manual rate. AD&D rates are almost exclusively established by the manual rate.

- Careful structure of the life benefits plan is a prime method of risk management.

- Having an appropriately modest noncontributory basic life plan is important to maximizing employee participation in the contributory supplemental life plan.

- Underwriters run tests on the RFP data to verify the validity and accuracy of the information provided.

- Having complete and accurate experience and plan information is vital for the underwriter to conduct a thorough experience evaluation.

- A reinsurer's approval is required before the quote is issued if any of the plan elements exceed standard reinsurance guidelines.

- Credibility is the determining factor as to how much the actual experience is used in determining the projected needed rate.

- Manual rates are of primary importance in determining life rates in all but the largest case segments. Ensuring the accuracy of the manual rate is crucial for accurate pricing.

- Blending or melding of manual and experience rates is a standard technique in developing the needed rate.

- Assumptions and contingencies are common in the quote offer and are designed to mitigate the unknown factors in the risk evaluation process.

- RFP requests for longer rate guarantees are common and may be considered by the underwriter depending on all of the risk elements associated with the case and/or underwriting guidelines.

- The costs for administrative requests that are nonstandard for the insurer will be factored into any quoted price.

Endnotes

1. Kirner, Tom and Pete Silkowski, *Group Benefits Disability Specialist Course Handbook* (Erlanger, KY: The National Underwriter Company), p. 16-25.
2. Ibid., p. 16-5.
3. Ibid., p. 16-26.
4. Ibid., p. 17-2.
5. Ibid., p. 16-15.

Chapter 9

Group Life and AD&D Claims Process

This chapter can be used to inform policyholders about key information and processes that are necessary for the insurer to adjudicate claims. Communicating and reinforcing the key takeaways can help ensure prompt and efficient service on life, AD&D, dependent life, premium waiver, and accelerated benefits claims.

This chapter will outline the claims process for Group Life and Accidental Death & Dismemberment (AD&D) insurance. The information required to file a claim and the claims process, including the use of internal insurance company resources, will be addressed.

The Group Life and AD&D Claims Process

The claims process for life insurance has three major steps: intake, decision, and payment. The process is not overly complicated, as it is usually very clear that the insured has died. However, there can be complicating factors, especially in group insurance where eligibility issues may come into play or when the employee is filing a waiver of premium claim. As discussed in Chapter 5, most group term life products contain a waiver of premium provision. The life policy may also contain an accelerated death benefit option, which allows a covered employee with a terminal illness to receive partial proceeds while still alive. With AD&D coverage, there can be a question about the nature of the accident and the covered loss.

The submission of a loss of life claim on a group life/AD&D policy differs from a group medical or disability claim in that the claimant is not submitting the claim. With the death of the employee, the beneficiary or appointed executor submits the necessary claim documentation to the insurer. With the death of a dependent, the employee submits the documentation. Claims examiners are trained on how to proceed through the claims process with persons who have recently suffered the loss of a loved one.

The submission of a premium waiver claim or an AD&D casualty loss does require the employee-claimant to submit the necessary information to the insurer. Some insurers who have long-term disability (LTD) coverage in addition to life/AD&D may not require a resubmission of information for a waiver of premium claim if that information has already been submitted under the Short Term Disability (STD).

Claim Time Frames

Insurers encourage the beneficiary or the employee-claimant to submit the necessary documentation as quickly as possible. Not submitting a claim within the preferred timeframe established by the insurer does not disqualify a person from submitting a valid claim. Insurers hold reserves in the event that a claim is submitted months or even years after the date of death.

The insurer is bound by the Employee Retirement Income Security Act (ERISA) of 1974 to adjudicate a claim within 90 days of receipt of a complete proof of loss. Complete Proof of Loss means the insurer has all the information necessary in order to make a claim determination (perfected claim).

Most insurers require a premium waiver claimant to submit proof of loss within 12 months of the initial date of disability. As time passes and the claimant's condition changes, trying to determine disability and the degree to which the claimant was/is disabled can get more difficult. Thus, timely submission of disability waiver claims is recommended. A sample waiver claim form from UNUM Life Insurance Company of America, is shown in Appendix 9A.

Many insurers require that proof of loss on an AD&D claim be submitted within 90 days of the accident, provided the claimant or beneficiary is able to do so. Inability to provide the proof of loss within the 90 days will not preclude payment of the claim.

If a claim is denied, the beneficiary has 60 days to request a written appeal. Once all the facts and additional information of the appeal are received, the insurer is required to make a decision on the appeal within 60 days of the receipt of all necessary appeals documentation.

Many states require that the insurer start paying interest on the claim amount after a certain period of time, regardless of whether or not the beneficiary has submitted all the necessary documentation.

Claim Intake Process

Intake starts when the insurer receives a completed claim form. Claims examiners refer to this as a "perfected" claim form.

Insurance companies allow several options by which a claim may be submitted, including a:

- paper form mailed in using the U.S. Postal Service;

- paper form faxed to the insurer;

- electronic form e-mailed to the insurer;

- electronic form completed online at the insurer's Web site;

- form information provided over the telephone (telephonic intake).

The claim form itself can be somewhat daunting at first because of its sheer size. A bereaved or disabled person presented with a multi-page form can be easily overwhelmed. However, a producer working with the employee can help ensure the form is filled out completely. A sample claim form from Assurant Employee Benefit Group is shown in Appendix 9B.

The loss of life claim form requires three basic information types: employer, deceased (employee or dependent), and beneficiary. Additional information may also be necessary and will be described.

Employer Information to Process a Claim

Employer information is required as the policy/contract is between the employer and the insurer. The insurer involves the employer in the claims process to validate that the employee was eligible and enrolled for the coverage at the time of the loss. The employer is also involved to determine if evidence of good health was required of the employee and that the administration of the evidence process was properly executed.

Information required includes:

- employer name;

- employer address and telephone number;

- policy number and type(s) of insurance;

- enrollment card on contributory coverage;

- beneficiary designation form.

This information is used by the insurer to identify the policy. The insurer will need to review the terms of the policy to ensure what benefits are payable. Note that there may well be more than one policy on the deceased employee, especially if the employer had supplemental life and/or AD&D in addition to basic life insurance. The insurer will also need to confirm that the policy (or policies) was in force on the date of death.

Employee Information to Process a Claim

Employee information will generally be furnished by the employer. This basic information will include:

- deceased (or disabled) employee's name;

- employee's Social Security number;

- employee's address;

- employee's earnings and basis (hourly, salaried, etc.);

- date of birth and date of death.

This information is used to ensure the employee was covered under the policy as well as to determine the amount of benefits payable. There most likely will be additional questions posed. These can vary by insurer but can include such items as:

- date hired or effective date of insurance;

- date last worked;

- occupation;

- date of accident (if applicable).

These are used in addition to the basic information items by the insurer to determine the insurer's liability.

Beneficiary Information to Process a Life Claim

Beneficiary information is required by the insurer. This will typically include the beneficiary's:

- name;

- address and telephone number;

- Social Security number (SSN);

- date of birth;

- relationship to the insured;

- bank or financial institution if the claim will be paid by electronic transfer.

This information is necessary so the insurer will know to whom to make payment. There will also be statements required to be signed by the beneficiary. These can include a certification of tax number (SSN), authorization to release information (should the insurer need medical records), and possibly a HIPAA release. The Health Insurance Portability and Accountability Act of 1996 (HIPAA) among other aspects protects an individual's privacy when it comes to health matters. When an insurance company needs to contact a claimant's physician for information on the claimant's health condition, the insurance company must first obtain permission from the claimant or claimant's family in the form of a HIPAA release.

There will most likely be information about the form of payment as well. Besides lump sum arrangements, most insurers will offer a method of depositing funds in a bank account for the beneficiary to draw upon, either by check or debit card. If the policy provides for some sort of periodic payment of proceeds, this will be asked as well.

Some insurers offer beneficiary assistance services. If this service applies, a representative will contact the beneficiary. If the beneficiary wants assistance in determining how to use the claim assets, the representative will likely ask for a great deal more information relating to the beneficiary's finances and financial goals.

Additional Information to Process a Life Claim

In addition to all of this information, there will also be a fraud warning as required by state regulation. Some insurers will have all the warnings for the various states on the claim form.

The insurer will always require a copy of the death certificate. A copy of the enrollment card with beneficiary designation is required as well, usually administered and kept by the employer. In cases where the insurer provides the beneficiary designation service, the insurer would maintain the beneficiary information and the employer is relieved from this duty.

One of the most important things to note is that whatever the format of the claim form, a *complete* claim form is an absolute requirement. Missing information in any of the above categories will delay payment of the claim.

Upon receipt of the claim form, many insurers may have a claim department representative contact the beneficiary. This may be necessary to gather additional information (as in the case of an accident) or simply as a service measure.

Additional Information for AD&D Loss of Life

The AD&D policy has exclusions, and the insurer will investigate each accident claim to ensure that an accident has occurred and to determine if any exclusions apply to the claim. If there is a claim under the supplemental life policy, the insurer will investigate to determine if the suicide exclusion applies.

In addition to the information already described, the insurer will typically require the following information, according to the nature of the accident:

- Police and/or accident report

- Coroner's and/or autopsy report

- Proof that the accident occurred on a recognized public conveyance (for common carrier or double indemnity provision)

Additional Information for Waiver of Premium or AD&D Casualty

Exclusions may also apply to a casualty loss (loss of limb or sight) under the AD&D policy. Moreover, appropriate medical information is needed to determine the precise extent of the claimant's incapacity, since payment is based on the contractually defined impairment or loss. The additional information often required for an AD&D casualty loss includes:

- hospital and/or medical records;

- doctor(s) report(s).

Waiver of premium claims also require extensive medical information to determine if the claimant meets (or continues to meet) the insurer's definition of total disability. The policy language typically requires the claimant to be disabled to the extent that the claimant cannot perform any occupation (called "any occ") for wage or profit. This can be a somewhat complicated determination, so medical information about the claimant's medical condition is critical. Note that the insurance company will not ask the attending physician if the claimant is disabled. Under ERISA, only the insurance company as claim fiduciary of the plan has the authority, indeed responsibility, to make that determination.

The date of disability is an essential element in determining when the claimant completes the required waiver elimination period. Typically, this period is from 180 to 270 days, beginning with the first day not worked due to the disability and after which the claimant is eligible for benefits. The additional information often required for a waiver of premium claim includes:

- waiver of premium claim form (can be the insurer's disability claim form);

- medical records;

- doctor(s) report(s), including diagnosis and prognosis;

- Independent Medical Exam (IME).

A payment to an accelerated benefit claimant may require an attending physician's statement about the prognosis and life expectancy of the claimant if not already indicated in the physician reports. If the claimant has already been approved for Waiver of Premium, then such a physician's statement would be redundant.

The Claim Decision Process

The claim decision or adjudication process commences upon receipt of complete documentation. Usually, the decision is straightforward. In those situations in which the eligibility of the employee is in doubt, the examiner has additional resources in the insurance company to call upon. Aside from eligibility issues, the reasons to call upon other resources include:

An unclear benefit amount.

- For example, a times earnings schedule in which the salary has recently changed and evidence should have been submitted for the increase in coverage but was not. In this situation, the insurer may pay the life insurance coverage that was in effect prior to the salary change. Another example could be a times earnings schedule when the salary is simply not clear. In this case, the insurer will need payroll records from the employer to determine what exactly the earnings were at time of death.

An accidental death.

- The insurer may need police reports in the case of a motor vehicle accident. In most states, driving while intoxicated is a felony offense and the insurer's policy might not pay an AD&D benefit in this situation.

An accelerated benefit claim.

- In the situation in which the insured has been diagnosed with a terminal illness, the insured and insured's family might want to take advantage of a policy provision to pay a partial benefit while the insured is still alive. To do so, the insurer will require medical documentation that the illness is terminal.

A waiver claim due to a disability.

- Waiver claims can be complicated due to the difficulty in determining the presence of a disability severe enough to prevent the insured from performing at any occupation.

The disability claim form is typically more complicated (see Appendix 9A for a sample disability waiver claim form). There could be quite a bit of back and forth between the insured and the insurer before the final determination is established.

The claims examiner can count on the following resources to help him/her arrive at a decision:

Legal Department

- Contested claims are likely to involve litigation. The examiner may consult with the insurer's own legal department to ensure the company has a sound position for approval or denial.

Clinical resources

- Some claims—including waiver claims, accelerated death benefit claims, and AD&D claims—will involve medical information. The examiner may use the expertise of staff physicians and/or nurses to assist with the analysis and interpretation of such information.

- Special investigative units

  - A few claims are going to be fraudulent. While the actual occurrence of life insurance fraud is considered relatively small, insurance companies investigate claims of a suspicious nature. The examiner may involve the company's special investigative unit if there is reason to suspect some sort of fraud.

The claim examiner will review all documentation to determine if the claim is payable. Recall that the examiner (and insurance company) is a claim fiduciary under ERISA and, as such, has a duty to ensure the plan is administered "prudently" for the sole benefit of the plan's "participants and their beneficiaries" by "following the plan documents."

The examiner also has a responsibility to the insurance company to ensure benefits are paid correctly. Companies routinely require examiners to be 95 percent to 99 percent accurate in life claim adjudication.[1]

Claims files are routinely audited by insurance companies to ensure their examiners and processes are as accurate and timely as possible.

Key decisions will be reached for the following items:

Policy and applicable provisions were in force at incurral date of claim.

- This means premium payments are up to date. Employers who are habitually late with premium payments can cause claim delays. Claims systems in use today are integrated with an insurer's premium receipt and accounting systems. Premiums overdue by some specific period (which can vary by insurer) will trigger an electronic hold on the claims system, which prevents an examiner from issuing a claims payment. Switching from one insurer to another may also be the cause of a claim being denied, as the policy may not have been in force on the date of death or disability.

The decedent was eligible for coverage.

- The decedent must have been in an eligible class and properly enrolled for coverage. If coverage underwriting rules required Evidence of Insurability (EOI), there must be documentation of an approved EOI. If the date of death is during any sort of coverage extension, there must be proper notification and documentation.

The claim amount will be determined:

- The amount of coverage must be verified. When times salary schedules are involved, payroll records may be requested for verification of the claim amount. If the amount of insurance was increased at a recent annual enrollment, for example, the examiner must determine if proper procedures were followed for the increase. If the payment requires interest to be added to the face amount, the examiner must ensure the proper interest is credited.

The beneficiary to receive payment will be determined.

- While at face value, determining to whom to pay the life insurance proceeds sounds simple, the reality can be far different. First, the group insurance company, unlike individual insurance, may not even have a record of who the beneficiary is. Many carriers rely on the policyholder to maintain beneficiary designations.[2] Marriages and divorces can also create beneficiary designation issues. The insured may have failed to update for life changes, or the record keeping may have been done inadequately.

- Additionally, the beneficiary must be legally competent to receive the death proceeds. For example, a minor is not legally qualified. The insurer may have a facility of payment provision in the policy to address this. The facility of payment provision permits the insurer to make monthly payments to any person or institution who has assumed responsibility for the minor. Once the minor's legal guardian makes claim on behalf of the minor beneficiary, the provision ends.[3] This provision also permits the insurer to make payments from the life proceeds to an individual who has paid funeral costs for the deceased.[4]

Claim Payment and Communication

The claim decision is communicated to the individual making claim for the policy proceeds. Generally, a decision will be made and communicated within 5 to 10 days after receipt of complete information.[5]

If the decision is a denial, under ERISA the denial must contain procedures to contest the claim. This includes the option to have an independent review of the claim decision. Most importantly, the denial must be communicated in writing to the individual making the claim.

If the claim is payable, the examiner will contact the claimant as standard procedure for many companies. This involves a discussion of the way in which the proceeds will be paid:

- Lump sum check

- Deposit in an interest-bearing checking account

- Some other settlement option as specified in the policy itself

    - Other settlement options can have income tax consequences. Income tax issues are covered in Chapter 10.

Producers can have a great effect on how well claims decisions turn out. The following are recommendations for producers:

1. Make sure eligibility is clearly defined, understood by the employer, and properly administered.

2. If there is an eligibility waiting period, make sure the employer is properly notifying new employees of their need to make a decision upon their completion of the waiting period.

3. If evidence of insurability (EOI) is required for any portion of life face amounts, ensure the employer understands how to administer it.

4. Ensure that the employer understands the importance of administering beneficiary designations and changes to them.

5. For life amount schedules that are based on earnings, ensure records are properly kept of salary changes. Note that if an employee's salary increase causes the face amount to exceed the guaranteed issue limit, the employee often must submit evidence of insurability for the excess over the guaranteed issue amount.

6. Arrange for the employer's staff handling plan administration to get instruction from the appropriate insurer's staff to clear up any questions and to reinforce proper procedures.

7. Make sure that all employee beneficiary designation or enrollment cards are current and up to date.

    The insurer is required by law to pay the claim to the beneficiary last designated. However, community property states such as Texas and California require that 50 percent of the claim proceeds be paid to the current spouse even if not the named beneficiary. This averts legal situations where current and ex-spouses contend the claim or where the named beneficiary is deceased.

    An updated beneficiary designation form:

    •   Ensures the claim proceeds go to the one intended by the decedent.

    •   Reduces claim processing time by having a clear payment path and avoids legal challenges that will slow up the process.

8. On transfer of carriers, avoid pitfalls by completing the following actions:

    •   Check if anyone is grandfathered for an insurance benefit. If so, obtain in writing the new carrier's acceptance of the grandfathered terms. Include a written list of those individuals who are grandfathered. For example, if a group of employees is allowed by a new carrier to maintain an older, more generous age reduction schedule, this should be clearly stated in the form of an "administrative letter" from the new carrier, which should become part of the new policy.

    •   Ask the employer if there is anyone not actively at work. If so, help the employer ascertain the status of such employees. If it appears the absent individual may evolve into a waiver of premium claim, determine how the old carrier wants to handle premium payments while the person is away from work. If premium is not paid during the individual's elimination period for the waiver, it could jeopardize coverage.

    •   Check if any employees have designated a trust as beneficiary. If so, ensure that the new carrier will accept such designations. Some carriers don't accept trusts. The same applies with anyone who has assigned coverage. Assignment of coverage is sometimes arranged by high wage earners as a means of estate planning and those assigning benefits are often principals or officers in the policyholder's company. So it is worthwhile investigating whether or not the insurer will accept a trust as beneficiary.

    •   Finally, make sure there is no gap in coverage between the carriers.

Appeals Process

A claim denial letter explains to the beneficiary or the insured the reasons for the denial. Applicable policy provisions are typically cited. Missing information that may have caused the denial will be described. The letter also describes the process to follow if the denied person wants to file an appeal of the decision.

The denial letter also states the claimant's rights under the ERISA appeals process. These include the right to:

- appoint a representative or adviser to assist with the appeal;

- review the documentation relating to the claim decision;

- provide additional information, ask questions, or make comments in writing.

Key Takeaways

- Insurers offer a variety of methods by which a life/AD&D claim can be submitted.

- A completed claim form along with supporting documentation is required in order for the claim adjudication process to be completed. Missing information will delay processing of the claim.

- Beneficiaries and employees are entitled to appeal a claim denial as dictated by ERISA.

- Insurers are required to make timely claim decisions as dictated by ERISA.

- Claims examiners can rely on a host of resources to help them to make a decision.

- A claim denial must be communicated to the claimant in writing.

- Producers can assist in ensuring proper life/AD&D claim adjudication.

- The type of information required to process a claim varies depending on whether it is in regards to loss of life, a casualty loss, or waiver of premium.

- Ensuring that all employees have their beneficiary designations up to date is vitally important.

- The initial date of disability is a key date in determining the approval date for a waiver of premium request.

- The disability claim form is typically more complicated than a death claim form.

- Claims files are routinely audited by insurance companies to ensure their examiners and processes are as accurate and timely as possible.

Endnotes

1. Landry, Kimberly, "Large-Case Group Life Practices," *LIMRA.com/abstracts* (Windsor, CT: LL Global, September 18, 2009), p. 15.

2. Brown, Cheryl, "Assignment of Group Life Coverage and Administration of Beneficiary Designations," *LIMRA.com/abstracts* (Windsor, CT: LL Global December 3, 2008), p. 6.

3. Beam, Burton T, *Group Benefits: Basic Concepts and Alternatives,* 10th Edition (Bryn Mawr, PA: The American College Press, 2004), p. 558.

4. Ibid., p. 83.

5. Landry, op. cit., p. 14.

Appendix 9A: Example of Disability Waiver Claim Form

DISABILITY CLAIM FORM

The Benefits Center
P.O. Box 100158, Columbia, SC 29202-3158

Pacific Time Zone   Toll-free: 1-877-851-7637   Fax: 1-877-851-7624
All Other Time Zones Toll-free: 1-800-858-6843   Fax: 1-800-447-2498
Call toll-free Monday through Friday, 8 a.m. to 8 p.m. (Eastern Time).

For use with policies issued by the following Unum Group ["Unum"] subsidiaries:

Unum Life Insurance Company of America   Provident Life and Accident Insurance Company
The Paul Revere Life Insurance Company

OUR COMMITMENT TO YOU

We understand that a disabling illness or injury creates emotional, physical and financial challenges, and we want to do whatever we can to help you. You have our commitment to provide you with responsive service and to be understanding and sensitive to your circumstances during the claim process.

INSTRUCTIONS

When should you use this claim form?

Use this claim form to submit a disability claim to Unum. This form should be used for the following types of claims only:

- Long Term Disability

- Any combination of the following: Long Term Disability, Individual Disability and Life Insurance Waiver of Premium. If you are covered for more than one of these products, this is the only form you need to complete.

Who is responsible for completing this claim form?

The information provided on this claim form will be used to evaluate your eligibility for disability benefits. Please provide complete and legible responses to ensure your claim is processed as quickly as possible. Please enclose any additional information you feel will assist us in the evaluation of your claim.

- **Employee/Individual Statement (pages 4-7):** Please complete this section of the claim form and fax it to 1-877-851-7624 (Pacific time zone) or 1-800-447-2498 (all other time zones). If you prefer, it may be mailed to the address noted above.

- Please complete the name and date of birth fields at the top of every page for easy identification purposes in case the pages become separated.

- **Direct Deposit Request (page 8):** Please complete this form is you wish to have your Long Term Disability benefits deposited directly into your bank account.

- **Authorization to Share Information with Third Parties (page 9):** If you wish to give us permission to share the details of your claim with a third party (such as your spouse, child, sibling, friend, etc.), please sign and date this form and fax it to 1-877-851-7624 (Pacific time zone) or 1-800-447-2498 (all other time zones). If you prefer, it may be mailed to the address noted above.

- **Employee/Individual Authorization (last page):** Please sign and date this form and provide a copy to your attending physician. Fax the completed form to 1-877-851-7624 (Pacific time zone) or 1-800-447-2498 (all other time zones) or mail it to the address noted above.

- **Employer Statement (pages 10-12):** Please give this section of the claim form to your employer and ask him/her to complete, sign and date the form. Your employer should fax the completed form to 1-877-851-7624 (Pacific time zone) or 1-800-447-2498 (all other time zones) or mail it to the address noted above.

- **Attending Physician Statement (pages 13-15):** Please complete Part I of this statement, then give this section of the claim form to the physician or treating provider primarily responsible for your care. Ask him/her to complete Part II and fax the completed form to 1-877-851-7624 (Pacific time zone) or 1-800-447-2498 (all other time zones). If s/he prefers, it may be mailed to the address noted above.

Questions?

If, at any time, you have questions about the claim process or need help to complete this form, please call the above toll-free number. Our Contact Center is staffed with experienced professionals who can be contacted from 8 a.m. to 8 p.m. Monday through Friday.

DISABILITY CLAIM FORM
The Benefits Center
P.O. Box 100158, Columbia, SC 29202-3158
Pacific Time Zone   Toll-free: 1-877-851-7637   Fax: 1-877-851-7624
All Other Time Zones Toll-free: 1-800-858-6843   Fax: 1-800-447-2498
Call toll-free Monday through Friday, 8 a.m. to 8 p.m. (Eastern Time).

Instructions (continued) / Claim Fraud Statements

Fraud Warning

For your protection, the laws of several states, including Alaska, Arizona, Arkansas, Delaware, Idaho, Indiana, Louisiana, Maine, Maryland, New Mexico, Ohio, Oklahoma, Rhode Island, Tennessee, Texas, Virginia, Washington, and West Virginia require the following statement to appear on this claim form:

Any person who knowingly and with the intent to injure, defraud or deceive an insurance company presents a false or fraudulent claim for payment of a loss or benefit or knowingly presents false information in an application for insurance is guilty of a crime and may be subject to fines and confinement in prison.

Fraud Warning for California Residents
For your protection, California law requires the following to appear on this claim form:
Any person who knowingly presents a false or fraudulent claim for the payment of a loss is guilty of a crime and may be subject fines and confinement in state prison.

Fraud Warning for Colorado Residents
For your protection, Colorado law requires the following to appear on this claim form:
It is unlawful to knowingly provide false, incomplete, or misleading facts or information to an insurance company for the purpose of defrauding or attempting to defraud the company. Penalties may include imprisonment, fines, denial of insurance, and civil damages. Any insurance company or agent of an insurance company who knowingly provides false, incomplete, or misleading facts or information to a policyholder or claimant for the purpose of defrauding or attempting to defraud the policyholder or claimant with regard to a settlement or award payable from insurance proceeds shall be reported to the Colorado Division of Insurance within the Department of Regulatory Agencies.

Fraud Warning for District of Columbia Residents
For your protection, the District of Columbia requires the following to appear on this claim form:
WARNING: It is a crime to provide false or misleading information to an insurer for the purpose of defrauding the insurer or any other person. Penalties include imprisonment and/or fines. In addition, an insurer may deny insurance benefits, if false information materially related to a claim was provided by the applicant.

Fraud Warning for Florida Residents
For your protection, Florida law requires the following to appear on this claim form:
Any person who knowingly and with intent to injure, defraud or deceive any insurer, files a statement of claim or an application containing false, incomplete or misleading information is guilty of a felony of the third degree.

Fraud Warning for Kentucky Residents
For your protection, Kentucky law requires the following to appear on this claim form:
Any person who knowingly and with intent to defraud any insurance company or other person files a statement of claim containing any materially false information or conceals, for the purpose of misleading, information concerning any fact material thereto commits a fraudulent insurance act, which is a crime.

Fraud Warning for Minnesota Residents
For your protection, Minnesota law requires the following to appear on this claim form:
A person who files a claim with intent to defraud or helps commit a fraud against an insurer is guilty of a crime.

Fraud Warning for New Hampshire Residents
For your protection, New Hampshire law requires the following to appear on this claim form:
Any person who, with a purpose to injure, defraud, or deceive any insurance company, files a statement of claim containing any false, incomplete, or misleading information is subject to prosecution and punishment for insurance fraud, as provided in RSA 638.20.

Fraud Warning for New Jersey Residents
For your protection, New Jersey law requires the following to appear on this claim form:
Any person who knowingly and with intent to defraud any insurance company or other persons, files a statement of claim containing any materially false information, or conceals for the purpose of misleading, information concerning any fact, material thereto, commits a fraudulent insurance act, which is a crime, subject to criminal prosecution and civil penalties.

DISABILITY CLAIM FORM
The Benefits Center
P.O. Box 100158, Columbia, SC 29202-3158
Pacific Time Zone   Toll-free: 1-877-851-7637   Fax: 1-877-851-7624
All Other Time Zones Toll-free: 1-800-858-6843   Fax: 1-800-447-2498
Call toll-free Monday through Friday, 8 a.m. to 8 p.m. (Eastern Time).

Instructions (continued) / Claim Fraud Statements

Fraud Warning for New York Residents

For your protection, New York law requires the following to appear on this claim form:
Any person who knowingly and with the intent to defraud any insurance company or other person files an application for insurance or statement of claim containing any materially false information, or conceals for the purpose of misleading, information concerning any fact material thereto, commits a fraudulent insurance act, which is a crime, and shall also be subject to a civil penalty not to exceed five thousand dollars and the stated value of the claim for each such violation.

Fraud Warning for Pennsylvania Residents

For your protection, Pennsylvania law requires the following to appear on this claim form:
Any person who knowingly and with intent to defraud any insurance company or other person files an application for insurance or statement of claim containing any materially false information or conceals for the purpose of misleading, information concerning any fact material thereto commits a fraudulent insurance act, which is a crime and subjects such person to criminal and civil penalties.

Fraud Warning for Puerto Rico Residents

For your protection, Puerto Rico law requires the following to appear on this claim form:
Any person who knowingly and with the intention of defrauding presents false information in an insurance application, or presents, helps, or causes the presentation of a fraudulent claim for the payment of a loss or any other benefit, or presents more than one claim for the same damage or loss, shall incur a felony and, upon conviction, shall be sanctioned for each violation with the penalty of a fine of not less than five thousand dollars ($5,000) and not more than ten thousand dollars ($10,000), or a fixed term of imprisonment for three (3) years, or both penalties. If aggravating circumstances are present, the penalty thus established may be increased to a maximum of five (5) years; if extenuating circumstances are present, it may be reduced to a minimum of two (2) years.

DISABILITY CLAIM FORM
The Benefits Center
P.O. Box 100158, Columbia, SC 29202-3158
Pacific Time Zone   Toll-free: 1-877-851-7637   Fax: 1-877-851-7624
All Other Time Zones Toll-free: 1-800-858-6843   Fax: 1-800-447-2498
Call toll-free Monday through Friday, 8 a.m. to 8 p.m. (Eastern Time).

EMPLOYEE/INDIVIDUAL STATEMENT (PLEASE PRINT)

A. Information About You

Last Name   Suffix   First Name   M

Date of Birth (mm/dd/yy)   Social Security Number   Gender
                                                                                           ☐ Male
                                                                                           ☐ Female

Home Address

City   State   Zip
                                                                                          -

Home Telephone Number   Cell Telephone Number

The state in which you work   Preferred e-mail address (for confirmation purposes only)

Employer Name

Language Preference   ☐ English ☐ Spanish

Please check all types of coverage you have with Unum.

☐ Short Term Disability   ☐ Long Term Disability   ☐ Individual Disability   ☐ Life Insurance   ☐ Voluntary Benefits Disability

☐ Voluntary Benefits Cancer/Critical Illness   ☐ Voluntary Benefits Accident   ☐ Voluntary Benefits MedSupport

Are you currently self-employed? ☐ Yes ☐ No | Do you work for another employer? ☐ Yes ☐ No

If yes, employer name: | Telephone Number

B. Information About the Condition(s) Causing Your Disability

1. For **illness**, answer the following questions then go to #4:

What is the name of your medical condition? | What were your first symptoms?

Describe when you first noticed the symptoms. | Date you were first treated by a physician (mm/dd/yy):

2. For an **injury**, answer the following questions then go to #4:

What is the name of your medical condition?

Describe where and how the injury occurred.

Date the injury occurred (mm/dd/yy): | If related to a motor vehicle accident, was an accident report filed? ☐ Yes ☐ No | Date you were first treated by a physician (mm/dd/yy):

3. For **pregnancy**, answer the following questions then go to #4:

What is your expected delivery date?

Were there any complications causing you to stop work prior to your expected delivery date? ☐ Yes ☐ No | If yes, please explain:

Have you already delivered? ☐ Yes ☐ No | If yes, what type of delivery? ☐ Vaginal ☐ C-Section | If yes, date of delivery:

CL-1019 (02/12)   4

DISABILITY CLAIM FORM
The Benefits Center
P.O. Box 100158, Columbia, SC 29202-3158
Pacific Time Zone   Toll-free: 1-877-851-7637   Fax: 1-877-851-7624
All Other Time Zones   Toll-free: 1-800-858-6843   Fax: 1-800-447-2498
Call toll-free Monday through Friday, 8 a.m. to 8 p.m. (Eastern Time).

EMPLOYEE/INDIVIDUAL STATEMENT (Continued)

Employee/Individual's Name (Last Name, Suffix, First Name, MI)   Date of Birth (mm/dd/yy)

4. For **all medical conditions**, answer the following questions:

What specific duties of your occupation are you unable to perform due to your medical condition?

Have you been treated for this condition(s) in the past? ☐ Yes ☐ No	If yes, when and by whom?
Is your condition related to your occupation? ☐ Yes ☐ No If no, go to Section C.	If yes, please explain:

Have you filed a Workers' Compensation claim? ☐ Yes ☐ No   If no, do you intend to file a Workers' Compensation claim? ☐ Yes ☐ No

C. Information About Your Disability

Date last worked (mm/dd/yy):	Number of hours worked on date last worked:	Date you were first unable to work due to this medical condition (mm/dd/yy):

D. Information About Physicians, Hospitals and Medications: This information will assist us in the evaluation of your claim.

Please provide the following information about all your current medical treatment providers (physicians, hospitals, physical therapists, etc). If you are being treated by more than two, please use a separate sheet of paper and include it with this form.

1.
Provider Name   Mailing Address   (   )
                                                                          Telephone No.
Specialty   City   State   Zip   (   )
                                                                          Fax No.
Date of First Visit (mm/dd/yy)   Date of Next Visit (mm/dd/yy)

2.
Provider Name   Mailing Address   (   )
                                                                          Telephone No.
Specialty   City   State   Zip   (   )
                                                                          Fax No.
Date of First Visit (mm/dd/yy)   Date of Next Visit (mm/dd/yy)

Please list any recent (within the last 12 months) hospital visits/admissions. If you have had more than two, use a separate sheet of paper and include it with this form.

1.
Hospital   Address   Date of Visit/Admission (mm/dd/yy)
Procedure   City   State   Zip   Date of Discharge (mm/dd/yy)

2.
Hospital   Address   Date of Visit/Admission (mm/dd/yy)
Procedure   City   State   Zip   Date of Discharge (mm/dd/yy)

Please list all current medications. If you have more than five, use a separate sheet of paper and include it with this form.

Prescription Name	Dosage/Frequency	Prescribing Physician	Pharmacy Name
1.			
2.			
3.			
4.			
5.			

** unum®**

DISABILITY CLAIM FORM
The Benefits Center
P.O. Box 100158, Columbia, SC 29202-3158
Pacific Time Zone   Toll-free: 1-877-851-7637   Fax: 1-877-851-7624
All Other Time Zones   Toll-free: 1-800-858-6843   Fax: 1-800-447-2498
Call toll-free Monday through Friday, 8 a.m. to 8 p.m. (Eastern Time).

EMPLOYEE/INDIVIDUAL STATEMENT (Continued)

Employee/Individual's Name (Last Name, Suffix, First Name, MI)   Date of Birth (mm/dd/yy)

E. Information About Other Disability Income: This information is important to ensure the accuracy of your disability benefit calculation.

You may be receiving income from other sources that could reduce your benefit from Unum. Please indicate what other income benefits you are eligible to recei
or are receiving as a result of your disability and complete the information requested.

Other Source of Income	Eligible to Receive	Receiving	Amount	Benefit Begin Da
Short Term Disability	☐ Yes ☐ No ☐ Unknown	☐ Yes ☐ No ☐ Unknown		
State Disability Plan (CA, HI, NJ, NY, PR, RI)	☐ Yes ☐ No ☐ Unknown	☐ Yes ☐ No ☐ Unknown		
Workers' Compensation	☐ Yes ☐ No ☐ Unknown	☐ Yes ☐ No ☐ Unknown		
Motor Vehicle Insurance	☐ Yes ☐ No ☐ Unknown	☐ Yes ☐ No ☐ Unknown		
Third Party Settlement/Income	☐ Yes ☐ No ☐ Unknown	☐ Yes ☐ No ☐ Unknown		
Social Security/Disability	☐ Yes ☐ No ☐ Unknown	☐ Yes ☐ No ☐ Unknown		
Social Security/Family	☐ Yes ☐ No ☐ Unknown	☐ Yes ☐ No ☐ Unknown		
Social Security/Retirement	☐ Yes ☐ No ☐ Unknown	☐ Yes ☐ No ☐ Unknown		
Unemployment	☐ Yes ☐ No ☐ Unknown	☐ Yes ☐ No ☐ Unknown		
Pension/Disability	☐ Yes ☐ No ☐ Unknown	☐ Yes ☐ No ☐ Unknown		
Pension/Retirement	☐ Yes ☐ No ☐ Unknown	☐ Yes ☐ No ☐ Unknown		
Canada Pension	☐ Yes ☐ No ☐ Unknown	☐ Yes ☐ No ☐ Unknown		
Public Employee Retirement System	☐ Yes ☐ No ☐ Unknown	☐ Yes ☐ No ☐ Unknown		
State Teachers Retirement System	☐ Yes ☐ No ☐ Unknown	☐ Yes ☐ No ☐ Unknown		

F. Information About Your Return-to-Work

Have you returned to work? ☐ Yes ☐ No   If yes, indicate information below.
Part Time (mm/dd/yy):   Full Time (mm/dd/yy):   Hours per week:

If you have not returned to work, when do you expect to return?
Part Time (mm/dd/yy):   Full Time (mm/dd/yy):   ☐ Unknown

G. Information About Your Family: This information is important to assist us in determining if your family may be eligible for other benefits.

Marital Status: ☐ Single ☐ Married ☐ Widowed ☐ Divorced ☐ Domestic Partner ☐ Separated

Spouse/Partner's Name	Spouse/Partner's Date of Birth (mm/dd/yy)	Is he/she employed ☐ Yes ☐ No

List your dependent children who are under age 25 (include additional sheets if necessary).

Name	Date of Birth (mm/dd/yy)	Attending School
		☐ Yes ☐ No
		☐ Yes ☐ No
		☐ Yes ☐ No

H. Information About Income Tax Withholding: The following information will ensure your benefit is taxed appropriately according to Federal and State regulation

TAX INFORMATION
If you do not know if you are covered under a fully-insured or self-funded plan, please contact your employer for assistance.
- **For Fully-Insured Plans** – If your request for benefits is approved, should Unum withhold Federal and/or State Income Taxes from your benefit checks?
  Federal Income Tax: ☐ Yes ☐ No If yes, how much should be withheld from each check? (whole dollar amount) $_____
  Minimum Withholding: $20/week for Short Term Disability and $88/month for Long Term Disability.
  State Income Tax: ☐ Yes ☐ No If yes, how much should be withheld from each check? (whole dollar amount) $_____
- **For Self-Funded Plans** – Attach a copy of your completed W-4 for accurate calculation of Federal and State income taxes. **Note:** If not provided, we are required by law to withhold 25% of your benefit for Federal Income Tax and the maximum withholding amount for State Income Tax.

DISABILITY CLAIM FORM
The Benefits Center
P.O. Box 100158, Columbia, SC 29202-3158
Pacific Time Zone   Toll-free: 1-877-851-7637   Fax: 1-877-851-7624
All Other Time Zones   Toll-free: 1-800-858-6843   Fax: 1-800-447-2498
Call toll-free Monday through Friday, 8 a.m. to 8 p.m. (Eastern Time).

EMPLOYEE/INDIVIDUAL STATEMENT (Continued)

Employee/Individual's Name (Last Name, Suffix, First Name, MI)   Date of Birth (mm/dd/yy)

Fraud Warning: For your protection, Arizona law requires the following to appear on this claim form:

Any person who knowingly and with the intent to injure, defraud or deceive an insurance company presents a false or fraudulent claim for payment of a loss or benefit or knowingly presents false information in an application for insurance is guilty of a crime and may be subject to fines and confinement in prison.

Fraud Warning: For your protection, New York law requires the following to appear on this claim form:

Any person who knowingly and with the intent to defraud any insurance company or other person files an application for insurance or statement of claim containing any materially false information, or conceals for the purpose of misleading, information concerning any fact material thereto, commits a fraudulent insurance act, which is a crime, and shall also be subject to a civil penalty not to exceed five thousand dollars and the stated value of the claim for each such violation.

I. Signature of Employee/Individual

I have read and understand the fraud notices listed on this form. I also acknowledge that should my claim be overpaid for any reason it is my obligation to repay any such overpayment. The above statements are true and complete to the best of my knowledge and belief. **(Your signature is required for benefit consideration.)**

X
_____   _____
Signature   Date

Reminder: Please sign and date the Authorization (last page of this claim form).

DISABILITY CLAIM FORM
The Benefits Center
P.O. Box 100158, Columbia, SC 29202-3158
Pacific Time Zone   Toll-free: 1-877-851-7637   Fax: 1-877-851-7624
All Other Time Zones Toll-free: 1-800-858-6843   Fax: 1-800-447-2498
Call toll-free Monday through Friday, 8 a.m. to 8 p.m. (Eastern Time).

DIRECT DEPOSIT REQUEST: To be completed by the Employee.

Please provide the information requested below by completing the appropriate section of this form. Once completed, sign and date the form and mail or fax it to address or fax number indicated above. Your request will be processed promptly.

A. Information About You

Last Name   First Name   M

Address

City   State   Zip

Social Security Number   Home Telephone Number

B. Information About How to Set-up or Change Your Direct Deposit

☐ Set-up Direct Deposit   ☐ Change Direct Deposit Account
Bank/Financial Institution Information
Name

Address

City   State   Zip

Type of Account   ☐ Checking **(Required: Please attach a voided check imprinted with your name)**
                   ☐ Savings
                       Bank Routing Number   Personal Account Number

Direct Deposit Cancellation Request Please complete this section thirty days in advance if you wish to cancel your direct deposit agreement.

☐ Cancel my direct deposit agreement   Effective Date

C. Signature of Individual

X _____   _____
Signature   Date

Frequently Asked Questions About Direct Deposit

· **What is Direct Deposit?**
  Direct deposit is a safe and easy way to have your benefit payment deposited directly into your checking or savings account. Unum will electronically transfer the money into your bank account on a monthly schedule.
· **Reasons to use Direct Deposit**
  − It's safe – no more lost or stolen checks
  − It's convenient
  − It's reliable
  − It saves time
· **How do I sign-up for Direct Deposit?**
  Just complete the top section of this form and mail or fax it to us. Please print clearly so we are able to verify your account numbers accurately.
· **What if I change financial institutions or want to stop my direct deposit?**
  It's simple!! To change financial institutions, please complete this form and attach a voided check imprinted with your name. To stop your direct deposit, please complete this form or provide the information on our secure website, unum.com.
· **When can I expect the money to be in my account?**
  Because this can vary from person-to-person, please discuss the details with your claims specialist and your financial institution.
· **What if I have questions?**
  Please call our toll-free Direct Deposit Customer Service line at 1-800-413-7671. There are knowledgeable and courteous representatives available to answer your questions, Monday through Friday, 8 a.m. to 4 p.m. Eastern Time.

Unum is a registered trademark and marketing brand of Unum Group and its insuring subsidiaries.

CL-1019 (02/12)   8

DISABILITY CLAIM FORM
The Benefits Center
P.O. Box 100158, Columbia, SC 29202-3158
Pacific Time Zone   Toll-free: 1-877-851-7637   Fax: 1-877-851-7624
All Other Time Zones Toll-free: 1-800-858-6843   Fax: 1-800-447-2498
Call toll-free Monday through Friday, 8 a.m. to 8 p.m. (Eastern Time).

You are not required to sign this Optional Authorization. However, if you would like us to communicate with a family member, friend or other third party about your claim, we recommend completing the information below. Please sign and date the form as indicated and mail or fax it to the address or fax number indicated above.

Optional Authorization to Disclose Information to Third Parties

To assist in the evaluation or administration of my claim(s), I authorize Unum Group, its subsidiaries and duly authorized representatives ("Unum") to share personal health and financial information relating to my claim with the family members, friends, and/or other third parties listed below:

My Spouse: _____
             (Name)   (Telephone Number)

Other Family Member: _____
         (Name / Relationship)   (Telephone Number)

Other person: _____
         (Name / Relationship)   (Telephone Number)

I authorize Unum to leave messages about my claim on my voicemail / answering machine.
☐ Yes ☐ No

I understand that information about my claim may include information about my health and that such information about my health may be related to any disorder of the immune system including, but not limited to, HIV and AIDS; use of drugs and alcohol; and mental and physical history, condition, advice or treatment, but does not include psychotherapy notes.

I do not wish the following information about my claim to be shared (leave blank if not applicable):

_____

I further understand that the information is subject to redisclosure and might not be protected by certain federal regulations governing the privacy of health information.

I may revoke this authorization in writing at any time except to the extent Unum or the authorized recipient of my information has relied on it prior to receiving my notice of revocation. I may revoke this Authorization by sending written notice to the address above.

This authorization is valid for the shorter of two (2) years or the duration of my claim. I may request a copy of the Authorization and a copy shall be as valid as the original.

_____   _____
Employee Signature   Date

_____   _____
Printed Name   Social Security Number

I signed on behalf of the claimant as _____ (indicate relationship). If Power of Attorney Designee, Personal Representative, Guardian, or Conservator, please attach a copy of the document granting authority.

CL-1019 (02/12)   9

DISABILITY CLAIM FORM
The Benefits Center
P.O. Box 100158, Columbia, SC 29202-3158
Pacific Time Zone   Toll-free: 1-877-851-7637   Fax: 1-877-851-7624
All Other Time Zones Toll-free: 1-800-858-6843   Fax: 1-800-447-2498
Call toll-free Monday through Friday, 8 a.m. to 8 p.m. (Eastern Time).

EMPLOYER STATEMENT - To be completed by the Employer (PLEASE PRINT)

A. Information About the Employer

Employer Name

Employer's Phone Number

Employer Address

City   State   Zip

Prior LTD Carrier Name | Prior LTD Carrier Employee Effective Date | Prior LTD Carrier Policy Termination Da

B. Information About the Employee

Employee's Name (Last Name, Suffix, First Name, MI)

Employee's Address

City   State   Zip

Employee Telephone Number   Social Security Number   Date of Hire (mm/dd/yy)

Please check all types of coverage this employee has with Unum and indicate the effective date of his/her coverage.
☐ Short Term Disability _____   ☐ Long Term Disability _____   ☐ Individual Disability _____
☐ Life Insurance _____ Premium paid thru date _____   ☐ Voluntary Benefits Disability _____
☐ Voluntary Benefits Cancer/Critical Illness _____   ☐ Voluntary Benefits MedSupport _____

Short Term Disability Policy Number	Division Number	Class Number	Division Description / Class Description		
Long Term Disability Policy Number	Division Number	Class Number	Division Description / Class Description		
Individual Disability Policy Number	Division Number	Class Number	Division Description / Class Description		
Life Insurance Policy Number	Division Number	Class Number	Division Description / Class Description	Basic Life Amount	Supplemental Life Amou

Date Last Worked (mm/dd/yy): | Number of hours worked on date last worked:
Days/Week _____ Hours/Day _____ | Regular Work Schedule
Hours/Week _____

Check off regular work days: ☐ Sunday ☐ Monday ☐ Tuesday ☐ Wednesday ☐ Thursday ☐ Friday ☐ Saturday

If this is a Section 125/Cafeteria plan, indicate which option of coverage this employee has chosen.
Previous Plan Year   Current Plan Year

Date of Open Enrollment (mm/dd/yy) _____ Option _____   Date of Open Enrollment (mm/dd/yy) _____ Option _____

C. Information About the Employee's Occupation

Occupation Title (please include a copy of the employee's job description):

Primary duties of the employee's occupation on date last worked:

Employee's Pre-disability Work Status: ☐ Full-time ☐ Part-time ☐ Exempt ☐ Non-exempt ☐ Bargaining ☐ Non-bargaining

Did the employee's occupational duties and/or hours change due to disability or medical condition prior to his/her last day worked? ☐ Yes ☐ No
If yes, please explain:

Has employee returned to work? ☐ Yes ☐ No | If yes, date (mm/dd/yy):   ☐ Full Time ☐ Part Time | Hours Per Week:

Has the employee's employment been terminated? ☐ Yes ☐ No | If yes, termination date (mm/dd/yy):

CL-1019 (02/12)   10

DISABILITY CLAIM FORM
The Benefits Center
P.O. Box 100158, Columbia, SC 29202-3158
Pacific Time Zone   Toll-free: 1-877-851-7637   Fax: 1-877-851-7624
All Other Time Zones Toll-free: 1-800-858-6843   Fax: 1-800-447-2498
Call toll-free Monday through Friday, 8 a.m. to 8 p.m. (Eastern Time).

EMPLOYER STATEMENT (Continued)

Employee's Name (Last Name, Suffix, First Name, MI)   Date of Birth (mm/dd/yy)

D. Information About the Employee's Salary

How was the employee paid prior to date last worked? Please check all that apply and indicate the amount paid.

☐ Hourly	$ _____	☐ Semi-Monthly	$ _____
☐ Weekly	$ _____	☐ Bonuses	$ _____
☐ Bi-Weekly	$ _____	☐ Commissions	$ _____

Date paid through for (mm/dd/yy):
☐ Salary Continuation _____
☐ Vacation Pay _____
☐ Accrued Sick pay _____
☐ Other _____

Paid Time Off balance as of last day worked:

Sick Leave balance as of last day worked:

Does the employee have an ownership interest in this business? ☐ Yes ☐ No | If yes, what is the % of ownership? _____ %

Type of business: ☐ Regular Corporation ☐ S Corporation ☐ Partnership ☐ Sole Proprietorship

Other than payments under this policy, will the employee be receiving any other income from you, such as K-1 earnings, bonuses, commissions, salary continuation, PTO? ☐ Yes ☐ No

Financial Documentation: We are requesting this information so we can accurately calculate your employee's benefit. Please refer to the definition of earnings in your policy and provide us with the appropriate payroll information.

If your earnings definition is:	Then we need:
Salary Only/Current Earnings	Payroll records or paystubs for the 3 months just prior to disability
Bonus/Commissions Included	Payroll records for either 12 or 24 months (per your definition of earnings) just prior to disability
Other	Payroll documentation referenced in your definition of earnings (e.g. W-2, K-1, Schedule C, teacher contract, etc.)

E. Information Needed for Calculation of FICA

What percent of the Long Term Disability benefit is taxable? _____ %

[See IRS Publication *15-A Employer's Supplemental Tax Guide, Section 6, Sick Pay Reporting* and/or *IRS Revenue Ruling 2004-55* for more information on calculating the taxable percent.]

Note: We will assume the benefit is 100% taxable if this information is not provided.

What percent of the Individual Disability benefit is taxable? _____ %

[See IRS Publication *15-A Employer's Supplemental Tax Guide, Section 6, Sick Pay Reporting* and/or *IRS Revenue Ruling 2004-55* for more information on calculating the taxable percent.]

Note: We will assume the benefit is 100% taxable if this information is not provided.

Year to Date Earnings (from January 1 to the present for FICA Deductions) $_____

F. Information About Other Disability Income

Is employee eligible for:	Yes	No	If yes, weekly or monthly amount	Weekly	Monthly	Date benefits begin	Date benefits end
Salary Continuation	☐	☐	$	☐	☐		
Short Term Disability	☐	☐	$	☐	☐		
State Disability	☐	☐	$	☐	☐		
Other Disability Benefits	☐	☐	$	☐	☐		
Social Security Disability Insurance	☐	☐	$	☐	☐		
Public Employee Retirement System	☐	☐	$	☐	☐		
State Teachers Retirement System	☐	☐	$	☐	☐		
Workers' Compensation	☐	☐	$	☐	☐		

DISABILITY CLAIM FORM
The Benefits Center
P.O. Box 100158, Columbia, SC 29202-3158
Pacific Time Zone   Toll-free: 1-877-851-7637   Fax: 1-877-851-7624
All Other Time Zones Toll-free: 1-800-858-6843   Fax: 1-800-447-2498
Call toll-free Monday through Friday, 8 a.m. to 8 p.m. (Eastern Time).

EMPLOYER STATEMENT (Continued)

Employee's Name (Last Name, Suffix, First Name, MI)   Date of Birth (mm/dd/yy)

Is the claim the result of a work related injury or illness? ☐ Yes ☐ No | If yes, has a Workers' Compensation claim been filed? ☐ Yes ☐ No

If yes, name of Workers' Compensation carrier | Telephone Number

Address of Carrier | Fax Number

City | State | Zip

If a Workers' Compensation claim has been denied, please submit a copy of denial with this claim.

G. Information About Your Pension Plan: This information is necessary to ensure the benefit is calculated accurately. (Do not complete for a maternity claim.)

Do you have a pension plan? ☐ Yes ☐ No

If yes, what type? ☐ Defined benefit ☐ Defined contribution ☐ 401(k)/403(b) ☐ Profit Sharing ☐ Other: (specify)

Is the employee eligible for your pension plan?   ☐ Yes ☐ No   What percentage does the employee contribute?

If eligible, does the employee participate?   ☐ Yes ☐ No   _____ %

If yes, when is the employee eligible to withdraw from the plan?

H. Information About Your Rehire or Return-to-Work Program

If the employee is released to return to work in restricted duty, are you willing to discuss accommodations? ☐ Yes ☐ No

If yes, whom should we contact to discuss a return-to-work plan?

Name

Title | Telephone Number

FRAUD NOTICE: Any person who knowingly files a statement of claim containing false or misleading information is subject to criminal and civil penalties. This includes the Employer portion of the claim form.

I. Signature of Benefit Administrator (Please Print)

The above statements are true and complete to the best of my knowledge and belief.

Name of Person Completing Form

Title of Person Completing Form

Telephone Number | Fax Number | Employer Tax ID Number

E-mail Address

Signature
X

Date

DISABILITY CLAIM FORM
The Benefits Center
P.O. Box 100158, Columbia, SC 29202-3158
Pacific Time Zone   Toll-free: 1-877-851-7637   Fax: 1-877-851-7624
All Other Time Zones Toll-free: 1-800-858-6843   Fax: 1-800-447-2498
Call toll-free Monday through Friday, 8 a.m. to 8 p.m. (Eastern Time).

ATTENDING PHYSICIAN STATEMENT (PLEASE PRINT)

PART I: TO BE COMPLETED BY PATIENT

Name of Patient (Last Name, Suffix, First Name, MI)   Social Security Number

Date of Birth (mm/dd/yy)   Home Telephone Number

Employer Name

PART II: TO BE COMPLETED BY PHYSICIAN OR TREATING PROVIDER
Instructions: Please complete, sign and date this form. The purpose of this form is to assist us in making a disability determination. Please complete all questions on this form and provide copies of supporting reports, such as office notes, medical records, medication logs, consultations and/or testing. Be sure to sign and date this form in Section D.

A. Patient Information

| Date of first visit for this current condition(s) (mm/dd/yy): | Date of last office visit (mm/dd/yy): | Date of next office visit (mm/dd/yy): | Did you advise your patient to stop working? ☐ Yes ☐ No If yes, effective when? (mm/dd/yy): |

Has the patient been treated for the same/similar condition in the past?   ☐ Yes   ☐ No   ☐ Unknown

If yes, please provide treatment dates (mm/dd/yy): From _____ Through _____

| Is the patient's condition work related? ☐ Yes ☐ No ☐ Unknown | Patient's Height: | Patient's Weight |

What is the primary diagnosis that may impact your patient's functional capacity?

| Please include primary ICD Code or DSM-IV Multi-Axial diagnoses codes | ICD Code: |

| DSM-IV: I | II | III | IV | V |

What are the other diagnoses that may impact your patient's functional capacity?   ☐ NA

| Secondary Diagnosis: | ICD Code: |
| Secondary Diagnosis: | ICD Code: |

Has the patient been hospitalized? ☐ Yes ☐ No   If yes, date hospitalized (mm/dd/yy):   through (mm/dd/yy):

Was surgery performed? ☐ Yes ☐ No   If yes, what procedure was performed?   CPT Code: Date Surgery Performed (mm/dd/yy):

DISABILITY CLAIM FORM
The Benefits Center
P.O. Box 100158, Columbia, SC 29202-3158
Pacific Time Zone   Toll-free: 1-877-851-7637   Fax: 1-877-851-7624
All Other Time Zones Toll-free: 1-800-858-6843   Fax: 1-800-447-2498
Call toll-free Monday through Friday, 8 a.m. to 8 p.m. (Eastern Time).

ATTENDING PHYSICIAN STATEMENT (Continued)

Patient's Name   Date of Birth (mm/dd/yy)

B. Functional Capacity

If your patient **does not** have physical and/or behavioral health RESTRICTIONS (activities patient should not do) and/or LIMITATIONS (activities patient cannot do), please initial here _____ and go to **SECTION D.**

Please note: When considering a standard 8 hour workday with breaks (approximately every two hours) please quantify terms that may not b uniformly understood such as "prolonged", "repetitive", "light-duty", "heavy lifting", or "stressful situations". In addition, never means not at all, occasional means more than never but less than 33% of the time; frequent means 34-66% of the time, and constant means 67-100% of the tir

Physical Restrictions and/or Limitations

If your patient has CURRENT PHYSICAL RESTRICTIONS (activities patient should not do) and/or PHYSICAL LIMITATIONS (activities patien cannot do) list below. Please be specific and understand that a reply of "no work" or "totally disabled" will not enable us to evaluate your patier claim for benefits and may result in us having to contact you for clarification.

Please provide the duration of these restrictions and limitations. From (mm/dd/yy): _____ To (mm/dd/yy): _____

Behavioral Health Restrictions and/or Limitations

If your patient has CURRENT BEHAVIORAL HEALTH RESTRICTIONS (activities patient should not do) and/or BEHAVIORAL HEALTH LIMITATIONS (activities patient cannot do) please list below. Please be specific and understand that a reply of "no work" or "totally disabled" v not enable us to evaluate your patient's claim for benefits and may result in us having to contact you for clarification.

Please provide the duration of these restrictions and limitations. From (mm/dd/yy): _____ To (mm/dd/yy): _____

What diagnostic or clinical findings support your patient's restrictions and/or limitations as noted above?

What is your treatment plan? Please include all medications.

DISABILITY CLAIM FORM
The Benefits Center
P.O. Box 100158, Columbia, SC 29202-3158
Pacific Time Zone   Toll-free: 1-877-851-7637   Fax: 1-877-851-7624
All Other Time Zones Toll-free: 1-800-858-6843 Fax: 1-800-447-2498
Call toll-free Monday through Friday, 8 a.m. to 8 p.m. (Eastern Time).

ATTENDING PHYSICIAN STATEMENT (Continued)

Patient's Name

Date of Birth (mm/dd/yy)

C. Other Treating Providers, Facilities or Hospitals

Please provide complete name, contact information and specialty of any other treating physicians, facilities or hospitals.

Name	Specialty	City, State

D. Signature of Attending Physician

The above statements are true and complete to the best of my knowledge and belief.

Physician Name (Last Name, First Name, MI, Suffix) Please Print

Medical Specialty

Degree

Address

City

State

Zip

Telephone Number

Fax Number

Physician's Tax ID Number:

Are you related to this patient? ☐ Yes ☐ No
If yes, what is the relationship?

Signature of Physician

Date

X

DISABILITY CLAIM FORM
The Benefits Center
P.O. Box 100158, Columbia, SC 29202-3158
Pacific Time Zone   Toll-free: 1-877-851-7637   Fax: 1-877-851-7624
All Other Time Zones   Toll-free: 1-800-858-6843   Fax: 1-800-447-2498
Call toll-free Monday through Friday, 8 a.m. to 8 p.m. (Eastern Time).

EMPLOYEE/INDIVIDUAL AUTHORIZATION – FOR EMPLOYEE TO COMPLETE

Please sign and return this authorization to The Benefits Center at the address above. You are entitled to receive a copy of this authorization. This authorization is designed to comply with the Health Insurance Portability and Accountability Act (HIPAA) Privacy Rule.

Authorization

I authorize health care professionals, hospitals, clinics, laboratories, pharmacies and all other medical or medically related providers, facilities or services, rehabilitation professionals, vocational evaluators, health plans, insurance companies, third party administrators, insurance producers, insurance service providers, credit bureaus, the MIB Group, Inc., GENEX Services, Inc., The Advocator Group and other Social Security advocacy vendors, The Association of Life Insurance Companies (which operates the Health Claims Index and the Disability Income Record System), professional licensing bodies, employers, attorneys, financial institutions and/or banks, and governmental entities;

To disclose information, whether from before, during or after the date of this authorization, about my health including HIV, AIDS or other disorders of the immune system, use of drugs or alcohol, mental or physical history, condition, advice or treatment (except this authorization does not authorize release of psychotherap notes), prescription drug history, earnings, financial or credit history, professional licenses, employment history, insurance claims and benefits, and all other claims and benefits, including Social Security claims an benefits;

To the following persons: Unum Group and its subsidiaries, Unum Life Insurance Company of America, Provident Life and Accident Insurance Company, The Paul Revere Life Insurance Company, and persons who evaluate claims for any of those companies ("Unum"), employee benefit plans sponsored by my employer and any person providing services to, or insurance benefits on behalf of, such plans, and to anyor who provides services, including the evaluation of claims, related to benefits offered by Unum, my employer or the Social Security Administration ("Authorized Recipients");

For the purposes of evaluating and administering claims, including assistance with return to work. Unum also may rely on this authorization for one year, or as otherwise permitted by law, to disclose information about me to the Authorized Recipients so they may conduct health care operations, claims payment, administrative, and audit functions related to my benefit plans.

Information authorized for use or disclosure may include information which may indicate the presence of a communicable or non-communicable disease.

If I do not sign this authorization or if I alter or revoke it, Unum may not be able to evaluate my claim(s), whi may lead to my claim(s) being denied. I may revoke this authorization at any time by sending written notice to the address above. I understand that revocation will not apply to any information that is requested prior to Unum receiving notice of revocation.

The privacy protections established by HIPAA may not apply to information disclosed under this authorizatic but other privacy laws do apply. Information disclosed under this authorization may be redisclosed only as permitted or required by law, including state fraud reporting laws. For evaluation and administration of claim this authorization is valid for two years or the duration of my claim.

Insured's Signature   Date Signed

Printed Name   Social Security Number

I signed on behalf of the Insured as _____ (Relationship). If Power of Attorney Designee, Guardian, or Conservator, please attach a copy of the document granting authority.

CL-1019-AUTH (02/12)

Appendix 9B: Example of Loss of Life Claim Form

**Instructions for Filing a Group Life
(or Dependent Life) Claim**

To the Administrator:
A claim for Group Life Insurance benefits should be submitted to Assurant Employee Benefits as soon as notice is received that an employee/dependent or the employee's beneficiary is eligible for benefits.

Filing of a Claim
1. Along with the Group Employer Statement and Beneficiary Statement, we will also require:
2. Certified copy of the death certificate.
3. Enrollment application and beneficiary changes.
4. If the claim is incurred in the first three months of coverage, payroll records and/or other proof of active work will be required.

If the insured's death is the direct result of an accident, accidental death benefits may be payable if the policy provides accidental death.

If accidental death claim is being filed, attach all available supporting information such as the official investigative report (police, accident, fire, FAA, OSHA), medical examiner's report or newspaper clippings.

If the insured died outside of the United States or the beneficiary is living in a foreign country, call 1.800.451.4531 to speak to a claims representative.

The Group Claim should be returned immediately to:

Assurant Employee Benefits
Life Benefit Center
PO Box 419876
Kansas City, MO 64141-6876

Street address:

Assurant Employee Benefits
2323 Grand Boulevard
Kansas City, MO 64108

Fax number:

1.816.881.8967

Email:

LifeClaims@assurant.com

If you have any questions, please call our Group Life Benefits Team at 800.451.4531 and a representative will assist you.

Products and services marketed by Assurant Employee Benefits are underwritten and/or provided by Union Security Insurance Company. In this document, the terms "we," "us," "our," and the like, refer to each as applicable.

Assurant Employee Benefits Group Life Benefits PO Box 419876 Kansas City Missouri 64141-6876
T 800.451.4531 F 816.881.8967
LifeClaims@assurant.com www .assurantemployeebenefits.com

Life Claims Statement

 **ASSURANT** Employee Benefits

This form may be used for both **employee/member** and **dependent life** insurance claims.

To be completed by the Employer/Plan Administrator

Section A: Employer/Association Information

Name of Employer/Association _____

Policy number _____ Participation number _____ Account number _____

Employer address _____

Location where employed _____
        STREET   CITY   STATE   ZIP

        STREET   CITY   STATE   ZIP

Employer telephone number _____ Fax number _____

Web site address _____

Section B: Employee/Member Information *(Please complete for all claims.)*

The deceased is insured as: ☐ Employee ☐ Spouse ☐ Child ☐ Member

Full name of Employee _____
        LAST   FIRST   MIDDLE INITIAL

Social Security number _____ Date of birth _____ Date of death _____

Address _____
     STREET   CITY   STATE   ZIP

Hire date _____ Date insurance effective _____ Occupation _____

Annual salary _____ Date of last salary increase _____ Hours worked per week _____

Employee pay status: ☐ Hourly ☐ Salaried   Salary on last date worked: $_____ per ☐ Hr ☐ Wk ☐ Mo ☐ Yr

Reason for ceasing work: ☐ Disability ☐ Discharge ☐ Leave of Absence ☐ Resigned ☐ Retired

          ☐ Temporary layoff ☐ Vacation ☐ Other *(Please explain.)* _____

          Last date worked _____

Section C: Please complete for all Dependent Life Claims

Full name of deceased dependent _____
        LAST   FIRST   MIDDLE INITIAL

Social Security number _____ Date of birth _____ Date of death _____

Dependent's marital status: ☐ Single ☐ Married ☐ Divorced ☐ Legally separated

Full-time student? ☐ Yes ☐ No

Dependent's most recent employer _____

Last date worked _____

If dependent was disabled, please provide disability date _____

If you have any questions, please call our Group Life Benefits Team at 800.451.4531 and a representative will assist you.

Assurant Employee Benefits Group Life Benefits PO Box 419876 Kansas City Missouri 64141-6876
T 800.451.4531 F 816.881.8967
LifeClaims@assurant.com www .assurantemployeebenefits.com

Page 2 of 8
KC2176A (2/2011)

Name of employee/member _____
                                                    LAST   FIRST   MIDDLE INITIAL

Date of birth _____

Section D: Insurance Coverage/Claimed Information

Type(s) of insurance and amount(s) **being claimed**

☐ Basic Term Life $ _____
☐ Additional Contributory Life (Supplemental) $ _____
☐ Voluntary Life $ _____
☐ Dependent Life (Basic or Voluntary) $ _____
☐ Accidental Death $ _____
   ☐ Automobile Accident $ _____
   ☐ Higher Education $ _____
☐ Dependent Accidental Death $ _____
☐ Other *(Please specify.)* _____ $ _____

                                                   Total $ _____

Was evidence of insurability required on any of the coverage claimed? ☐ Yes ☐ No

Date last premium paid _____ Was insurance in force at date of death? ☐ Yes ☐ No

Section E: Payment Information — A copy of all beneficiary designations must be provided with the claim form.

Please provide the following information about the beneficiary(ies) your records reflect. Note that if this is for dependent coverage, the beneficiary is normally the employee. If there are more than three beneficiaries, please attach a sheet with additional names and information. Please list only primary beneficiary(ies).

Is there a beneficiary dispute? ☐ Yes ☐ No

Name of Beneficiary #1 _____
SSN/TIN* _____ Relationship to Deceased _____

Name of Beneficiary #2 _____
SSN/TIN* _____ Relationship to Deceased _____

Name of Beneficiary #3 _____
SSN/TIN* _____ Relationship to Deceased _____

*Social Security Number/Taxpayer Identification Number

Group Policyholder Statement completed by *(name of representative at employer or administrator that completed this form)*

_____
PLEASE PRINT

_____
SIGNATURE (REPRESENTATIVE OF POLICYHOLDER/EMPLOYER)   DATE

_____
EMAIL ADDRESS

I hereby certify that the information provided on this form is complete and accurate to the best of my knowledge and I have no financial interest in this claim.

Note: Please send all life claim documents to the Kansas City location. Please do not send claim information to our Clinton, Iowa location.

If you have any questions, please call our Group Life Benefits Team at 800.451.4531 and a representative will assist you.

Assurant Employee Benefits Group Life Benefits PO Box 419876 Kansas City Missouri 64141-6876
T 800.451.4531 F 816.881.8967
LifeClaims@assurant.com www.assurantemployeebenefits.com

Page 3 of 8
KC2176A (2/2011)

Beneficiary Statement

 **ASSURANT** Employee Benefits

To be completed by each beneficiary making claim.* *(Please print.)*	HOME OFFICE USE ONLY Claim # _____	PF opening balance $ _____

Employee/Member's name _____

LAST   FIRST   MIDDLE INITIAL

Date of birth _____ Social Security number _____ Policy number _____

Section F: Information about you, the beneficiary

Beneficiary's name _____

LAST   FIRST   MIDDLE INITIAL

Beneficiary's date of birth _____

Beneficiary's Social Security/Taxpayer Identification number _____

Beneficiary's address _____

STREET   CITY   STATE   ZIP

Daytime phone _____ Home phone _____

Email address _____

Beneficiary's relationship to Deceased _____

Is beneficiary a U.S. citizen? ☐ Yes ☐ No   If "No," the appropriate IRS Form W-8 will be required.

Are Accidental Death benefits being claimed? ☐ Yes ☐ No

If "Yes," please provide any additional supporting information including police report, Medical Examiner's report and newspaper articles.

*Primary beneficiaries only, unless contingent beneficiaries wish to make a claim.

IMPORTANT TAX INFORMATION

The Federal income tax laws require us to request that you provide us with your correct Social Security Number or Taxpayer Identification Number.

Please read and complete the following information in order to comply with the Federal income tax laws.

Certification

Under penalties of perjury, I certify that:

1. The number shown on this form is my correct Social Security/Taxpayer Identification number (or I am waiting for a number to be issued to me); and

2. I am not subject to backup withholding because: (a) I am exempt from backup withholding, or (b) I have not been notified by the Internal Revenue Service (IRS) that I am subject to backup withholding as a result of a failure to report all interest or dividends, or (c) the IRS has notified me that I am no longer subject to backup withholding; and

3. I am a U.S. citizen or other U.S. person.

NOTE: Certification Instructions – You must cross out item 2 above if you have been notified by the IRS that you are currently subject to backup withholding because of underreporting interest or dividends on your tax return.

The IRS does not require your consent to any provision of this document other than the certifications required to avoid backup withholding.

Your Signature _____ Date _____

Please print your name _____

Note: Your signature as signed above will also be used to verify your signature for ProviderFund® Account drafts.

If you have any questions, please call our Group Life Benefits Team at 800.451.4531 and a representative will assist you.

Name of employee/member _____
                                                      LAST   FIRST   MIDDLE INITIAL

Date of birth _____

Important note regarding payment of benefits: If you are a personal beneficiary whose share of the proceeds plus interest meets our requirements, a ProviderFund® account (an interest-bearing account) will be opened in your name if you so choose. ProviderFund® account drafts (similar to checks) will be supplied upon approval of the claim for benefits allowing you immediate access to your money. For more information, access our ProviderFund® brochure at http://www.assurantemployeebenefits.com/816/aebcom/forms/claims/k2796.pdf.

The Benefits of Choosing a ProviderFund® Account

Options: You are allowed the time you need to make important financial decisions and to decide the best options for your financial future during this critical and difficult period.

Secure: All amounts are fully protected and guaranteed by Union Security Insurance Company a company whose financial strength is rated A-(Excellent) by AM Best. These accounts are not insured by the Federal Deposit Insurance Corporation (FDIC).

Free: You will receive unlimited free drafts and monthly statements as long as your account is open.

Accessible: You may write drafts for any amount over $250 and up to your full balance at any time.

Interest: Your account earns interest the day the account opens. Interest is compounded daily and credited to your account on the 20th day of each month.

Service: You can call 800.451.4531, ext. 2802 during regular hours to speak with an Account Representative for assistance with your account. In addition, you can call a 24-hour toll-free line at 888.227.1308 for quick updates on your account.

Please choose your method of payment:
- ☐ I choose to participate in the ProviderFund® Account option. We will send you a supplemental contract to complete before we can set up your account.
- ☐ I prefer to receive a lump sum check.

Section G: Authorization to Release Information / Physician Information
(Note: If insured was on an approved waiver of premium claim this does not need to be completed.)

1. Occasionally in the processing of a claim it becomes necessary for us to contact an outside source for additional information. The legal representative or next of kin of the insured should sign the authorization below to avoid us having to obtain it at a future date.

    Upon presentation of the original or a photocopy of this signed authorization, I authorize any medical professional, hospital or other medical-care institution, insurance support organization, pharmacy, governmental agency, insurance company, group policyholder, employer or an agent, attorney, consumer reporting agency or independent administrator, acting on its behalf, to provide Union Security Insurance Company information concerning advice, care or treatment provided the insured named above or spouse or minor children thereof, any post-mortem examination reports including autopsy, toxicology and investigation. This may include information relating to mental illness, use of drugs or use of alcohol. I authorize any other insurance company to release policy and claim information. I also authorize any employer, group policyholder or benefit plan administrator to provide Union Security Insurance Company with financial or employment related information.

    I understand that the information authorized herein will be used by Union Security Insurance Company to evaluate a claim for insurance benefits and that I or any authorized representative will receive a copy of this authorization upon request. Information obtained will not be released to any person or organization EXCEPT to reinsuring companies, or other person or organization performing business or legal services in connection with the claim. This authorization is not governed by HIPAA, however, when necessary, I may be asked to execute a HIPAA authorization form, allowing Union Security Insurance Company to use and disclose protected health information.

    This authorization is valid from the date signed for the duration of the claim.

    Signature _____ Date _____

If you have any questions, please call our Group Life Benefits Team at 800.451.4531 and a representative will assist you.

Name of employee/member _____
                                             LAST   FIRST   MIDDLE INITIAL

Date of birth _____

2. List the name and address of the employee/dependent's primary physician.

Name	Address	Phone number	Dates treated	Conditions

BENEFICIARY INSTRUCTIONS

If the insured did not name a beneficiary or if a named beneficiary has predeceased the insured:
- Forward a certified copy of the death certificate for any named beneficiary who predeceased the insured.
- Payment of the life insurance benefits will be paid in the order as specified in the policy provisions of the contract.
- The next of kin must complete a Surviving Family Statement (Form KC2181A).

If the beneficiary is the estate:
- Payment of the life insurance benefits will be made to the executor/administrator of the estate. The executor/administrator is appointed by the probate court and is responsible for managing the insured's estate. Please note that a person named as the executor/administrator in the insured's last will and testament must be appointed by the court before payment can be made.
- The executor/administrator of the estate should complete the Claimant's Statement and provide a certified copy of the Letters of Testamentary or Letters of Administration issued by the probate court. The estate Tax Identification number, (not Social Security number) is required on the Claimant's Statement.

If the beneficiary is a minor:
- In order to receive payment of life insurance proceeds, a beneficiary must be of the age of majority, as determined by the state where the beneficiary resides. In most states, the age of majority is considered to be 18 years of age.
- If the beneficiary is under 18 years of age, then the parent or guardian of the minor beneficiary should complete and sign the Claimant's Statement. The proceeds will be deposited into a blocked ProviderFund® account until:
  - The minor beneficiary reaches the age of majority; alternatively,
  - Payment will be made to a court appointed guardian of the minor's estate. A guardian is appointed by the court and is responsible for managing the minor's estate. A copy of the Letters of Guardianship of the minor's estate must be forwarded to our office.

If the beneficiary is a trust:
- When a trust or trust agreement is designated as the beneficiary, a copy of the following pages of the trust must be provided: **Face page of Trust, Trustee or Successor Trustee designation, Signature Page of Trust.**

If the insured's death is a direct result of an accident, accidental death benefits may be payable if the policy provides accidental death.

- If accidental death claim is being filed, attach all available supporting information such as the official investigative report (police, accident, fire, FAA, OSHA), medical examiner's report or newspaper clippings.

If you have any questions, please call our Group Life Benefits Team at 800.451.4531 and a representative will assist you.

Assurant Employee Benefits Group Life Benefits PO Box 419876 Kansas City Missouri 64141-6876
T 800.451.4531 F 816.881.8967
LifeClaims@assurant.com www .assurantemployeebenefits.com

Group Life Insurance Claim Statement    **ASSURANT** Employee
                                                                    Benefits

For your protection, certain state laws require the following to appear on this form.

WARNING: Any person who knowingly and with intent to injure, defraud, or deceive any insurance company or other person files an application for insurance or statement of claim containing any materially false information or conceals for the purpose of misleading, information concerning any fact material thereto, commits a fraudulent insurance act which is a crime and subjects such person to criminal and civil penalties.

In addition, any person who commits such a fraudulent act (or facilitates the act):

- may be prosecuted under state law (Alaska residents only).
- may be subject to fines and confinement in prison (Arkansas, California, and New Mexico residents only).
- is subject to penalties that may include imprisonment, fines, denial of insurance, and civil damages (Colorado residents only). Also, any insurance company or agent of an insurance company who knowingly provides false, incomplete, or misleading facts or information to a policyholder or claimant for the purpose of defrauding or attempting to defraud the policyholder or claimant with regard to a settlement of award payable from insurance proceeds shall be reported to the Colorado division of insurance within the Department of Regulatory Agencies.
- is guilty of a felony (Delaware, Idaho, Indiana, and Oklahoma residents only).
- is guilty of a felony of the third degree (Florida residents only).
- may be subject to penalties including imprisonment, fines or denial of insurance benefits (Maine residents only).
- may be found guilty of insurance fraud (Maryland residents only).
- is subject to prosecution and punishment for insurance fraud as provided in RSA638:20 (New Hampshire residents only).
- shall also be subject to a civil penalty not to exceed five thousand dollars and the stated value of the claim for each such violation (New York residents only).

It is a crime to knowingly provide false, incomplete, or misleading information to an insurance company for the purpose of defrauding the company. Penalties, include imprisonment, fines, and denial of insurance benefits (Virginia residents only).

Any person who knowingly and with intent to defraud any insurance company or person files an application for insurance or statement of claim containing any materially false information or conceals for the purpose of misleading, information concerning any fact material thereto commits a fraudulent insurance act, which is a crime and subjects such person to criminal and civil penalties (Pennsylvania residents only).

Pursuant to Section 403(d) and Regulation 95 of the New York Insurance Law, the following statement applies to our accident and health policies only: Any person who knowingly and with intent to defraud any insurance company or other person files an application for insurance or statement of claim containing any materially false information, or conceals for the purpose of misleading, information concerning any fact material thereto, commits a fraudulent act, which is a crime, and shall also be subject to a civil penalty not to exceed five thousand dollars and the stated value of the claim for each such violation.

If you have any questions, please call our Group Life Benefits Team at 800.451.4531 and a representative will assist you.

**HIPAA Authorization for Release
of Protected Health Information – Life**

 **ASSURANT** Employee Benefits

Insured/Member name _____ SS no. _____

Address _____ City _____ State _____ Zip code _____

Individual who is the Subject of Protected Health Information _____

Policy no. _____ Partici pation no. _____ Account no. _____ Certificate no. _____

Persons/categories of persons <u>providing</u> the information: Entities possessing the information identified below, including physicians, any provider of medical services, pharmacy, pharmacy benefits manager, or any pharmacy-related services entity, insurance company, Social Security Administration, governmental agency, vocational provider or employer having medical information with respect to any physical or mental condition of the Individual referenced above.

Persons/categories of persons <u>receiving</u> the information: Union Security Insurance Company or Union Security Life Insurance Company of New York ("Companies").

I hereby authorize the use or disclosure of protected health information regarding the Individual referenced above, as described below:

Description of information to be disclosed: Records concerning medical advice, care or treatment. This may also include, but is not limited to: information relating to use of drugs or use of alcohol; post-mortem examination reporting, including autopsy, toxicology and investigation reports; accident reports made by ambulance, law enforcement and paramedics; other insurance carriers or a prior life insurance carrier or life insurance policy and related claim information; and financial or employment-related information.

The sole purpose of this disclosure is for the adjudication of a claim for life insurance benefits under the Policy referenced above.

I understand the following:

- I have the right to refuse to sign this authorization; however, if I refuse to sign this authorization, I understand that the Companies may not be able to gather the information necessary to determine if I am eligible for coverage or benefits under one of the Companies' insurance policies. I understand that a photocopy or facsimile of this authorization is as valid as the original. Upon request, I may receive a copy of this authorization.
- This authorization is voluntary. I may revoke it any time by writing Assurant Employee Benefits, Privacy Office, PO Box 419052, Kansas City, MO 64141-6052. Any such revocation will not affect any actions that Companies took before receipt of the revocation.
- Federal law requires that we inform you that the information that we collect may, under certain circumstances, be re-disclosed by us to third parties and thus no longer protected by federal law. Oklahoma only – we are required to inform you that **the information authorized for release may include information which may indicate the presence of a communicable disease or noncommunicable disease.**
- I understand that any information obtained by this authorization may be used and disclosed by HIPAA and non-HIPAA plans.
- The authorization is effective from the date signed below until a final adjudication of the claim for life insurance benefits is reached or 24 months from date of signature, whichever comes first.

_____   _____
SIGNATURE OF INDIVIDUAL OR PERSONAL REPRESENTATIVE   DATE

Printed name of personal representative _____

Relationship to insured/member _____
(e.g. LEGAL GUARDIAN, EXECUTOR, ADMINISTRATOR, OR NEXT-OF-KIN)

YOU MAY REFUSE TO SIGN THIS AUTHORIZATION

Please make a copy of the signed Authorization for your records. Then please mail or fax the completed and signed Authorization for processing to the appropriate address below, attention Life Claims:

Assurant Employee Benefits, 2323 Grand Boulevard, Kansas City, MO 64108-2670
Fax no. 816.881.8967

Union Security Life Insurance Company of New York,
Administered by: **Assurant Employee Benefits**, 2323 Grand Boulevard, Kansas City, MO 64108-2670
Fax no. 816.881.8967

Products and services marketed by Assurant Employee Benefits are underwritten and/or provided by Union Security Insurance Company. In New York, insurance products are underwritten by Union Security Life Insurance Company of New York, which is licensed in New York and has it's principal place of business in Syracuse, New York.

Assurant Employee Benefits Group Life Benefits PO Box 419876 Kansas City Missouri 64141-6876
T 800.451.4531 F 816.881.8967
LifeClaims@assurant.com www .assurantemployeebenefits.com

Page 8 of 8
KC2176A (2/2011)

Chapter 10

Taxation of Group Term Life Insurance

This chapter is designed to provide conceptual understanding of taxation relating to Group Life and Accidental Death & Dismemberment (AD&D) products. It is not designed as a tax guide or to provide tax advice. Beneficiaries of group life and/or AD&D proceeds or employee recipients of group life and/or AD&D proceeds are responsible for any taxes related to those proceeds and should consult a qualified tax adviser.

Insurance professionals can use the information in this chapter to deepen their understanding of how taxation impacts the structure of, operation of, and benefit payments from group life/AD&D insurance plans. Because taxation potentially impacts the nature of the benefits as well as impacts employees' take-home pay, the information can prove very valuable when creating the overall plan design.

When discussing taxation of group life insurance, insurance professionals know that life and AD&D insurance proceeds are generally not taxable to the beneficiary as income. However, there are some quirks in group insurance related to taxation. The owner of the group life insurance contract is typically the employer as policyholder and plan sponsor. There are some tax rules for the owner/employer. Taxes also have an effect on the insured/beneficiary. Producers who work with many group customers should be aware of Internal Revenue Code (IRC) Section 79, which deals with life insurance taxation. This section of the tax code will be covered in some detail.

Income Taxes on Claim Payments

The following death benefits paid to beneficiaries are typically not taxed:

- Employee life claims

- Employee AD&D claims

- The final balance of accelerated death benefits (after employee has died)

The following benefit payments made to an employee are typically not taxed:

- Accelerated death benefits (while employee is still alive)

- Dependent life/AD&D claims

- AD&D claims for things such as loss of limb or sight, hearing, cognitive impairment, etc.

Life proceeds to an employee's beneficiaries are not taxable for federal income tax. Group life insurance proceeds paid as an accelerated death benefit are not taxable for income tax to a dying claimant, but they may be subject to state income taxes. If an employee made any investment earnings from accelerated death proceeds, the earnings on the proceeds would be taxable as ordinary income. Because there are no income taxes (there is no witholding tax) on life/AD&D proceeds, group insurers are not required to have the beneficiary complete an Internal Revenue Service (IRS) Form W-9.

Estate Taxes

Depending upon the deceased employee's taxable estate, group term life proceeds may need to be included and thus subject to estate tax. Some employees will execute an absolute assignment of the life coverage to a trust to eliminate the estate tax inclusion.

Impact of Taxation on Risk Selection

Unlike group disability, where tax structure could potentially impact an underwriter's risk selection evaluation, tax structure on group life/AD&D has minimal impact on the willingness of an underwriter to quote on and accept a group. The likelihood of an employee turning down supplemental life coverage solely because of the additional tax income on their pay caused by imputed income is minimal and would have a minimal impact on projected participation in the supplemental life plan.

State Premium Tax

State premium tax is the responsibility of the group insurer to collect and pay to each state in which it conducts group life and AD&D business. The insurer culls out the tax from the premium collected from policyholders and remits it to the proper taxing authorities in each respective state. The tax is calculated as a percentage of the premiums collected, ranging from 1.75 percent to 3.00 percent, depending on the state.

The underwriter accounts for the tax when establishing the premium rates. The tax is built into the premium rates the employer/employees pay and is therefore transparent to them.

Deductibility of Group Premiums

Employers in general can deduct the premiums they pay on group term life/AD&D insurance for employees as a normal business expense, just like the cost of rent, salaries, or utilities.[1] This is for noncontributory coverage or the employer's share on contributory coverage. The employee's contributions towards premium payment cannot be taken as a normal business expense by the employer. However, for the premiums to be deductible, it is expressly stated in some states' regulations that the employer cannot be the beneficiary of the policy. Nor can the employee's contributions towards premium be considered a deduction for the employee's own income tax purposes.

Imputed Income

Congress modified the federal tax code in the 1980's to apply an imputed income tax to group life insurance plans. The idea was to prevent employers from using the group life plan as a means of providing highly compensated employees with "tax free" benefits in the form of high amounts of life insurance coverage, particularly where there is a wide disparity from the coverage provided for the rank-and-file employees. As such, imputed income is a mechanism designed to ensure greater equality in the amount of group life insurance coverage among all the enrolled employees.

Employees must pay taxes on life insurance premiums paid on their behalf for face amounts over $50,000. The employer includes the premiums as "imputed income" on the employee's Form W-2. The imputed income is included as part of taxable income for both federal income tax and FICA (Social Security and Medicare) taxes. Currently, imputed income tax is not charged at the state or local levels.

AD&D and dependent life amounts are not added to the employee's life amounts to establish the $50,000 imputed income cap. For example, if an employee had a life face amount of $40,000 and an AD&D face amount of $40,000, the employee's life amount would not be considered imputed income. Noncontributory dependent life coverage has a separate imputed income cap.

IRC Section 79

The Internal Revenue Service (IRS) in IRC Section 79 established the $50,000 cap for life premium being excluded from employees' taxable incomes. The rules are somewhat complex, and are covered here in some detail, since the rules apply to both structure of the plan and to an insured's individual situation.

Plan Structure to Qualify for $50,000 Exemption

First, the plan itself must meet strict IRS guidelines:

1. The life proceeds cannot be an "income" benefit. Since most group life is term insurance that does not build a cash value, this isn't a major consideration.

2. With few exceptions, the group plan must cover a minimum of ten employees. Dependents are not included in comprising this minimum. Exceptions to this rule will be described later.

3. Individuals must not be able to "select" amounts of coverage in lieu of taxable compensation. However, having a set schedule that permits employees to select from a menu of coverages (such as times earnings schedules) is allowed.

4. The employer must be the policyholder. This precludes individual insurance that is issued to an employee.

5. There is also a complicated "straddle rule" that will be addressed later in this chapter.

Figure 10-1 provides an excerpt from *IRS Publication 15B* regarding these conditions for exclusion.

Excluding Taxable Premium

In order for the plan to allow up to a $50,000 exemption relating to the imputed income, the plan must not be discriminatory. That is, it cannot favor key employees. Key employees are defined by the IRS as:

• An officer of the company earning more than $100,000 a year.

• A person owning 5 percent of the company.

• A person owning 1 percent of the company with an annual income of more than $150,000.[2]

Figure 10-1. Conditions for Exclusion Excerpt

Group-Term Life Insurance Coverage

This exclusion applies to life insurance coverage that meets all the following conditions:

- It provides a general death benefit that is not included in income.

- You provide it to a group of employees. See <u>The 10-employee rule</u>, later.

- It provides an amount of insurance to each employee based on a formula that prevents individual selection. This formula must use factors such as the employee's age, years of service, pay, or position.

- You provide it under a policy you directly or indirectly carry. Even if you do not pay any of the policy's cost, you are considered to carry it if you arrange for payment of its cost by your employees and charge at least one employee less than, and at least one other employee more than, the cost of his or her insurance. Determine the cost of the insurance, for this purpose, as explained under <u>Coverage over the limit</u>, later.

Source: *IRS Publication 15B, Employer's Tax Guide to Fringe Benefits* (Washington, DC: Department of Treasury, Internal Revenue Service, 2012), pp. 12–13.

To be considered nondiscriminatory:

- 70 percent of employees must benefit from the plan.

- 85 percent of employees who are covered by the plan must not be key employees.

- Eligibility and benefits must not be set up in such a way as to benefit key employees over other employees.

- The plan must meet the discrimination tests in a cafeteria or Section 125 plan.[3]

Individual Qualification for $50,000 Exemption

Section 79 defines who can be included as an employee for partial exclusion (first $50,000 not consider imputed income) of group term life insurance costs as follows:

- An employee "under common law" is a worker who does services for the employer, and the employer has the right to control what the employee does and where the employee does it.[4]

- A full-time life insurance agent who is a "current statutory employee" is an employee.[5]

- A former employee who has met either of the definitions of employee above. [6]

- A "leased" employee who has provided service to the policyholder on a substantially full-time basis for at least a year if the services were performed under the policyholder's primary direction or control.[7]

The IRS also allows the employer to exclude certain employees in determining if the plan meets the nondiscrimination test. These are employees with less than three years of service, part-time and seasonal employees, foreign workers whose income is from sources outside of the United States, and union employees who are covered by a separate plan through the union.[8]

The IRS does permit a plan with less than ten employees covered to take advantage of the partial exclusion if all aspects of one of the following two conditions are met:

Condition 1 has three elements: [9]

1. If evidence of good health is required, it is a "medical questionnaire," such as an Evidence of Insurability (EOI) form, that is completed by the employee and no physical examination is necessary.

2. All full-time employees are eligible. Or, if EOI is required, all who had EOI accepted by the insurer are covered. Even if an employee who is eligible has his/her EOI rejected by the insurer, so long as the other employees are covered, this element is met.

3. The face amount for employees is either a set percentage of pay for all covered employees or some other form in which "no coverage bracket can exceed 2½ times the next lower bracket, and the lowest bracket must be at least 10% of the highest bracket."

Figures 10.2 and 10.3 provide examples of schedules that would and would not meet Element 3 of Condition 1.[10]

The Figure 10-3 schedule fails to meet the requirements for a small group exclusion, since the president's face amount is more than 2½ times the manager's and the clerical employees' face amount is less than 10 percent of the president's. To make the schedule meet IRS requirements, the president's face amount should be reduced to $187,500, or 2½ times the manager's. Alternatively, the other coverage amounts could be increased to $400,000 and 100,000 for the manager and clerical employees, respectively.

Figure 10-2. Schedule for Under-10 Group that Meets IRS Requirements	
President	$150,000
Manager	75,000
Clerical employees	35,000

Figure 10-3. Schedule for Under-10 Group that does NOT Meet IRS Requirements	
President	$1,000,000
Manager	75,000
Clerical employees	35,000

Condition 2 also has three elements:[11] One of the three elements must be met.

1.   There are employees of more than one company covered by the plan. Such a plan could exist under a multiple-employer welfare trust or an association plan.

2.   The plan is part of a program to cover a union or an "organization that carries on substantial activities besides obtaining insurance."

3.   Evidence of insurability does not impact the employee's eligibility or the amount of insurance.

The IRS apparently recognizes that insurers' underwriting rules could affect the above conditions, since the IRS permits the employer to not count as employees any one of the following:

•   Employee age 65 or older

•   Part-time employees working 20 hours or less

•   Employees in the waiting period of the policy, so long as the waiting period is not over 6 months[12]

Imputed Income with Multiple Plans

Occasionally employers will have more than one group term life program. In that event, how the policies are treated for Section 79 depends on whether they are with one insurer or two different insurers. If multiple policies are with one insurer, they are combined for the purposes of Section 79 testing for discrimination compliance. If an employee had coverage with the same insurer for noncontributory basic life coverage of $10,000 and supplemental (employee-pay-all) coverage of $70,000, the amount of imputed income would be $30,000 ($10,000 basic + $70,000 supplemental − $50,000 exclusion).

However, the regulations do permit the employer to treat each policy on its own if the costs and coverage can clearly be separated. If multiple policies are with different insurers, they must be treated separately.

Regardless of how they are treated, the amounts are combined for Section 79 purposes at the individual employee level. Under Section 79, the cost of the first $50,000 of coverage is not taxed to the employee. Because all group term insurance provided by an employer that qualifies under Section 79 is considered to be one plan, this exclusion applies once to each employee. [13.] For example, an employee who has a basic life amount of $25,000 with an insurer and a supplemental life amount of $100,000 with the same insurer has a total of $125,000 in coverage. The first $50,000 qualifies for the exclusion of premium. The remaining $75,000 of coverage results in computed income to the employee that is taxable as income.[14]

An employee who has $25,000 of basic life with insurer "A" and has elected $125,000 of supplemental life with insurer "B" has $150,000 in group coverage. The $25,000 under insurer "A" is under the $50,000 imputed income cap-no tax applies. The first $25,000 of supplemental life with insurer "B" is tax exempt with $100,000 being considered for imputed income calculation and taxable under IRC Code 79.

If an employee had group term life with two different employers, the employee is required to combine both policies. There is only one $50,000 exclusion, so the employee combines the face amounts on both policies, subtracts $50,000 (the exclusion), and then figures the imputed income on the remainder using Table I rates (Figure 10-4). It is the employee' responsibility, not each employer, to report the correct imputed income to the IRS for income tax purposes.

To recap, any group term life insurance program that qualifies under IRC Section 79 lets employees receive up to $50,000 in coverage at no tax cost to the employee. If the employer's plan has amounts over that, any employee who has a face amount greater than $50,000 has "imputed income". This income must be included on the employee's W-2. It should also be noted that the employer's plan must permit any employee who so chooses to reject insurance amounts that result in imputed income.

Employees for Whom the $50,000 Exemption Does Not Apply

Clearly, owners and partners are not employees and therefore do not qualify for the exclusion at all. In other words, the full cost of insurance for these individuals is "income." In addition, Subchapter S shareholders with greater than 2 percent stock ownership anytime during the year do not qualify as employees and therefore do not get the premium exclusion.[15]

Dependent Life Imputed Income

Noncontributory dependent life amounts of $2,000 or less are considered de minimus and therefore there is no imputed income applicable. However, for face amounts in excess of $2,000, there is imputed income on the entire amount of the premiums paid for the coverage. If a spouse's dependent life face amount was $10,000, the tax on imputed income is the full $10,000, not $8,000 where one would assume the first $2,000 to be "tax free." The imputed income is calculated using Table I rates for the dependent's age.

However, if the dependent life is purchased by the employee with "after-tax" dollars, there is no imputed income.[16] "After-tax" means that the premium is being paid with employee earnings that have already been taxed, rather than a "pretax" premium that might be run through a Section 125 plan.

An employee who has dependent life on a domestic partner, same sex or different, is taxed on the full amount of the value of the insurance (unless the partner is also a dependent of the employee based on IRS dependency rules).[17]

Just as for employees, AD&D insurance for dependents is not considered life insurance, so therefore there is no imputed income.[18]

When Imputed Income Can Apply to a Voluntary Plan

A voluntary or supplemental life insurance program that is fully paid for by the employee may still be subject to Section 79. In other words, even if the employee pays the cost of most of the insurance, it may result in imputed income.

Often, insurers use age banded rates for supplemental and voluntary programs. The IRS has established "Table I" as a set of age banded rates for determining the applicability of the imputed income exemption. If the insurer's rates are such that one employee pays a rate above the Table I IRS rates and one employee pays a rate below Table I IRS rates, the rates are said to "straddle" Table I rates. The straddling, by regulation, causes the plan to be subject to the imputed income regulation.[19]

Example of Straddling Table I

Employee 1 is 35 years old and has chosen supplemental life. His premium rate is $.08 per thousand. His monthly premium is below Table I rates (see Figure 10-4). Employee 2 is 60 years old and also has supplemental coverage. Her monthly premium rate is $.70 cents per thousand. Since Employee 1's rate is below Table I and Employee 2's rate is above Table I, the premium rates straddle the table, and thus the entire program is subject to inclusion in the imputed income calculation, regardless of who pays the premium.

Amount of Imputed Income

The amount of imputed income the policyholder must calculate on a covered individual is based on the IRS Table I rates shown in Figure 10-4. The policyholder must do this calculation for each month the employee is covered and has imputed income. Once the calculation is done, a withholding deduction for the tax on the imputed income is typically taken from the employee's pay.

Figure 10-4. IRS Table I Rates	
Cost Per $1,000 of Protection for One Month	
Age	Cost
Under 25	$ .05
25 through 29	.06
30 through 34	.08
35 through 39	.09
40 through 44	.10
45 through 49	.15
50 through 54	.23
55 through 59	.43
60 through 64	.66
65 through 69	1.27
70 and older	2.06

Source: *IRS Publication 15B, Employer's Tax Guide to Fringe Benefits*
(Washington, DC: Department of Treasury, Internal Revenue Service, 2012), p. 14.

Calculating the Imputed Income

Imputed income is computed using the following formulas:

Imputed Income (Monthly) = [(FA − $50,000) × TI/$1,000] − EE

Imputed Income (Annualized) = [(FA − $50,000) × TI/$1,000 × 12] − EE

Where:

FA = Face amount

TI = Table I rate

EE = Employee's Contribution

Example 1: Imputed Income Calculation with Noncontributory Coverage

Jennifer is 44 years old and has $75,000 in group term life coverage that is paid entirely by her employer, of which $25,000 is considered as imputed income. Her monthly imputed income is calculated as follows:

Imputed Income (Monthly) = [(FA − $50,000) × TI/$1,000] − EE

= [($75,000 − $50,000) × $.10/$1,000] − $0

= ($25,000 × 0.0001) − $0

= <u>$2.50</u>

Assuming the amount of imputed income remained the same throughout the tax year, her annual imputed income would be $30.00 (12 × $2.50) upon which she is liable for income tax. The $30.00 would be added to her reported regular wages for income tax purposes.

Example 2: Imputed Income Calculation with Straddling

Ann is 40 years old, has basic group term life coverage of $75,000, and contributory supplemental life coverage of $200,000 for which she pays the entire premium. The plan has rates that straddle the Table I rates, and therefore the supplemental plan is subject to the imputed income calculation. She paid $192 for the year for the supplemental plan. Her annualized imputed income is calculated as follows:

$$\text{Imputed Income (Annualized)} = [(FA - \$50,000) \times TI/\$1,000 \times 12] - EE$$

$$= [(\$275,000 - \$50,000) \times \$.10/\$1,000 \times 12] - \$192$$

$$= (\$225,000 \times .0001 \times 12) - \$192$$

$$= \$270 - \$192$$

$$= \underline{\$78}$$

The $78.00 would be added to her reported regular wages for income tax purposes.

For all of the examples above, the amount of imputed income is included on the employee's Form W-2 and the employee will pay income tax on it. Additionally, the imputed income is subject to FICA taxes (Social Security and Medicare).

Also bear in mind that owners, partners, and Subchapter S shareholders entire life amounts paid for by the employer (plus supplemental and voluntary if the rates straddle) are considered imputed income.

Thus, an employee, owner, partner, and Subchapter S shareholder all may have imputed income which results in income tax and FICA tax liability at any life benefit level. However, in no event will the employer be required to pay the employee's portion of FICA. The employer also has no federal unemployment tax (FUTA) liability on imputed income amounts. [20]

Key Takeaways

- Life insurance proceeds are not included in income for the beneficiary if paid in a lump sum. Proceeds that are paid out in some form of yearly or installment benefit resulting in interest income are taxable as income.

- Employees may elect to have an assignment of benefits to a trust to avoid estate tax liability. However, not all insurance carriers permit assignments.

- When changing carriers, if there are employees who have made trust assignments, make sure the new carrier will accept them.

- Group term life insurance paid for by an employer can result in imputed income for an employee. The IRS permits the first $50,000 of face amount to be excluded from tax for employees who meet the IRS definition of "employee."

- Owners, partners, and Subchapter S shareholders have imputed income on the full amount of any employer-paid group term life.

- Individuals who have imputed income are liable for federal income tax and FICA tax. However, the employer is not liable for the employer's share of FICA and FUTA.

- Dependent life plans may be subject to imputed income if coverage amounts are over $2,000 and if they are fully paid by the employer. If coverage is over $2,000 and employer-paid, the full amount of dependent life and Table I rates are used to compute imputed income. A domestic partner's life premiums, based on Table I rates, are fully included in the employee's wages.

- Dependent life paid by the employee with after-tax dollars is not subject to imputed income.

- Supplemental and voluntary life programs, even if fully employee paid, may need to be included in imputed income if the rates straddle Table I rates.

Endnotes

1. *Publication 535, Business Expenses* (Washington, DC: Department of Treasury, Internal Revenue Service, 2012), p. 18.
2. Publication 15B, Employer's Tax Guide to Fringe Benefits (Washington, DC: Department of Treasury, Internal Revenue Service, 2012), p. 13.
3. Ibid.
4. Ibid., p. 8.
5. Ibid., p. 11.
6. Ibid.
7. Ibid.
8. Ibid., p. 13.
9. Ibid., p. 12.
10. Chandler, Darlene K., J.D., CLU, ChFC, The Group Life Insurance Handbook, (Erlanger, KY: The National Underwriter Company, 1997), pp. 68–70.
11. *Publication 15B, Employer's Tax Guide to Fringe Benefits*
    (Washington, DC: Department of Treasury, Internal Revenue Service, 2012), p. 12.
12. Ibid., p. 12.

13. Beam, Burton T., *Group Benefits: Basic Concepts and Alternatives*, 10th Edition (Bryn Mawr, PA: The American College Press, 2004), p. 173.

14. "Group-Term Life Insurance," *IRS website*, *http://www.irs.gov/govt/fslg/article/0,,id=110345,00.html* (accessed July 12, 2012).

15. *Publication 15B, Employer's Tax Guide to Fringe Benefits* (Washington, DC: Department of Treasury, Internal Revenue Service, 2012), p. 12.

16. Ibid., p. 13.

17. Laffie, Leslie, "Domestic Partner Benefits Taxable to Employee," *Journal of Accountancy* (American Institute of Certified Public Accountants, July 2001).

18. *Publication 15B, Employer's Tax Guide to Fringe Benefits* (Washington, DC: Department of Treasury, Internal Revenue Service, 2012), p. 5.

19. "Group-Term Life Insurance," *IRS website*, *http://www.irs.gov/govt/fslg/article/0,,id=110345,00.html* (accessed July 12, 2012).

20. *Publication 15B, Employer's Tax Guide to Fringe Benefits* (Washington, DC: Department of Treasury, Internal Revenue Service, 2012), pp. 12–13.

Chapter 11

Premium Payment Methods

In today's challenging economic environment, employers are looking wherever they can to save money and to maximize their cash flow, especially when it comes to their group benefits plan. This chapter will focus on potential premium payment alternatives of which a policyholder might be able to take advantage and which can save the policyholder money and/or maximize cash flow. Insurance professionals will find they are better able to meet client needs when they are versed in and able to offer these various nontraditional payment options.

Many nontraditional premium payment methods may be thought of as antiquated and have faded from the current group life market. Because many of the arrangements are complex and require a significant commitment of manpower for both the insurer and policyholder, they can be impractical to implement or not worthwhile. However, there may be situations where a nontraditional premium payment method is still a sound option.

Traditional Premium Payments

Most Group Life and Accidental Death & Dismemberment (AD&D) policyholders remit premium to the insurer on a monthly basis. The premium is due on the first day of each month of coverage, but all contracts provide a 31-day grace period. The grace period is designed to enable the policyholder to collect any contributions from the employees and to have time to generate a self-reported bill or to provide the insurer with the information to create a bill for the policyholder. There is no charge for cash flow loss by the insurer for the standard 31-day grace period.

For ease in billing administration, carriers sometimes allow policyholders to remit premium on a quarterly or semiannual basis. The premium is remitted at the beginning of the period and a "true up" of the actual coverage amounts for each month is done at the end of each quarter or half year. Typically, this accommodation is done for smaller policyholders who may not have the staff to produce the monthly premium bills and premium. Premium is still payable in advance of the coverage period, which, in part, makes these other-than-monthly payment methods unpopular.

Rates/Premium

Employee life and AD&D premiums are almost always charged at a rate per $1,000 of coverage. On plans where each employee has the same flat benefit, such as $10,000 per employee, a charge per employee can be accommodated since each employee's individual amount of premium is the same.

Dependent life premium can be billed by family unit or for spousal coverage, which can be charged at a rate per $1,000 of coverage. When charged as a family unit, a rate per employee who has dependent coverage is charged, regardless of the number of family members. When there is a substantial spouse schedule, many underwriters prefer to have a rate per $1,000 of coverage with a separate per-unit charge for dependent children.

Employer Role in Bill Creation

The policyholder plays a pivotal role in creating an accurate monthly premium bill and in collecting and remitting the group life premium. On a self-accounting, or *self-administered* premium arrangement, the employer reports the amount that should be remitted to the insurer by creating the monthly bill. The insurer trusts the policyholder to be truthful and accurate in reporting the premium amount due. Occasionally, the insurer will send a company auditor to the policyholder's headquarters to review the self-reporting billing process for accuracy.

With direct or home office accounting or list billing premium arrangements, the employer compiles the billing information and has the insurer calculate the monthly premium. Typically, direct billing is reserved for smaller policyholders who may not be equipped to deal with the group insurance billing process, particularly with additions and deletions of employees.

Many policyholders use a payroll service in calculating the deductions that should be taken from the employees' pay for life/AD&D premium contributions. The payroll service compiles the information needed to complete the billing statement and furnishes it to the policyholder.

The behind-the-scenes compilation of the payroll data might look as shown in Figure 11-1.

| Figure 11-1. Supplemental Life Extract Example | | | | | | |
Employee Name	Annual Earnings (Rate of Pay)	Salary Multiple Elected	Age	Amount of Insurance (A)	Rate Per $1,000 (B)	Monthly Premium Contribution (A × B ÷ $1,000)
Smith	$55,098	3	55	$166,000	$.66	$109.56
Jones	30,965	2	55	62,000	.66	40.92
Henry	79,864	2	47	160,000	.37	59.20
Peale	37,000	1	33	37,000	.11	4.07
Robinson	27,765	1	33	28,000	.11	3.08
Velez	61,007	2	27	123,000	.11	13.53
Rooney	39,765	1	38	40,000	.23	9.20
O'Leary	42,870	3	62	129,000	.66	85.14
Kendrick	44,087	1	26	45,000	.11	4.95
D'Onofrio	51,808	3	44	156,000	.23	35.88

The policyholder uses the compiled payroll data to complete the billing form or structured shell provided by the insurer. The bill separates each line of coverage and is often subdivided by class of employees and/or employee locations. Figure 11-2 provides a simple illustrative billing statement.

In our simple example, the payment of the full $4,854.15 for all lines of coverage is expected. Some carriers assess a charge for late payment of a premium (beyond the grace period) and assess a fee if full payment is not received.

Most of the billing shells are in an electronic spreadsheet format requiring the self-administering policyholder to fill in the necessary information. The spreadsheet completes the calculations, much like TurboTax completes the calculations for a taxpayer. The billing statements also have an area for adjusting previous months' billing statements with addition and deletions of insured persons being a very common adjustment.

Figure 11-2. Billing Statement

Monthly Premium Statement for: <u>September</u>   Policyholder: <u>ABC Company</u>

Account Number: <u>xx00yyzz</u>

	Number of Insureds	Covered Monthly Volume (A)	Rate (B)	Monthly Premium (A × B ÷ $1,000)
Basic Life				
	226	$2,260,000	$0.24	$ 542.40
Basic AD&D				
	226	$2,260,000	$.045	$ 101.70
Supplemental Life				
	4	Under 25 $ 211,000	$ .08	$ 16.88
	18	25 – 34 605,000	.11	66.55
	43	35 – 44 2,069,000	.23	475.87
	37	45 – 5 2,432,000	.37	899.84
	41	55 – 6 3,007,000	.66	1,984.62
	11	65 – 74 287,000	1.59	456.33
	3	75 and over 108,000	2.87	309.96
Total	157			$4,210.05
			All Lines Total Premium Due	$4,854.15

There are a variety of remittance methods available to policyholders such as Automated Clearing House (ACH), wire transfers, credit or debit card, lockbox, or even a hardcopy paper check via postal service. Carriers have different requirements and options, often varying by customer size.

Alternative Premium Payments

"Alternative funding arrangements that are intended to improve cash flow [for the policyholder] are designed either to postpone the payment of premiums to the insurance company or to keep the funds that would otherwise be held in reserves until the insurance company needs them."[1] Nontraditional premium payment or plan funding in the group arena is typically associated with group medical and dental plans because of the significantly higher premiums associated with these coverages. These cash flow vehicles include:

- Administrative Services Only (ASO)

- Claims Services Only (CSO)

- Cost-plus agreement

These arrangements typically do not work well with group life insurance because they represent a potential shift in liability and fiduciary responsibility. They work well on coverage where the credibility of the experience is high and claims tend to emerge in a more predictable fashion. Wide swings in claims are much more likely on life coverage than on health coverage. Since budgeting for plan claims and expenses by the employer is essential in these arrangements, they are typically reserved only for cases with credible and predictable historic experience.

Group life coverage claims are low-frequency events with limited experience credibility. However, there are arrangements that can be established under a group life plan wherein qualified policyholders may be granted alternative cash flow options.

Qualifications for Nontraditional Premium Payment Arrangements

Insurers differ in the qualifications they may require of a policyholder before an offer of a cash-flow vehicle is made, but a few general rules of thumb apply universally. The underwriter needs to ensure the client:

- Has a proven track record of paying premium accurately and on time.

- Has the financial rating and wherewithal to pay plan liabilities in the event the policyholder agrees to take on some of those plan liabilities.

- Has the ability to budget for unanticipated swings in claim activity.

- Meets minimum size requirements, usually based on premium and/or lives, to qualify for an alternative cash flow option. These are established by underwriting guidelines.

- Is aware of the new and/or increased responsibilities the client is assuming, especially if this is the first time the client has entered into such a cash-flow arrangement.

- Has the capability to take on plan administration duties in exchange for improved cash flow.

Deferred Premium Arrangement or Extended Grace Period

This method of improving a policyholder's cash flow works well for group health and life policyholders. In this cash flow arrangement, there is no shift in liability from the insurer to the client. However, the underwriter will undoubtedly load the rate to account for the cash flow loss the insurance company will experience. Since insurers invest premiums that are not used to fund plan liabilities, this investment loss must be accounted for and charged accordingly. Generally, the insurer will charge an additional 0.5 percent to 2.0 percent of the premium per month of extended grace.

It is important to note that insurers cannot extend beyond a 90-day deferral of premium in order to comply with statutory requirements of being able to categorize the owed premium as an asset.

Some carriers have policyholders sign an agreement in which they acknowledge that they understand the arrangement into which they have entered and are aware of all premium payments due at policy termination.

The deferral of premium enables the policyholder to realize a cash flow advantage at the onset of the relationship with the insurer. After the premium delay is established, the premiums lag for the length of the deferral, as shown in Figure 11-3.

Figure 11-3. Premium Deferral Schedule	
ABC Company 60-Day Premium Deferral	
Premium Due Date	*Premium Payment for:*
March	None
April	None
May	March
June	April
July	May
August	June

A premium deferral allows the policyholder to:

• Use the funds otherwise due as premium for other purposes.

• Invest the delayed funds in hopes of earning a higher investment return than the insurer is charging for the privilege of delaying the premium.

On contributory plans, underwriters routinely offer to extend the standard 31-day grace period to 45 days without loading the rates. This allows the policyholder time to collect the employee contributions, particularly if there are multiple locations from which premiums are collected. The thought is that the policyholder should not be charged for cash flow loss simply because of an administrative process that takes time.

At the termination of the policy, which includes changing carriers, most insurers require that all due and unpaid premium be remitted immediately. It is incumbent upon the policyholder to be aware of and recall this financial responsibility at policy termination. The policyholder will need to budget for the deferred number of months of due and unpaid premiums instead of one month.

Retrospective Rating Method

A retrospective rating or "participating" (par) plan enables a policyholder to participate in the financial outcome of the group plan and be eligible for a potential refund. While this is not a cash flow program in the strictest sense, it does enable the policyholder to reap the rewards of having better-than-expected experience.

In today's group life environment, the vast majority of cases are on a "nonparticipating" basis. This means that regardless of the financial result of the case at year's end, the policyholder is not eligible to participate in a potential refund process. In 2008, only 4.2 percent of group life face amounts were reported as being on a participating basis. This compares to 26.9 percent a decade earlier.[2]

A retrospective rating method is most often applied to group medical and dental plans, but can also include life coverage. AD&D coverage is typically not part of a par arrangement since claims are so unpredictable that it would be fair to neither the insurer nor the policyholder. A retrospective rating method is more suited for medical and dental plans where claims experience has a greater propensity for consistency from year to year. Because group life claims are of low frequency, applying a retrospective rating method to life insurance alone may produce wide swings in results from year to year. To avoid these swings, many carriers require a minimum number of lives, such as 500 or 1,000, to even consider a participating life plan.

A retrospective rating arrangement can be quite involved, but in essence, it is really an accounting mechanism. A year-end accounting is done, typically within 60 days after the completion of each policy year. If the annual premium paid exceeds the costs for claims, reserves, and expenses, the policyholder may be eligible for a refund of the difference. If the costs for claims, reserves, and expenses exceed the premium collected for the policy year, then a deficit is charged to the policyholder's account.

Deficits can be accrued over policy years and are usually retired by surpluses that are generated in successive policy years. Note that the insurer does not ask for any additional premium at the end of the policy year if the case is in a deficit position. If the case terminates in a deficit position, the insurer does not charge the policyholder for the accumulated deficit. Because of the potential for the policyholder to leave the insurer in a deficit, having had the advantage of a potential refund throughout, the insurer will typically increase the risk charge in the expenses.

Figure 11- 4 shows a very simple example of how a retrospective accounting that produced a potential refund might look.

Figure 11-4. Retrospective Rating Methods Resulting in a Refund	
Annual paid premium	$310,000
Paid claims	$200,000
Change in reserves	2,200
Expenses	41,800
Total claims, reserves, and expenses	244,000
Policy year result	$ 66,000

The potential refund in Figure 11-4 is $66,000 since total liabilities of $244,000 were that much less than the $310,000 in collected premium. Before any refund is sent to the policyholder, the underwriter will first apply the generated $66,000 surplus to any outstanding plan liabilities, including any prior accumulated deficits. Figure 11-5 provides an example of a deficit that is carried from a previous year.

Figure 11-5. Year-to-Year Retrospective Accounting			
	Year 1	Year 2	Year 3
A) Annual paid premium	$310,000	$ 315,000	$320,000
B) Paid claims	200,000	286,000	231,000
C) Change in reserves	2,200	4,700	3,300
D) Expenses	41,800	42,300	42,700
E) Policy year result (A-[B+C+D])	$ 66,000	$(18,000) deficit	$43,000
F) Accumulated results	$ 66,000***	$(18,000)*	$25,000**
G) Potential refund amount	$ 66,000	$0	$25,000

*Assumes the previous year's surplus was refunded.
**$43,000 surplus − $18,000 accumulated deficit = $25,000 surplus
***Assume policyholder took full $66,000 in refund.

In Figure 11-5, had the policyholder cancelled at the end of Year 2, the policyholder would have left with a deficit of $18,000. The insurer does not collect the balance of accumulated deficit at cancellation. However, if this policyholder were to reengage the insurer again at some point in the future, it is very likely the insurer would require the policyholder to make good on the $18,000 deficit before agreeing to accept the group insurance application.

Carriers vary in how they charge interest on accumulated deficits or underfunded reserves. The interest is charged on the deficit to account for the resulting investment income loss and is collected along with the deficit itself from annual surplus that emerges in the future.

The retrospective accounting can be quite involved, and because of that, underwriters prefer to offer this arrangement to policyholders with staff who are experienced in such accounting processes. For example, in a year that produces a surplus, any initially calculated surplus amounts that are to be refunded to the policyholder must be refigured to account for the state premium tax that did not have to be charged in the expenses.

Claim Stabilization Fund

Insurers often entice a participating policyholder to leave some or all of a policy year surplus in a special account with the insurer called the Claim Stabilization Fund or Reserve. This account is also known as Premium Stabilization Reserve or Fund, Premium Deposit Account, Premium Reserve Fund, or simply a Special Fund. The Special Fund offers the policyholder several advantages from a cash flow perspective:

- Insurers offer attractive interest rates for amounts left on deposit.

- Unlike a bank account where the employer would have to pay tax on ordinary interest, interest is credited tax free, provided the funds are used to pay plan expenses.

- The policyholder can use the funds to offset deficits generated in a plan year(s) or can use the funds to provide employees with a premium holiday.

The Special Fund also increases the underwriter's flexibility when evaluating the experience for a prospective rate change. The Special Fund:

- serves to protect against unforeseen losses or potential deficits;

- allows the policyholder to use Special Fund money to pay for what might otherwise be a rate increase;

- enables the policyholder to enrich the plan of benefits and fund any increased cost with the Special Fund.

In some cases, the policyholder may want to leave a surplus on deposit because the company doesn't have the means to distribute individual refunds to all the employees who contributed toward the premium.

Insurers vary in the way in which they credit the Special Fund interest. Some carriers may show the interest as a credit to case expenses or reserves, while others may apply the interest as a dividend to the Special Fund. Some carriers credit the Special Fund based on a monthly balance while others apply an interest rate to the average of the Special Fund balance at the beginning of the plan year with the Special Fund balance at the end of the Plan Year. Figure 11-6 provides an illustrative example of how a Special Fund can be used to stabilize a participating plan's experience over the course of time. Assume the insurer credited the Special Fund at a 2.5 percent mean interest rate.

Figure 11-6. Plan with Stabilization Fund.

	Year 1	Year 2	Year 3
A) Annual paid premium	$310,000	$ 315,000	$320,000
B) Paid claims	200,000	286,000	281,000
C) Change in reserves	2,200	4,700	3,300
D) Expenses	41,800	42,300	42,700
E) Policy year result A-[B+C+D])	$ 66,000	$ (18,000) deficit	$(7,000) deficit
F) Special Fund left on deposit, plus interest	$ 50,000*	$ 51,025**	$ 33,763***
Plan accumulated results	$ 50,000	$ 33,025**	$ 26,763***

* <u>Year 1</u> – Policy year surplus was $66,000. The policyholder decided to take $16,000 in refund and leave $50,000 on deposit in the Special Fund.

**   Year 2 – The policy year ended in an $18,000 deficit. The underwriter was able to offset this $18,000 deficit entirely with money from the Special Fund. The Special Fund earned $1,025 in dividends over the course of Year 2, applying a formula of:

     Interest = [(Beginning Balance + Year-End Balance) ÷ 2] × Interest Rate
         = {[$50,000 + (50,000 – 18,000)] ÷ 2} × .025
         = <u>$1,025</u>

The Special Fund on deposit before applying the deficit is $51,025 ($50,000 + $1,025). Applying the $18,000 deficit leaves a balance of $33,025 ($51,025 – $18,000) remaining in the Special Fund.

***<u>Year 3</u> – The policy year ended in a $7,000 deficit. The underwriter was able to offset this $7,000 deficit entirely with money from the Special Fund. The Special Fund earned $738 in dividends over the course of Year 2, applying a formula of:

     Interest = [(Beginning Balance + Year-End Balance) ÷ 2] × Interest Rate
         = {[$33,025 + (33,025 – 7,000)] ÷ 2} × .025
         = <u>$738</u>

The Special Fund on deposit before applying the deficit is $33,763 ($33,025 + $738). Applying the $7,000 deficit leaves a balance of $26,763 ($33,763 – $7,000) remaining in the Special Fund.

Premium Holiday

If a policyholder decides to leave surplus amounts on deposit with the insurer, a participating plan Special Fund may enable a policyholder to take a premium holiday. A premium holiday is a period of time for which due premiums are paid from the Special Fund. The premium holiday is negotiated between the insurer and the policyholder with regard to the amount of holiday the policyholder wishes to "buy."

The policyholder is billed as normal, but the refund/surplus is internally transferred by the insurer to credit the policyholder's account as a premium payment. The holiday applies to both employer and employee contributions to the plan, including contributions for supplemental life premiums. No payroll deduction is made from the employees' pay for the month(s) of the premium holiday. A premium holiday can provide a morale boost for employees enrolled in a voluntary or supplemental life plan. In fact, the prospect of a premium holiday can act as a selling point for enrolling employees into the supplemental life program.

Retrospective Premium Agreement

A retrospective premium agreement is a way for a policyholder who believes that the rates being charged are too high to prospectively request a lower rate be paid. In turn, the policyholder acknowledges additional premium liability if the rates were not too high. It is commonly called a "retro" or a "call" arrangement because the insurer can retroactively collect additional premium at the end of the policy year.

A retro differs from a participating rating method in that it is directly tied to the premium rates that are to be charged on a monthly basis. The term "retro" can be confusing because it can apply in a participating (retrospective rating method) plan or in a nonparticipating plan, but in most cases, it is arranged in a participating plan. The agreement document will clearly state the terms and conditions under which the insurer can invoke the call balance of the due but unpaid premium.

Nonpar Retro

Although it is relatively rare, a nonparticipating retro agreement can be executed, particularly in situations where both insurer and policyholder want to continue the relationship with each other but have a disagreement about rates that cannot be resolved.

The nonpar retro agreement is typically based on a mutually agreed-upon loss ratio. If the year-end loss ratio is lower than the agreed-upon loss ratio, then no call or additional premium is due to the insurer. If the year-end loss ratio comes in higher than the agreed-upon loss ratio, then the insurer is entitled to additional premium.

In many retro agreements, there are caveats that limit the amount of additional premium the insurer can collect with the retro call. For example, the agreement may limit the call to 10 percent of the premium or to a flat dollar amount.

Nonpar Retro Example

Agreement: If the incurred loss ratio exceeds 83.0 percent, then the insurer is entitled to collect up to an additional 10 percent of the annual premium.

Assume:

A) Annual paid premium	$310,000
B) Paid claims	$190,000
C) Change in reserves	$2,200
D) Incurred loss ratio ([B + C] ÷ A)	62.0%

In this example, the incurred loss ratio is 62.0 percent, which is lower than the established tolerable loss ratio of 83.0 percent. The underwriter believed that $.83 of every premium dollar, or $257,300 ($310,000 × .83), was needed to cover claims and reserves. Only $192,200 ($190,000 + $2,200) was actually needed, or $.62 of every premium dollar. Therefore, the retro call for additional premium is not invoked.

However, if the case had incurred a loss ratio of 85.0 percent, where $.85 of every premium dollar needed to be allocated for claims and reserves, then the underwriter could have invoked the retro call.

$310,000 × 85% = $263,500 actual incurred claims and reserves

$310,000 × 83% = 257,300 tolerable

$ 6,200 underfunded

Retro call maximum: 10% × $310,000 = $31,000

According to the retro agreement formula, the insurer could call up to $31,000 in additional premium. The actual amount of underfunding is $6,200, so that is the amount the insurer can call. Any previous policy year surplus or underfunding is immaterial because this is a nonparticipating arrangement.

Participating Retro

The same principles that apply in a nonparticipating retro also apply in a participating arrangement. The difference is that the potential call amounts may be tied to prior years' accumulated deficits, if that is how the retro agreement is structured. Sometimes the retro call amount is not tied to prior years. A common retro structure is to allow the collection rates to be 10 percent less than the contract rates, the rates to which the insurer is entitled in the event the plan is underfunded at policy year-end. The insurer may establish contract rates and collection rates in the agreement. These two rates would be applied to the total volume reported throughout the policy year to determine the potential retro call amount.

Contract rate: $.240

Collection rate: $.216

Another way to set up the agreement is to apply a percentage to the premium collected throughout the year. In order to collect the full 10 percent retro, the insurer would have to call 11.1 percent ($1.00 \div .90$) of the premium in order to collect the full value of the premium. Calling 10 percent of a premium that has already been reduced in the collection phase would understate the retro call. The full retro amount is due as soon as it is billed. There is no grace period on a retro call.

Figure 11-7 provides an example of a participating retro agreement. It assumes that the insurer can collect up to 11.1 percent of the current year premium and that accumulated deficits can also be called up to the point that the 11.1 percent maximum is reached.

Figure 11-7. Participating Retro Example		
	Year 1	**Year 2**
A) Annual paid premium at collection rate	$297,000	$ 320,000
B) Paid claims	286,000	274,000
C) Change in reserves	4,700	1,900
D) Expenses	42,300	42,700
E) Policy year result (A-[B+C+D])	$(36,000) deficit	$1,400 surplus
F) Potential refund amount	$ 0	$ 0***
G) Potential retro call at contract rate (A × 11.1%)	$ 32,967	$ 35,520
H) Amount of actuals retro call	$ 32,967	$ 1,633**
I) Accumulated policy year results (H + E)	$ (3,033) deficit*	$ 0

*Year 1 – The policy year ended in a $36,000 deficit at the retro collection rates. The policyholder was not eligible for a refund due to the deficit. The retro calculation enabled the insurer to collect an additional $32,967 ($297,000 × 11.1%) in premium. The $32,976 retro call was due right after the annual accounting was completed. Despite the retro call that was applied against the deficit, the net result was an accumulated deficit of $3,033 ($36,000 – $32,967) to be recouped from future potential surpluses and/or retro calls.

** Year 2 – The policy year ended in a surplus of $1,400. This $1,400 was applied to the previous accumulated deficit of $3,033 to reduce the deficit to $1,633. The insurer was entitled to collect up to $35,520 ($320,000 × 11.1%), but only needed to collect $1,633 to retire the deficit completely. The account was at zero balance at the end of Year 2 after the $1,633 retro premium was remitted.

***Policyholder not eligible for $1,400 surplus as a refund because of accumulated deficit. Surplus of $1,400 was applied before retro was called.

Security Requirements for Retros

Because there is a risk that the policyholder may not be able to come up with the owed premium at the call, the underwriter may require the estimated value of the call be secured with a letter of credit or other means. This security is most likely to be required of a policyholder with marginal or unclear finances or of a policyholder who has demonstrated difficulty in paying bills to vendors on time.

Flex Funding or Cost-Plus Arrangement

A flex funding plan is also known as a cost-plus arrangement or life minimum premium plan. This arrangement is reserved for only the largest and/or most sophisticated of group life policyholders. The arrangement affects the plan benefits, the way in which premiums are paid, and the way in which reserves are established and held. Many of the principles of a minimum premium plan typically associated with group medical and dental apply.

The premise of the arrangement is for the policyholder to have the protection and services provided through a traditional life plan yet paying for claims only as they surface. Rather than paying a full monthly premium, the policyholder remits only the amount needed for expenses to administer the plan. When claims are paid, the insurer issues a bill and collects a premium for the value of the life claims that have been paid. The positive cash flow the customer realizes by paying for claims only as they surface can be significant where claim frequency is low.

Plan Benefits Structure

A traditional policy is issued by the insurer to the policyholder, and the customary liability and responsibility implicit in the group contract apply in a flex funded arrangement. However, because of the nature of the plan, a waiver of premium provision may not apply. Instead, the insurer typically agrees to provide coverage to disabled employees on a Death Benefit Only (DBO) basis. AD&D benefits are typically not run through a flex funded program.

A waiver of premium claim is an underwriting reserving event rather than an actual payment. Because an actual claim payment has not been made on the disabled employee, there is no amount for which to bill the policyholder. The DBO arrangement provides coverage for disabled employees as long as the employer continues to carry them on the coverage roster (and remits expense premium for them), but after case termination, the insurer has no further obligation to cover the disabled employees.

Reserves

Since a full traditional premium is not collected, the means for the insurer to have funds to pay for Incurred-But-Not-Reported (IBNR) liability at policy termination is necessary. There are a variety of ways to arrange for funding of the reserves, and carriers vary in the options that they offer. Options include the following:

- The policyholder pays a monthly premium for the value of the reserve. This is a very modest charge compared to the full monthly premium that would exist in a traditional premium arrangement.

- The policyholder funds the value of the reserve up front and leaves the reserve on deposit with the insurer in the form of an interest-bearing Special Fund. At case termination, the insurer would determine the final reserve need. If reserves were more than sufficient, the insurer may return the excess to the policyholder in the form of a refund.

- The policyholder signs a promissory note agreeing to remit the full value of the IBNR reserve need at case termination. Insurers may require that the note be secured with a letter of credit, depending on underwriting guidelines.

- The insurer accepts a signed hold-harmless agreement in which the policyholder relinquishes the insurer from any responsibility for claims that may emerge after the policy has terminated.

Case Expenses

The policyholder remits a monthly premium for case expenses. In most cases, the expenses represent only about 10 percent to 25 percent of a full traditional premium. A rate per $1,000 of coverage and/or a charge based on the number of insureds may be applied. Expenses include the customary charges for case administration and profit as a base and may vary by month as claims emerge to account for:

- claim handling charges (may be charged separately as claims arise, depending on insurer);

- state premium tax on claims and the premium collected as case expenses;

- commissions.

The expense percentage for flex funded cases will typically run higher than a comparable traditional plan because of the increased administrative costs and the insurer's cash flow loss.

Cap Rate or Stop-Loss Rate

In effect, stop-loss protection is provided in a flex funded arrangement to protect the policyholder from the extraordinarily wide claim swings that can occur in life insurance. A cap is established to limit the amount of payments to the amount the policyholder would have otherwise paid in a traditionally funded plan.

A rate is established as if the case were traditionally funded. The monthly reported volume is multiplied by this rate to generate a monthly "cap." The cap limits the amount the policyholder has to pay in claims that emerge during a month, thus enabling a more predictable budget for plan benefits. The policyholder pays the remainder of the claim to the insurer in the subsequent month(s) if still under the cap. Carriers vary in how they apply the cap mechanism.

The cap is accumulated from month to month for a full policy year. Any "unused" cap amount from previous months is added to the most current month's cap. At the beginning of a new policy year, a new cap is established. Typically, deficits or accumulated amounts owed from previous years are collected in the subsequent policy year. An accounting comparing the total accumulated cap to incurred claims is made at the end of each policy year. Figure 11-8 provides an illustrative example of how the cap can apply in a 4-month view of a policy year.

Figure 11-8. Applying a Cap

	April	May	June	July
A) Cap rate	$.26	$.26	$.26	$.26
B) Monthly volume	$87,000,000	$89,500,000	$84,300,000	$85,700,000
C) Monthly cap (A × B ÷ $1,000)	22,260	23,270	21,918	22,282
D) Accumulated monthly cap	22,620*	45,890	67,808	90,090
E) Claims & conversions	0	82,000	0	0
F) Payment to insurer	0	45,890**	14,192***	21,918****

*April – In the first month of the plan, there were no claims incurred. The cap premium for April was $22,620 and since there were no claims charged to the cap, $22,620 rolled over to next month to be added to the accumulated cap.

**May – In the second month of the plan, there was $82,000 in incurred claims. The cap premium for May was $23,270 ($89,500,000 × $.26 ÷ $1,000). The accumulated cap premium for May was $45,890 ($22,620 + $23,270). The policyholder's maximum payment up to the accumulated cap is $45,890, and this amount (plus state premium tax) is remitted to the policyholder as part of May's premium. The policyholder is responsible for paying the remaining $36,110 ($82,000 – $45,890) claim payment when there is available cap space. This is a great example of how the cap protected the policyholder from having to pay the full $82,000 claim and allowed for more favorable budgeting.

***June – In the third month of the plan, there were no incurred claims. The cap premium for June was $21,918 ($84,300,000 × $.26 ÷ $1,000). The accumulated cap premium for June was $67,808 ($45,890 + $21,918). The remaining $36,110 from the May claims is reduced under the accumulated cap by $14,192 ($82,000 – 67,808). The policyholder remits $14,192 to the insurer, the amount allowed to be collected under the cap. There remains $21,918 ($82,000-$45,890 -$14,192) to be collected for the claim if cap space exists in July.

****July – In the fourth month of the plan, there were no claims incurred. The cap premium for July was $22,282 ($85,700,000 × $.26 ÷ $1,000). The accumulated cap premium for June was $90,090 ($67,808 + $22,282). The accumulated cap allows for the remaining outstanding balance of $21,918 in claims to be collected since the accumulated cap of $90,090 is over the accumulated claims of $82,000. The policyholder remits $21,918 ($82,000 – $45,890 – $14,192) in premium. The May claims have been fully retired.

Billing for Claims

The insurer bills each month for expenses to operate the case. In months in which claims are charged, the insurer may add the claim charges to the bill if claim handling expenses are being charged separately. The applicable state premium tax is included in the claims and claim handling charges. The standard 31-day grace period for the collection of the monthly premium applies to expenses and payments for incurred claims.

Key Takeaways

- Alternative methods of paying premium can be advantageous to a policyholder and helpful in retaining a client for the insurer.

- Nontraditional premium arrangements do come with increased risk to both the policyholder and the insurer.

- Careful screening is conducted by the underwriter to ensure that a policyholder qualifies for the nontraditional payment of premium.

- Nontraditional premium arrangements are offered more frequently to larger policyholders.

- Most nontraditional premium arrangements require a significantly greater commitment in manpower to administer for both policyholder and insurer.

- A Special Fund can increase underwriting flexibility when it comes to projected rate increases, since the underwriter may have a surplus from which to draw on an underfunded case.

- It is crucial for policyholders to understand the full extent of their financial responsibilities before entering into a non-traditional premium arrangement with an insurer.

Endnotes

1. Beam, Burton T. Jr. and John J. McFadden, *Employee Benefits*, Eighth Edition (New York, NY: Kaplan Publishing), p. 436.
2. "Table 7.3, Life Insurance Purchases, by Participating Status," *2009 Life Insurers Fact Book* (Washington D.C.: American Council of Life Insurers, 2009), page 68.

Chapter 12

Voluntary Life and AD&D Benefits

Today's environment is one in which employers are constantly strapped with the costs of employee benefits. This is primarily due to the seemingly never ending increase in the cost of health plans. Figure 12-1 demonstrates the increase in average health costs between 2001 and 2011.

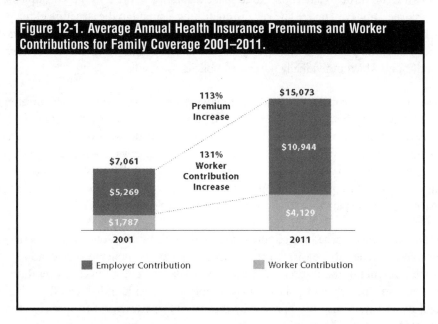

Figure 12-1. Average Annual Health Insurance Premiums and Worker Contributions for Family Coverage 2001–2011.

Source: *Employer Health Benefits 2011 Annual Survey* (The Kaiser Family Foundation and Health Research and Education Trust, September 2011), p. 1.

In this setting, using products that don't cost the employer more yet provide real value to employees is very attractive. The group life market has seen an increase in employee-pay-all plans in response to today's economic environment. Having knowledge of voluntary and supplemental life and Accidental Death & Dismemberment (AD&D) and being able to advise employers about their effective use is important for most group insurance professionals.

Voluntary and supplemental group term life insurance have been around a long time. They are essentially the same form of insurance, although carriers may call them by different names. The advantage to these employee-pay-all plans is that they permit the employer to offer relatively high amounts of life insurance at little or no cost to the employer. At times, the line between pure group voluntary and individually purchased life insurance offered through the employer is blurred. They are very different. To differentiate, we will call an employee-pay-all life insurance program that is an employer-sponsored group contract "voluntary" life, and we will call an employee-pay-all life insurance policy that is employer-sanctioned and marketed but issued to the individual employee "worksite" life insurance.

Worksite Insurance

Worksite supplemental life insurance is characterized by having individual policies sold to employees that the employees pay for through payroll deductions. The employer allows the insurance company access to the employees in order to sell its products. Often, the employee premiums are run through a Section 125 to make insurance payable with pretax dollars, which saves employees money in taxes. The key distinguishing element in the structure of the program from a group plan lies in the fact that the employer is not considered the policyholder. Rather, each individual who purchases the coverage is considered a policy owner. The employer is the conduit through which individually purchased policies are made.

These life/AD&D products are sold to employees usually with one-on-one meetings with agents of the worksite insurance carrier at the employer's premesis, usually during work hours. Employees are invited to attend these one-on-one meetings by the worksite insurance agent. The decision to accept the invitation and to purchase life/AD&D coverage is exclusively up to the employee and may or may not have the active endorsement of the employer. The one-on-one meetings often give the employee the opportunity to involve the insurance agent in constructing a life/AD&D coverage plan that is tailored to the employee's unique situation.

The amounts of coverage may require evidence of good health. Policies are generally issued on a guaranteed renewable basis, which means as long as the policy owner continues to pay the required premium, the insurer will continue to offer to renew the coverage. Rates can be changed only for the "class of policies" that is, not on a specific individual. Rate changes for a class of policies must also be approved by the state's Department of Insurance before being implemented.

The worksite products have an advantage for employees of being very flexible. The insurer may offer a range of types of products. Employees can select coverage plans that fit their situation and price point. Another plus over group voluntary insurance is that the policy is owned by the employee. The employee can continue coverage even after leaving the employer.

It should be noted that some worksite carriers also sell group voluntary products, such as voluntary life, voluntary AD&D, and short- and long-term disability.

Group Voluntary Life

Group voluntary life insurance is characterized by having a group policy sold to the employer who acts as the policyholder. Premium contributions are payroll deducted and can be run through a Section 125 plan. The employer selects the type of schedule offered from which employees can select coverage amounts. Some flexibility may be permitted the employee, be it in multiples of earnings or incremental amounts.

An employee terminating employment usually cannot continue the coverage, unless the policy offers some sort of portability or continuation provision. Further, dependent coverage customarily ends when the employee's coverage ends.

Group rates are based on the insurer's group experience manifested through the manual rates. On larger groups, insurers can take into account the experience of that particular employer group. The coverage is annual term, and the insurer can change rates or even terminate the coverage on renewal. Group voluntary insurance has an advantage in lower comparative administrative costs, which can translate into lower overall costs for the employees.

Comparison of Worksite to Group Voluntary

With worksite marketing, the employer provides the worksite agent the opportunity to meet with the employees to offer them a wide variety of insurance products. The employer does not choose the offerings. The agent may also provide the employees with information about the other group coverages the employer does offer, such as health insurance.

With group voluntary life/AD&D, the employer is the policyholder. The employer decides the plan of benefits, with any choices, to offer the employees. The solicitation is done by the producer, representatives of the group insurance company, or both in tandem. In any case, the employer will payroll-deduct the premiums. Frequently, there is a Section 125 plan set up through which premiums will be run.

Each employee who purchases a worksite product gets an individual policy. The employee is the policy owner with all the rights that the insurer bestows on policy owners. In group voluntary, the employee is merely a plan participant. The employee does not receive a policy. Rather, the employee receives a certificate or booklet that describes the coverage and the employee's rights, interests, and privileges related to the master policy held by the employer.

In worksite products, the insurance agent has a wide variety of offerings and benefit choices. Frequently, the worksite carrier can offer more than term life products on an individual basis, such as whole life and other permanent types of life insurance, accident coverage, disability coverage, cancer insurance, and critical illness insurance. Indeed, the list can be very comprehensive. Within each product, the agent has a wide range of benefit choices and price tags for each employee, allowing a great degree of customization.

With group voluntary, types of insurance have been preselected by the employer with the producer's assistance. The benefits have been preselected as well with whatever choices are made available. Rates have been set by the group insurance underwriter and the employee's cost is a function of these preset rates. Group voluntary life insurance is generally always term life insurance. The only customization related to the employee comes in the form of the preset choices from which the employee can select.

Since the employee is the policyholder of worksite life, the employee can continue the insurance upon leaving the employer simply by switching from payroll deduction to direct billing to the employee by the worksite insurer. This is in contrast to group voluntary. When an employee leaves the employer, his or her group coverage terminates. However, many group voluntary contracts permit the employee to convert or "port" some amounts of coverage.

Figure 12-2 summarizes the differences between worksite and voluntary insurance.

Figure 12-2. Comparison of Worksite to Group Voluntary Insurance	
Worksite	*Group Voluntary*
• The employer provides platform for insurer to market to employees.	• The employer acts as policyholder.
• Each employee who buys receives an individually tailored policy.	• Employees are covered as a member of the group and receive a booklet/certificate certifying coverage under the plan.
• There is a high degree of plan choice and price points.	• There is a limited degree of plan choice and price points.
• A variety of coverage types are offered besides term insurance.	• Term insurance is typically offered.
• The employee owns the policy regardless of employment status.	• Employee coverage is contingent upon remaining employed and eligible under the employer's plan.

Reason for Popularity of Group Voluntary

At first glance, it may seem worksite insurance with its individual polices enjoys all the advantages. Yet, group platform voluntary sales have been growing and are beginning to eclipse individual worksite sales.

Over the last decade, the mix of sales between group and individual platforms has shifted from predominantly individual plans to more and more group voluntary plans.* In 2010, group voluntary sales were $2.069 billion while individual sales were $2.634 billion, a difference of only $25 million. This is in comparison to sales of these offerings in 2006 at which time individual worksite sales were 57 percent individual and 43 percent voluntary according to Eastbridge Consulting.

"As we predicted a number of years ago, the voluntary market is becoming primarily one comprised of group platform products," says Gil Lowerre, president of Eastbridge. "Of the top 15 companies, all have some group products and most are predominantly group or hybrid plans."[1] Hybrid products are filed on a group platform but have some characteristics that are more common with individual plans.

Group Benefit producers or brokers are usually already handling the health insurance and employer-provided ancillary lines of insurance such as disability, basic life, and dental. Therefore, it is a small step to have the producer bring in the voluntary life and AD&D offerings, which for most benefit brokers, will be a group product. Eastbridge Consulting, who gathers and publishes proprietary data on the worksite and voluntary markets, offers the data shown in Figure 12-3. From this data, it can clearly be seen that producers who deal with employee benefits enjoy a distribution advantage.

Figure 12-3. 2009 Sales by Segment		
Segment	*2009 Estimated Sales ($000,000)*	*Percent of Total*
Benefit broker/producer	$2,826.8	52.4%
Career worksite agenzt	1,176.9	21.8%
Classic worksite broker	793.6	14.7%
Worksite specialist	421.8	7.8%
Occasional producer	177.9	3.3%
Total	$ 5,397	100%

Source: Lowerre, Gil, and Bonnie Brazzell, "Benefits Brokers Take Control," *Benefits Selling Magazine* (Erlanger, KY: Summit Business Media, September 2010), p. 28.

---

*Note: Eastbridge Consulting combines both group policy platform and individual policy platform sales in their research and reporting. The authors believe it is important to distinguish these types of offerings. They are very different with different distribution methods sold by different types of insurance carriers for the most part.

As most marketing professionals are aware, distribution is a key component of any sale. Having an advantage in distribution can make all the difference. However, in addition to distribution, group voluntary products have other advantages over worksite:

- Cost: While voluntary costs the employer little or nothing, it does cost the employee. Since voluntary products are on a group platform and have different (lower) commission structures, they enjoy a rather substantial cost advantage over individual worksite products.

- Administration: Group voluntary insurance has simpler administration than individual worksite insurance for the employer in many respects. The group carrier can simply bill the voluntary along with the other employer-paid coverages. Enrollment can be easier for the employer, since most group voluntary products are not sold in one-on-one meetings.

- Simplicity: Since the group voluntary offering is limited in both types of products and benefit choices within the product, they are inherently simpler. Fewer choices can quell employees' reluctance to buy out of fear of making the wrong choice.

Group term life voluntary insurance has been gaining an increasing share of the group term life market.[2] The reasons for this include the following:

Cost has to be the number one reason employers choose to offer voluntary (and worksite) products. Voluntary is chosen by the employer since it is employee-paid and costs employers little.

- There can be some administrative burden for the policyholder, but it is usually not a major issue, since all group insurance encompasses some administrative effort and costs for the employer.

- Voluntary life plans are typically included with the overall administration and operation of the group plan in general.

- The cost of group benefits, especially health benefits, has reached alarming levels. The average annual cost of health insurance today for a family is $15,073, of which $10,944 is employer-paid and $4,129 is employee-paid.[3] Group term life insurance, in contrast, has an average annual premium of $198 per person.[4] While it is relatively inexpensive, employers are highly motivated to contain all benefit costs and pass part of the costs to employees.[5] So, voluntary life at an average employee cost of $220 per year, or $18 per month, for nearly $78,000 in coverage is very reasonable.[6]

- Providing choice to employees has also been a strong motivator from employers. Employees have indicated they like having choices about the benefits they purchase.[7] The insurance industry has widely adopted the concept of voluntary benefits as a solution to the challenges of employee benefits. A full 67 percent of voluntary carriers believe employees are more enthusiastic about benefits when given choices.[8]

- The desire for employee recruitment and retention (loyalty) is another factor driving the growth of voluntary offerings.[9] Employers understand benefits are very important to employees. An attractive benefits package with an array of choices can help employers to recruit the best candidates for open positions. Good benefits help to secure employees' loyalty to the company. Since employers, however, view containing benefit costs as a primary concern, using voluntary simply makes sense.[10]

So, for several reasons, voluntary insurance (and its fraternal twin, worksite) has achieved robust growth. It is not likely that the factors propelling the growth of voluntary and worksite insurance will change in the near future. Producers will likely have more conversations with their employer-clients about voluntary and worksite life insurance offerings in the future.

Voluntary Challenges

Voluntary life and AD&D is not without its challenges for both policyholder and insurer. The main challenges are related to participation, the enrollment process, degree of risk, and ERISA implications.

Participation

Perhaps the largest issue in voluntary life/AD&D is employee participation or enrollment in the plan. Low or insufficient participation can quickly sink a group program due to its being predicated on adequate participation.

Good participation helps keep administrative costs under control by spreading fixed administrative costs, such as underwriting, policy issue, and billing, over a larger premium base. More importantly, good participation helps mitigate the risk of *antiselection* by ensuring a good cohort of younger, healthy participants to offset the potentially higher claims costs of older, less-healthy workers. Underwriters count on or hope for good participation when underwriting a voluntary group. Often, their quotes are conditional upon achieving some specified level of participation.

Importance of Enrollment

The enrollment process is carefully considered by the underwriter in the risk selection process as well as in the experience evaluation and pricing of the plan. If future enrollment processes are expected to be different than those currently in place, they must be accounted for in terms of risk management and premium cost. The greatest fear the underwriter has relating to enrollment is that the voluntary plan will not be able to sustain itself financially due to a poor *spread of risk* where only those at greatest risk of death or disability are likely to enroll.

Participation Requirements

Underwriters will typically establish a minimum enrollment or participation level for the voluntary plan. The participation factor is usually based on a percentage of employees who are eligible to enroll compared to those who have actually enrolled in the past or the percentage of those who are expected to enroll when the plan takes effect.

Many insurers establish a minimum participation of 20 percent to 25 percent of the eligible employees. If the current or projected participation level is below minimum underwriting guidelines, it may be a reason to not quote on the voluntary life and AD&D.

The underwriter is likely to adjust the formula rates based on projected employee participation in the plan. The most challenging element is what to do after accepting the risk and then having minimum participation levels not met at enrollment? Readjusting the rates upward to account for the increased risk is likely to drive participation downward as those who need the coverage least will be driven out by the increased cost. This can lead to the proverbial "death spiral," where ever-increasing rates on a diminishing enrollment reaches a level where enough premium can no longer be collected to cover all plan costs.

Determining the projected participation level at change in carriers is tricky. The underwriter will typically assume that the most current level of participation will follow the same level at change in carrier. The tricky part is projecting how successful the new insurer's enrollment tactics might be in increasing enrollment.

Risk

Risk is another challenge that is closely related to participation. Beyond the risk of low participation, there is simply the risk of offering too generous a plan that is overpopulated with employees with health conditions that lead to insufficient premium to cover premium waiver and death claims. This is classic antiselection.

Theoretically, the loads underwriters apply for participation account for antiselection risk. However, a group with a preponderance of unhealthy older workers may skew the risk profile in unfavorable ways, leading to excessively poor experience that can't be made up with rate loads. In these situations, the underwriter faces a difficult choice. The underwriter may raise rates. This frequently leads to the younger and healthier employees dropping coverage. The result is a worsening pool of insureds and the need for subsequent rate increases. This is the classic underwriting "death spiral" previously mentioned.

Rejecting a case below minimum participation levels and refusing to accept the policyholder on the books is often impractical. Another option to overcome insufficient participation risk is to see if the case can be reenrolled to get better overall participation. However, this too can have its downside. Reenrolling can result in opening up the plan to less than healthy employees opting to enroll which can adversely affect the loss experience of the plan. Then, too, there is no guarantee reenrolling will result in any better participation level or improved risk profile, leaving all in the same quandary. Finally, the underwriter has the option of leaving the insufficiently enrolled case alone and hoping for improvement. However, this is seldom the best choice as experience has shown over the years.

ERISA Implications

ERISA provides an exemption for plans that are employee-pay-all. The voluntary life plan may not fall under the auspices of ERISA if all of the following conditions are met:

1. The employer does not contribute to the cost.

2. The coverage/participation is voluntary.

3. The only administrative function provided by the employer is to collect premiums through payroll deduction.

4. No consideration is received by the employer other than compensation for administrative services performed.

Thus, it seems that group voluntary life is not covered by ERISA. However, with regulatory matters, few things are so simple. Many court jurisdictions have found group voluntary plans *do* fall under ERISA, as explained in the following quote from ERISA expert Ron Neyer:

> "ERISA does not govern the plan if all four of the above requirements are met, which appears relatively straightforward on the surface. However, failing to satisfy all requirements does not necessarily mean that ERISA applies. Courts must determine whether the plan was "established or maintained" by the employer when a voluntary plan falls outside of the safe harbor. Recent rulings have shown that ERISA plans can be easily created based on many different actions, including the employer's intent, oral representations, written representations in internally distributed documents, establishment of a fund to pay benefits, and the reasonable understanding of the employees."[11]

In this research report, group voluntary insurance was part of the subject matter, so it was not simply worksite insurance that was addressed.

As shown in Figure 12-4, insurers vary quite a bit in how they determine if ERISA applies.

Figure 12-4. How Carriers Determine ERISA Governance of Voluntary Products				
	Number of Companies			
	Life		Disability	
	Individual	Group	Individual	Group
Company requires the client (employer) to indicate ERISA-governance	5	5	6	6
Company determines ERISA-governance on a case-by-case basis	2	4	2	2
Company identifies all voluntary products as ERISA-governed	1	4	1	4
Company relies on the producer to work with the client (employer) to indicate ERISA-governance	0	1	0	1
Other	5	3	3	4
Not applicable: coverage is not offered	10	6	11	4

Source: Neyer, Ron, Interpreting ERISA Guidelines for Worksite Life and Disability Products (Windsor, CT: LIMRA, 2009), p. 2

In as much as the employer exercises significant control over the plan through the selection of benefit levels and the carrier, ERISA may be found to apply.[12] Employers may need to refer to legal counsel for advice on the applicability of ERISA regarding their group voluntary life/AD&D plan.

Voluntary Enrollment

Successful enrollment has long been considered the key to a viable voluntary plan. Effective enrollment usually has several beneficial outcomes for the plan:

- Participation increases, which helps in risk management of the plan.

- Costs of administering the plan are spread out over a larger premium base, thus holding down plan unit costs.

- Effective enrollment means more employees have a positive view of the plan, helping to meet employer objectives.

The underwriter usually has confidence in his/her company's ability to increase participation in the voluntary life/AD&D plan over the prior carrier's participation level. If the underwriter is not confident that projected participation minimums can be met after the sale, the underwriter may abstain from quoting.

Achieving a successful enrollment generally means the following have been accomplished:

- Plan designs and benefit levels that are attractive to employees at reasonable costs, which also provide value for their premium dollars.

- The plan is not overly generous so as to retain sound risk management.

- Appropriate communication about the plan and the enrollment process.

  - Employees need to be aware of what is being offered well in advance of the enrollment. Employees frequently will want to involve spouses and family members in determining the amounts of coverage. Advance communication allows this to happen.

  - Communicating about the voluntary life/AD&D enrollment too far in advance can cause employees to forget about it or have diminished interest.

  - Appropriate advance notice varies by policyholder circumstances, such as number of employees, number of locations, plan complexity, and employee knowledge of the benefits. Typically, 30 to 45 days advance notice is considered appropriate.

- An enrollment period of appropriate length.

  - Usually, the period is from 2 to 4 weeks.

  - Less than 2 weeks can make employees feel rushed and tend not to enroll.

  - Greater than 4 weeks can cause employees to lose their sense of urgency and fail to enroll out of forgetfulness.

- Employer support for the plan and the enrollment process. This includes:

  - communicating the employer's support for the plan;

  - helping the enrollment process by setting aside time for employees to enroll;

  - encouraging or requiring employees to attend enrollment meetings.

- Use of appropriate technology for enrolling employees.

  - For example, trying to use the Internet for enrollment processes with a technology-adverse group can backfire. Similarly, using old-fashioned paper enrollment with a technology-savvy group may result in a less-than-enthusiastic response.

- Technology use can include:

  - online enrollments;

  - laptop enrollments;

  - on-site kiosks;

  - use of interactive voice response (IVR) for phone enrollments;

  - use of Internet, both for communication and enrollment, including use of social media;

  - personalized enrollment statements/forms.

- Effective enrollers who:

  - are enthusiastic about the product, carrier, and the enrollment itself;

  - are knowledgeable about the product and the need for group life/AD&D insurance;

  - believe in the coverage themselves;

  - are compensated or recognized appropriately (so as to attract quality enrollers).

Usually, group voluntary enrollment is accomplished through meetings, simulcasts, and/or conference calls with a number of employees at once. Enrollment specialists are usually not employees of the policyholder, rather they are engaged by the insurer and/or producer. Insurers often have enrollers conduct the meetings, or the producers may perform this function. While these actions will not guarantee good enrollment participation, they will certainly help the cause.

Enrollment at Renewal

What to do about voluntary life enrollment at renewal time can be especially difficult. Many underwriters shy away from any renewal enrollment tactic other than that with standard evidence of insurability requirements. In most underwriters' judgment, the extra little bit of participation does not warrant the *antiselection* risk of an uncontrolled enrollment approach.

The underwriter may tie the renewal rate offered to a minimum participation level. If the minimum is not achieved at enrollment, the underwriter may reserve the right to reprice the case. This, of course, can lead to a "death spiral" of the voluntary plan.

To protect against antiselection, most life and AD&D policies require a late entrant to submit evidence of good health. A "late entrant" is a person who was previously eligible for coverage but declined it within the enrollment window and now wants to enroll in the plan. The risk is that the person is now enrolling because of contracting a potentially life-threatening or disabling condition.

Annual Enrollment

Many employers have an annual enrollment for their employee benefits. Generally, the focus is on benefits like health choices and 401k deductions. Some employers have life programs that permit a small increase in benefit levels, such as one increment without new evidence of insurability. However, these annual enrollments are not to be confused with an open enrollment. If a group program has an annual enrollment as in a Section 125 plan, the employees make their choices about life and AD&D coverage at the same time as health and disability coverage.

Open Enrollment

This is an enrollment without standard evidence of insurability requirements for late entrants. That is, unenrolled employees are permitted to join the plan at benefit levels up to the guaranteed issue amount or increment limit without any evidence of good health during the enrollment period. An open enrollment is sometimes part of the annual enrollment.

Because of the significant increase in risk associated with an open enrollment, it usually requires the underwriter's approval to authorize one. Previously declined late entrants with unsatisfactory evidence of insurability are generally not permitted to enroll in an open enrollment, although this varies by carrier.

An open enrollment may be used when a plan's participation is at unacceptable levels primarily due to a poorly administered initial enrollment. There are risks associated with an open enrollment, which include:[13]

- Anti-selection risk

  - Employees who did not previously enroll due to a known health condition now get a "free pass." Employees who previously did not consider coverage may have developed health problems that now make life insurance coverage extremely enticing.

- A change in the enrolled employee mix

  - If the open enrollment is successful, the mix of employees may change so much that the census characteristics used in both manual rates and experience underwriting may have significantly changed. If *step rates* are used on a manually rated case, this will not be as big an issue.

In order for an open enrollment to be successful, the proper environment should exist. A proper environment includes the following:[14]

- The employer has had other voluntary products with acceptable participation. This is an indication that voluntary products are accepted by employees and the employer supports voluntary offerings.

- The employer offers a limited number of choices. Too many choices can confuse employees and result in underenrollment.

- The employer actively supports the enrollment. This can be very important if the employer was not active with the prior enrollment that resulted in the poor participation.

- If past efforts have been less than successful, different enrollment methods are now being used. Chosen practices should be based on historic success or the belief that new tactics will improve participation.

Underwriters may place very specific requirements on any open enrollment, which may include the following:[15]

- There must not have been a previous open enrollment within some specified period of time. If a recent open enrollment was unsuccessful, there is less of a chance another one close in time will achieve the desired participation.

- The open enrollment period must be for a limited time. The underwriter does not want too much time for employees to get previously unplanned medical testing done and then enroll with a known health condition.

- Employees previously declined for unacceptable evidence may need to submit new evidence of insurability.

- Evidence will still be used on amounts exceeding the guaranteed issue limit.

- Minimum participation levels are specified. The underwriter reserves the right to increase rates if minimum participation is not achieved during the open enrollment.

The underwriter could even specify that if the targeted minimum participation is not reached, the carrier will not issue or renew the case.

- Benefit levels are not being increased. There could be an exception made if the previous benefit levels were so low as to not be enticing. Again, the underwriter is concerned about *antiselection*.

Open enrollments can be useful. The key is doing an open enrollment properly so as to minimize the antiselection and maximize participation. However, the opposite could occur, making a bad situation worse. Thus, there is sometimes reluctance on the part of the underwriter to approve an open enrollment.

Assessing Voluntary Life Participation

Before prescribing solutions to a plan with low participation or maintaining a plan with solid participation levels, the underwriter will need to gather information about the plan structure and its history. The underwriter will carefully evaluate historic participation patterns and assume the most current participation level to be a baseline starting point.

The underwriter will likely ask the following questions in order to apply assumptions to the current baseline participation:

How will the underlying basic life plan affect participation on supplemental life and AD&D?

- An assessment of the basic and supplemental life plan designs is usually done very early on to determine if an appropriate balance between the two plans exists. The underwriter checks to see if the amount of coverage, the choices in coverage, the GI limit, and plan maximum make sense between the two plans from a risk management perspective and from the employer-purchaser's point of view.

Does a rich basic life plan discourage employees from enrolling in supplemental?

- If the basic life plan is too rich, particularly in situations where employee salaries are unusually low or where employees have historically been reluctant to enroll in the voluntary plan, the underwriter needs to seriously consider how, if at all, the situation can be remedied to improve supplemental life participation.

How much can the average employee afford to spend on supplemental life and AD&D?

- The underwriter may look at the census data used for the manual rating to guesstimate the average employee salary. This exercise might even be done by class. This practice gives the underwriter additional insight into current enrollment and potential future enrollment relative to what employees might be willing to spend for life coverage.

- Information about employee costs for group medical, dental, and disability coverages is typically not available. A seasoned underwriter might make estimates about these costs and factor them into how it might impact employee funds available to purchase voluntary life insurance.

- How much the employee can afford may factor into the type of benefits schedule the underwriter deems appropriate for the voluntary life plan.

How will the enrollment process be different than that of the past?

- Changes in the historic enrollment process can impact projected plan participation positively or negatively. Projecting how a new enrollment process will affect actual enrollment is perhaps the most difficult element to assess for assumptions about plan participation and associated pricing. The underwriter will likely inquire about the details of the changes and guess how they will play out.

Will there be a new or different communication campaign to the employees?

- Effective communication is vital in a successful enrollment. The underwriter will project how the new communications campaign will impact enrollment and possibly take into consideration:

  - Employees' comfort with understanding the benefits as communicated. For example, one might expect more comfort in a white collar financial services industry than in a blue collar semi-skilled labor force.

  - If English is a second language for a significant portion of the employee population and translation services are required for the printing of the booklet/ certificate, the underwriter must factor this into enrollment projections. Having translation services tends to increase participation with employees for whom English is a second language, because they feel positive about the fact that the employer and insurer have gone out of their way to reduce the language barrier.

  - Hardcopy mailing of enrollment materials to the employees' homes can be effective, yet expensive. Hardcopy distribution of materials at the work location, particularly at an enrollment meeting, can also be very effective. Emailing the materials is nearly as effective, and in some cases, even more effective than hardcopy communication.

  - Novel ideas such as a benefits fair at the work location and/or holding a raffle for those who attend the enrollment meeting can be innovative ways to engage employees and get them to seriously consider enrolling into the voluntary life plan.

Will the policyholder actively endorse and communicate the value of the plan?

- Who endorses the plan and how they communicate their endorsement can be important and may be considered by the underwriter in projecting enrollment participation. For example, if union leadership endorses the voluntary life plan as a good value, this can have a profoundly positive impact on employee participation.

Will the policyholder allow and encourage the insurer's enrollment specialists access to the employees?

- How the enrollment specialists gain access to the employees must also be considered. If the employer has a single location and standard hours, access can be straightforward. However, specialists can be challenged where the policyholder has shift workers or a significant number of employees on the road or offsite.

- Multiple or remote locations must also be considered by the underwriter when assessing the potential effectiveness of the specialists. It may be cost-prohibitive for the specialists to travel to various locations. However, the use of technology has made access to information and the specialists themselves easier.

- A savvy policyholder may inquire about the qualifications and licensing of an insurer's enrollment specialists or sales reps before allowing them access to their employees.

Voluntary Life Enrollment Tactics

The underwriter establishes realistic expectations for an upcoming supplemental life enrollment. An increase of 10 percent to 15 percent over the previous enrollment is usually considered successful. If the tactics are reapplied in the subsequent year's enrollment, it is not likely to achieve the same percentage increases.

There are a number of enrollment tactics worth expanding upon, since they can have a direct bearing on plan pricing. Some of these tactics are used in conjunction with each other.

Step Rates versus Composite Rates

Because of the elective nature of supplemental life and AD&D where employees usually pay the full cost, underwriters routinely require the rates to be structured on a step-rated or age-bracketed basis. This is done to ensure the rates are fairly distributed based on age and to ensure maximum participation in the plan.

Some clients are resistant to step rates because of the increased complexity required to calculate the monthly billing report. It's not necessarily a deal breaker in terms of risk selection and is understandable with smaller policyholders. The underwriter may load the composite rate to account for the fact that the younger employees are less likely to enroll at the higher rate that is being driven by the older employees.

Personalized Enrollment Statements

Personalized enrollment statements or forms are an effective way to increase employee participation in a voluntary life plan where employees must make a choice related to the amount of coverage. The personalized statements are distributed or e-mailed to each individual employee, whether they currently participate in the plan or not.

The statement will customarily show the employee's name, age, class, salary, and current amount (if applicable) of coverage. The statement will also indicate if any GI limits are in place with a brief explanation of the evidence process that may be applicable to the employee. The plan may limit the number of salary multiples or increments the employee can elect without evidence, and this is customarily noted as well. Dependent life coverage may be included on the statement.

The key to the personalized enrollment form is that each of the employee choices along with a calculation of the associated monthly cost is done for the employee. It provides black and white figures to the employees, allowing them to focus on the choices rather than being frustrated by math calculations.

First-Time Buyers

Situations where the employer is offering voluntary life for the first time can be especially challenging to the underwriter in projecting enrollment participation, since no historic baseline exists. To ensure a desirable spread of risk among the insured population, the underwriter might consider:

- offering limited choices in coverage;

- a modest maximum benefit (which may be increased at renewal);

- a lower GI limit than might otherwise be in place (which also may be increased at renewal);

- applying "short-form" medical underwriting for enrollment in the plan.

Mergers and acquisitions are commonplace in the American economy and present difficulty in projecting participation when employees from previously different organizations are now merged together under one group voluntary life plan. Underwriters will often use the same enrollment techniques for mergers/acquisitions as they would in a first-time buyer situation.

Short-Form Medical Underwriting

Short-form medical underwriting is essentially an abbreviated evidence of good health process. Each employee who wants to enroll fills out a brief health questionnaire, which is significantly less comprehensive than a standard personal health statement. The insurer may conduct further investigation into a health status based on the way an employee responded to the limited number of questions. Carriers vary in their use of short-form medical underwriting, and certain states have limitations on its use.

In "death spiral" situations or in cases where all enrollment tactics have resulted in unsatisfactory enrollment participation, the underwriter may use short-form medical underwriting as a means of continuing to offer the voluntary life plan with reduced risk to the insurer.

Key Takeaways

- Voluntary products are a key resource for employers to provide a wide range of benefits to meet employees' needs at minimal cost to the employer.

- Group voluntary products are to be distinguished from individual worksite offerings.

- A proper enrollment process leading to good participation is the key to a successful group voluntary offering.

- The group voluntary offering, even though paid for entirely by the employee, may still be subject to ERISA. Carriers vary in their interpretation of ERISA guidelines.

- Annual enrollment and open enrollment are different types of enrollment, although an annual enrollment could be conducted as an open enrollment.

- Open enrollments for plans with poor participation are fraught with risks and should only be done with great care.

- Before prescribing solutions to a plan with low participation or maintaining a plan with solid participation levels, the underwriter will need to gather more information about the plan structure and its history.

- The employer plays a key role in the successful enrollment of a voluntary life plan.

- Timing related to enrollments, such as setting the duration of the enrollment period and timing the announcements, is critical to an enrollment's success.

- Enrollment practices should be selected based on historic success or the belief that new tactics will improve participation.

- First-time buyers and policyholders who have experienced a merger or acquisition can be very challenging for underwriters in terms of projecting voluntary life enrollment participation.

- Some worksite carriers also sell group voluntary products, such as supplemental life, supplemental AD&D, and short- and long-term disability insurance.

- Since voluntary products are on a group platform and have different (lower) commission structures than individual worksite policies, they enjoy a rather substantial cost advantage over individual worksite products.

- Worksite life products offer a significantly higher degree of individual customization than is usually available in a group life and AD&D voluntary plan.

Endnotes

1. Press Release (Avon, CT: Eastbridge Consulting Group, August 2, 2011), http://eastbridge.com/news/2011pr/pr8211.html (Accessed July 17, 2012).

2. *2010 U.S. Group Life Market Survey Summary Report*, *http://genre.com/sharedfile/pdf/GLMS201103-en.pdf*, (Stamford, CT: Gen Re Research, 2011), p. 7.

3. Employer Health Benefits 2011 Annual Survey, http://ehbs.kff.org/pdf/2011/8225.pdf (Chicago, IL: The Kaiser Family Foundation, September 2011), p. 1.

4. *2010 U.S. Group Life Market Survey Summary Report*, *http://genre.com/sharedfile/pdf/GLMS201103-en.pdf* (Stamford, CT: Gen Re Research, 2011), p. 3.

5. *8th Annual Study of Employee Benefit Trends* (New York, NY: MetLife, Inc., April 12, 2010), p. 14.

6. *2010 U.S. Group Life Market Survey Summary Report*, *http://genre.com/sharedfile/pdf/GLMS201103-en.pdf* (Stamford, CT: Gen Re Research, 2011), p. 4.

7. "*9th Annual Study of Employee Benefit Trends* (New York, NY: , 2011), p. 21.

8. Press Release (Avon, CT: Eastbridge Consulting Group, July 31, 2008), *http://www.eastbridge.com/news/2008pr/pr73108.htm* (Accessed July 17, 2012).

9. *9th Annual Study of Employee Benefit Trends* (New York, NY: 2011), p. 4.

10. Ibid., p. 10.

11. Neyer, Ron, Interpreting ERISA Guidelines for Worksite Life and Disability Products (Windsor, CT: LIMRA, 2009), p. 2

12. Kirner, Tom and Pete Silkowski, Group Benefits Disability Specialist Course Handbook (Erlanger, KY: The National Underwriter Company, 2007), pp. 15-17.

13. Ibid., p. 15-15.

14. Ibid., p. 15-15.

15. Ibid., p. 15-16.

Chapter 13

How Insurers Differentiate and Add Value

Group life insurance is fairly straightforward. Policy terms and language are driven by state regulation. So many states have enacted the NAIC Model Bill on contract provisions that there is not a great deal of difference among insurers on life contracts. Death benefits are fairly cut and dried; it is not much more complicated than "you die, we pay." With Accidental Death & Dismemberment (ADD) insurance, there can be some differences in the triggering events and the sums paid for an accidental loss. However, the differences among major carriers are not large, especially when compared with group health plans.

So, how do insurers go about differentiating themselves? After all, if there were no differences, group term life would simply be an absolute commodity. Most true commodities, such as crushed rock, fuel oil, and lumber, are differentiated by price. Although convenience of buying and perhaps ease of delivery make a difference, the "add-on services" are what really make one supplier preferable to another. So also, insurers go to great lengths to differentiate themselves.

This chapter will present various ways in which Group Term Life and AD&D carriers differentiate their life and AD&D products. It permits a look beyond the mere price or rate in determining the best insurance carrier fit for the producer's client. Group life and AD&D products have evolved to go well beyond "you die, we pay." So as not to fall behind their competition, carriers are quick to copy a newly introduced contract provision or service that appears to meet a perceived need in the marketplace.

Buyers of group life/AD&D products usually find that carriers may be different based on their risk tolerance, rate guarantee period, ease of doing business, level of service, and optional add-ons.

Risk Tolerance

Not all carriers have the same risk tolerance. In fact, this area can vary widely. Figure 13-1 provides examples of just how much carriers can vary on maximum life benefits. Notice that there is a wide spread. Although this illustrative chart is just for a certain segment of employers—those with 51-99 employees—there is just as much variation in all size segments. Other factors such as industry, occupation, geographic location, and even persistency history (number of carriers over some set period of time) can affect the benefit levels offered by insurers. Guaranteed issue limits will similarly vary by carrier. So too, will evidence of insurability requirements. The implications are that a client may not fit the risk parameters of all carriers based on the client's criteria.

Figure 13-1. Variation of Life Benefits Among Carriers

Case Size: 51 to 99 employees

Company	Basic Term			Voluntary Term		
	Minimum	Maximum	Average	Minimum	Maximum	Average
Company A	$125,000	$175,000	$150,000	$100,000	$100,000	$100,000
Company C	$200,000	$220,000	$210,000	$ 50,000	$ 50,000	$ 50,000
Company F	$ 10,000	$300,000	—	$ 10,000	$ 50,000	—
Company G	—	—	—	—	—	$ 50,000
Company H	$100,000	$400,000	$250,000	$100,000	$140,000	$120,000
Company I	$ 0	$400,000	Varies	$ 50,000	$ 50,000	$ 50,000
Company J	$200,000	$400,000	$275,000	$ 50,000	$100,000	$ 50,000
Company K	—	—	—	—	—	—
Company L	$ 20,000	$300,000	$ 50,000	$ 80,000	$100,000	$ 80,000
Company M	—	—	—	—	—	$ 50,000
Company N	$175,000	$350,000	$250,000	$ 25,000	$ 50,000	$ 50,000
Company O	NA	NA	NA	NA	NA	NA
Company Q	—	$175,000	—	—	$ 50,000	—
Company R	$150,000	$180,000	$165,000	$ 80,000	$ 80,000	$ 80,000

Source: Shah, Aditya, "Underwriting Guidelines for Group Term Life Insurance," http://www.limra.com/abstracts/abstract.aspx?fid=5210 (Windsor, CT: LL Global, 2005), p.2.

Rate Guarantee

Rate guarantees that insurers are willing to offer can vary. A rate guarantee of two years may be standard, but carrier practices are not all alike. A carrier's risk tolerance for a rate guarantee beyond two years may be influenced by the policyholder's size (annual premium or covered lives), industry, and/or historic experience.

Rate guarantees are a risk management issue, because many unforeseen things can happen over the course of the rate guarantee period that will affect the experience of the case. For example, the employer could experience greater than normal turnover, changing the employee census mix. Or, the employer could suffer financial pressures that might affect the experience, particularly the waiver of premium claims. There could be some emergence of a disease (think of HIV or the H1N1 flu, for examples) that affects mortality, particularly if the insureds travel extensively. At the very least, each employee covered at the start of the rate guarantee is that much older at the end of the rate guarantee period, and age affects mortality.

Figure 13-2 provides a chart that outlines some common rate guarantee practices among carriers for the large case segment of insurance. Carriers' practices will vary just as widely in all segments of the market.

Figure 13-2. Common Rate Guarantee Practices in the Large Case Segment

Question: In the 1,000+ life market, what is your estimate of how often carriers are willing to offer a rate guarantee of the following durations?

Rate Guarantee Duration	Answers (9 carriers responding)				
	Never (0% of 2008 cases)	Sometimes (1–49% of 2008 cases)	Often (50–99% of 2008 cases)	Always (100% of 2008 cases)	NA
2–3 years	0	0	3	5	1
4–5 years	0	7	1	0	1
6 years	3	5	0	0	1
More than 6 years	2	6	0	0	1

Source: Landry, Kimberly, "Large Case Group Life Practices," http://www.limra.com/abstracts/abstract.aspx?fid=10204,(Windsor, CT: LL Global, 2009), p. 20.

Ease of Doing Business

All carriers try to be easy for producers and employers to work with. There are key differentiators beyond contract provisions, including ease of quoting, clarity of RFP response, flexibility, and responsiveness.

Ease of Quoting

Differences do exist among carriers related to how accurately and completely they respond to all elements of the request for proposal (RFP) and how timely they are with the response. There are differences in staff talent, depth, and experience relating to group life coverage. Some group representatives (reps) are better equipped than others at knowing the questions to ask the producer to ensure the underwriter has complete information to accurately underwrite and rate the risk and issue the quote. A rep may be more comfortable in handling medical or disability aspects of the RFP than life aspects. Other reps may undervalue the life portion of an RFP and not give as much emphasis to it as to other lines of coverage. Some group reps may lack experience and not understand completely all the factors in underwriting, which can make a difference.

Not all underwriters are the same. Some underwriters will do a more complete job than others, often due to time constraints, experience, or work load. Carrier underwriting guidelines vary and may preclude or limit their ability to respond to or meet all RFP bid specs. In such cases, the underwriter and rep together will typically develop an alternative they hope will be acceptable to the producer and prospective policyholder.

Providing a proposal within the requested timeline may seem straightforward. Most carriers will try to provide a proposal by the deadline, and the vast majority do provide timely responses. However, like any other business, communication breakdowns can occur and cause delays. The reps' and underwriters' time constraints and workloads may cause an RFP to fall through the cracks. Some proposals may be ranked higher than others in importance for the insurer due to the characteristics of the employer/client. For example, carriers specializing in large groups of 1,000 or more lives may not get excited about a 20-life case. Conversely, carriers specializing in smaller cases may not have the interest in or capacity for a 5,000-life case. Carriers may have industry limitations as well, based on underwriting guidelines, risk assessment, and appetite for risk. Some carriers are very enthusiastic about public groups, such as municipalities. Other carriers might have these same groups on their "exception quote only" list. The latter carrier is not going to bend over backwards for a group the carrier doesn't really want to do business with. Thus, when an RFP appears in an underwriting shop and it is not their bailiwick or normal course of business, delayed responses can occur.

Clarity of RFP Response

Not all RFP proposals are the same. Carriers who are unable to meet some of the specifications of the RFP may provide a proposal, but it may not be exactly what was requested. Sometimes the reasons are explained, and sometimes they are not. Another consideration is the presence of any conditions or contingencies attached with the proposal. For example, an underwriter may not be completely comfortable with the RFP data provided and may provide a quote that is conditional upon receipt of final enrollment data.

Not all underwriters will approach a case in the same way. There will be differences across carriers and even amongst the underwriters of the same staff. Insurers do train their underwriters to provide a consistent response, but underwriting is an art more than a science. Each individual underwriter's perception of the data and the risk it implies, their tolerance for risk, their authority limits, and their experience with underwriting cases are unique.

Flexibility and Responsiveness

A key question a producer must ask is, "Am I getting a thoughtful, complete, and accurate proposal and rate, or am I getting a boilerplate response with little attention paid to expressed client concerns?" Obviously, working with the insurer's group representative is the key to ensuring the client is getting the best possible proposal response.

The ability and willingness of a carrier to work with a prospective policyholder in filling specific requests is important. Not all carriers exhibit the same degree of flexibility on a case, which is a function of a myriad of factors. For example, the underwriter may be quoting the insurer's absolute rock bottom price with no room to move further on any other element of the case.

Insurers vary in their flexibility for customizing contract provisions that may require state filing of the language. In this regard, policyholder expectations should and can be managed. If unique, duplicate, or special contract language is required, causing the state filing of that language, it is probably not reasonable to expect most carriers to be willing to do a single case filing on a relatively small group. Single case filing requires time and it can be relatively expensive for the insurer. So, if a carrier is willing to do this at all, it will generally be on larger cases and the underwriter will need to consider building the cost of the filing into the premium rates. It is an essential part of the RFP process to identify the need for state filing, not only for pricing purposes but also to ensure that booklet/certificates can be issued to the employees on a timely basis since state filing can be time-consuming.

Producers should also gauge the accessibility of insurer sales and service representatives to respond to employer inquiries. Being responsive to questions, especially any posed in the RFP, is a good indication of the carrier's interest in the RFP. Responsiveness in the RFP process is generally indicative of the level of responsiveness after the sale.

Carriers have differences in what they consider to be prudent plan designs. For example, assume a high guaranteed issue limit is requested in an RFP that is beyond a carrier's risk capacity. In the past, the underwriter would sometimes simply respond by issuing a "decline to quote" (DTQ) or would quote their "standard" rather than the requested G.I. limit. However, in today's hypercompetitive market most group representatives don't want to come back to the producer with a DTQ or unfulfilled bid specs. The issued quote may come back with benefit levels or rates and contingencies that are considered uncompetitive, but at least the insurer has provided a valid response to the RFP. Despite having provided a knowingly uncompetitive quote on some element of the RFP (especially plan design), there may be other aspects in which the issued quote is better than the competition and may keep the carrier in the running.

All carriers need a consistent data set to produce accurate rates and a thorough RFP response. Carriers vary in their minimum data requirements in order to respond to an RFP, including identified services requirements.

Case installation and plan administration at change in carrier can vary. There are differences between carriers, especially affecting supplemental/voluntary cases. Participation and enrollment requirements and capabilities must be considered in the RFP stage. For example, some carriers may require new enrollment cards, while others may be willing to take the prior carrier's enrollment card. If ease of enrollment is essential and is stated in the RFP, the carrier who accepts prior carrier enrollment cards likely has a leg up on the competition. However, administrative elements such as enrollment card administration are often not stated in the bid specifications.

How different carriers make use of technology and processes can make a difference. Insurer practices that can minimize use of employer resources may be of interest. Having the employer's Human Resource staff actively engaged in the enrollment can be a burden. Typically, electronic enrollments or the use of technology to assist employees to enroll will be specifically stated in the RFP. Leveraging the use of technology in enrollment and plan administration can separate a carrier from the pack.

The quality and clarity of communication and enrollment materials makes a difference in enrollment results. The RFP specs may indicate the manner and nature of the communications. For example, the RFP may state that the carrier must provide personalized enrollment statements that are to be mailed to each eligible employee's home address. Since mailing costs can be considerable, this requirement will undoubtedly be highlighted in the quote issued as there is likely to be a pricing implication associated with it. Carriers can tout the effectiveness of their communications and processes by citing their enrollment track record in the quotation.

Carrier responsiveness and timeliness to issue the policy and booklet/certificates can sometimes be important, particularly if a policyholder has had problems with punctuality in the past. If this is an issue, the RFP will typically state the expectation that booklet/certificates will be delivered within "x" number of days of the effective date of coverage.

The quality and clarity of the administration manual can make a big difference in the ongoing administration of the plan. While the administration manual is rarely mentioned in the RFP, most carriers are eager to provide a sample if one is requested, either in hardcopy or in electronic form. For policyholders with limited staff resources to support the group plan's administration, the administrative manual and its ease of use can be a slight distinguishing factor.

How effectively and quickly carriers respond to problems and resolve issues is an important difference. Simple things like accessibility of insurer sales and service representatives to respond to employer inquiries can be important. Carrier accessibility and responsiveness may appear as requirements in an RFP, but these are difficult to quantify, much less to be used as a competitive advantage. In this arena, a carrier's previous performance with the broker as well as the insurer's reputation for service in the marketplace usually carries more weight than any words written in a quote letter.

Occasionally, a "performance guarantee" may be a requirement in the RFP, especially for larger policyholders. A performance guarantee is a written agreement between the insurer and the policyholder whereby the insurer guarantees they will meet certain established service-related performance criteria. Failure to meet these minimums results in the policyholder receiving cash or its premium equivalent from the insurer. A performance guarantee on life/AD&D coverage is infrequent and is most often included with the group health coverages. The most common elements on group life/AD&D that can be subject to a performance guarantee are:

- timely delivery of the booklet/certificate and policy;

- accuracy rates of claim payments;

- wait times and call abandonment rates if the carrier provides telephonic claims or other services; and

- enrollment rates.

Ongoing Carrier Services

Billing methods and services also vary among carriers. Billing methods may be very different. Some carriers on small cases require list billing or home office billing. Some carriers will not do any list billing. Internet billing is becoming more popular, but not all carriers provide it. Methods or options for remitting premiums vary by carrier and may vary by case size. It is important to match a client's capabilities and needs with the service the carrier is willing and able to provide. The carrier who is willing to provide home office or list billing to a large client where other carriers are reluctant to do so may find this a competitive advantage if billing is one of the policyholder's "hot buttons".

Contractual Services and Distinctions

There are services and benefits to employees and their dependents that come with a group life/AD&D contract besides the proceeds from a death or disability claim. These may include the assignment of benefits, accelerated death benefits, conversion privileges, portability, waiver of premium, and coverage continuation.

Assignment of Benefits

An assignment of benefits is a written notice whereby an employee assigns controlling rights and interest in the policy proceeds to a third party. This permits the assignee to determine things such as who the beneficiary will be. Assignment enables the covered employee to use his/her interest in the group policy as an asset. It often is used by employees to remove proceeds from estate. Not all carriers permit assignments.

Accelerated Death Benefits

An accelerated death benefit contract provision enables a terminally ill employee or dependent to receive a portion of proceeds from the group life plan while still alive. The concept is to provide claims funds to a person who very likely has extraordinarily high medical expenses. It is also called a living benefits option or the accelerated benefit. The accelerated death benefit is not applicable to AD&D. Most group life contracts today are issued with an Accelerated Death Benefit provision. Carriers differ in the life expectancy requirement as well as maximum payment to the terminally ill person.

Conversion Privilege

With a conversion privilege, an individual's group coverage or portions thereof that is terminating may be converted to an individual policy without providing evidence of insurability. Conversion can apply to amounts lost due to ADEA age reductions. Conversion privileges are required by state law, but there can be differences among carriers as to how they are administered. How much is convertible can vary based on the individual's situation and specific contract provisions. The type of policy and coverage amounts with the conversion can also vary. Carriers vary in the rates they charge on the individual conversion policy to the person converting. Some carriers charge the policyholder's experience in the experience-rating process based on the amount of coverage converted by individual insureds. (See Chapter 7 for details)

Portability

Portability is an option that allows employees to continue group life coverage (not AD&D) at group rates. The employer buys this as an add-on to the group term life contract. It may also be available to dependents (if dependent life exists), although carriers are not all alike relating to dependents. The usual requirements for an employee to "port" coverage can include the following:

- The employment ends before the employee reaches normal retirement age or the employee is no longer eligible for coverage.

- The group policy is still in force.

- Evidence of insurability is submitted and approved, although most carriers do not require evidence.

Once ported, coverage continues usually until the employee:

- picks up life coverage under another group plan;

- reaches some stated age limit; or

- no longer pays the required premium.

Carriers vary in how they administer and bill the portability policy to those who have ported and most carriers are well-versed in the process.

Waiver of Premium

The waiver of premium provision allows for continued employee and dependent life insurance coverage without payment of premiums while the employee is disabled. Requirements can vary but commonly include the following:

- The employee must be within a certain age range at the date of disability, usually below age 60 or 65.

- There is a maximum duration of waiver, subject to certain age limitations.

- The employee must be disabled for a specific period of time, such as a waiting period of 6 or 9 months, before the employee qualifies for the waiver.

- The employee must meet the definition of disabled such as being unable to perform any occupation. This definition may be different from the standard STD or LTD definition.

The waiver of premium may be extended to include waiving premiums for dependent coverage while the employee is disabled. The waiver applies only to the disabled employee, not to disabled dependents. Coverage amounts while on waiver are subject to the plan's ADEA age reductions.

The Waiver of Premium provision is one of the more scrutinized life contract provisions since the limitations and restrictions are aimed at older employees-those most likely to become disabled. Carriers have a very wide range of offerings and most are nimble at matching the right schedule with the policyholder's price point.

Coverage Continuation

The continuation of coverage provision allows coverage to continue for a period of time if the employee is not an active employee for certain specified reasons. Rules related to coverage continuation can vary but commonly include the following:

- Coverage continues only so long as premium payments are kept up to date.

- Continued coverage terminates when the group policy terminates.

- The coverage is subject to age reductions.

- The provision must be equally applied to all employees (by class).

The continuation of coverage provision is an employer option that is subject to underwriter approval. Conversion is generally available when the continued coverage period ends. Allowable reasons and durations may vary among carriers. Figure 13-3 shows common reasons and typical durations for each.

Figure 13-3. Reasons and Durations for Continued Coverage Provisions	
Reason	*Typical Duration*
Documented leave of absence	Duration of 3 to 6 months beginning with the last day of the month following the month in which leave commenced.
Military leave to enter active military service	Duration up to 8 or 12 weeks
A layoff due to lack of work	Duration ending the last day of month following month in which lay-off commenced
Employment status change from full-time to part-time	Duration ending the last day of third month following date in which change occurred
Leave of absence under the Family and Medical Leave Act	Duration up to 12 weeks, or longer if required by state law, following the date the insurance would have terminated
Absence due to sickness or injury	Duration ending the last day of a period of 12 months starting when first absent

Value-Added Services

In part due to intense competition and in part due to carriers trying to get the discussion on something other than price/rate, a host of added services are available on group term life insurance. The value-added services found in the policy itself, such as the seatbelt benefit, are discussed in Chapter 5. Some additional services may not be explicitly stated in the contract, but may be provided administratively. Other services are optional and can be added to the contract for additional cost by the employer. Examples of value-added services include employee assistance programs, funeral planning, bereavement counseling, beneficiary designation management, estate planning, and travel assistance.

Employee Assistance Programs

Employee Assistance Programs (EAPs) are not new. Many health insurers have been offering them for years. However, life carriers have begun to offer EAPs with group term life. These programs can differ greatly. EAPs can arrange for a grieving loved one or a newly disabled employee to be engaged with a host of support services. A common variation is telephonic counseling versus face to face meetings. There is a very large difference in the quality and effectiveness of the program among carriers. If face to face meetings are included there can be differences in number of visits allowed. The life carrier will generally outsource these programs to a third-party provider. The cost will be built into the life rate in most cases.

Virtually all group medical and disability carriers have EAP programs established, so extending them to life/AD&D coverage is a natural fit.

Funeral Planning

Some carriers offer funeral planning services through third-party vendors for assistance to the family of the deceased insured or even to the living insured in prearranging one's own funeral. Services may include assistance in finding a funeral home, finding out about funeral costs, and even researching and negotiating the best possible prices for a cemetery plot and casket.

Bereavement Counseling Services

Many group life insurers make professionally licensed counselors available to family members of the deceased insured for assistance with the bereavement process. The availability and extent of the services vary by carrier. This unquestionably goes far beyond the "you die, we pay" adage that had been the historic refrain of group life/AD&D.

Beneficiary Designation Management

Not all insurers keep records of beneficiaries, since employers typically handle the day-to-day administrative duties and retain the enrollment cards. Some carriers will perform beneficiary designation management for an add-on price. Others may provide it as a courtesy service to the policyholder, in which case the cost will be built into the life rates. This service would specifically be requested by the producer in the RFP to alert insurers that it is of interest or is a requirement.

Will Preparation and Estate Planning

Some carriers are beginning to offer will preparation and estate planning services through third-party vendors. The majority of Americans (55 percent) do not have wills,[1] and this can cause some difficulties for surviving family members, especially with the premature death of a primary income earner. This is an undervalued benefit of which many employees are not aware, which is available to them through the group life contract. Carriers vary in the depth and level of services offered.

Travel Assistance

Travel assistance encompasses a host of services for covered individuals who are traveling. These services can include prescription filling, finding appropriate health services, coordination with one's primary care physician, and even repatriation of the remains of the deceased who dies abroad. Services are provided by a third-party vendor. Services provided can vary by carrier. The price can be an add-on or built into the rate.

Many of the value-added services offered by group life/AD&D insurers are not considered of great value to the majority of employees, in part due to American culture being uncomfortable with contemplating death or potentially catastrophic events. However, these value-added services can be of the utmost value to an insured and his/her family at the time of greatest need.

Key Takeaways

- Not all carriers are alike. Even though the group term life/AD&D policies are similar, there can be large differences in services and add-ons.

- Not all underwriters will approach the same case in the same way. How carriers approach risk in terms of benefit maximums, guaranteed issue limits, use of medical underwriting, and rate guarantees will be different.

- The rate guarantee length reflects the carrier's tolerance for risk and projections about the policyholder's future plan performance.

- Insurers' reputations for ease of doing business will vary.

- Part of the reason carriers differ in response to a specific RFP may be the characteristics of the employer itself.

- Administration services offered by group life insurers are not all the same. Matching a client's needs with carrier capabilities is an essential producer duty.

- Carriers can offer a range of add-on services, many of which are provided by third-party vendors. Add-on services may include employee assistance programs, funeral planning, bereavement counseling, beneficiary designation management, estate planning, and travel assistance.

- There may be an explicit additional charge for add-ons, or the cost may be built into the life/AD&D premium rate.

- Carriers vary in the rates they charge on the individual conversion policy to the person converting.

Endnotes

1. "Majority of American Adults Remain Without Wills," Lawyers.com
(http://press-room.lawyers.com/Majority-of-American-Adults-Remain-Without-Wills.html, Accessed July 31, 2012)
(New York, NY: April 3, 2007).

Chapter 14

Issues In Changing Carriers

This chapter addresses some of the issues that can arise when a Group Life/AD&D policyholder decides to switch to a new carrier. None of these issues are insurmountable nor are they a reason not to switch carriers. Insurance professionals can avert trouble and ensure a smooth transition if they are aware of the potential challenges.

Group life policyholders switch carriers for the same reasons any consumer switches brands. A primary driver is to seek a better value for the premium dollar. As with a new brand, the provider is not likely to have precisely the same product or service as the predecessor. Perhaps new products or services are what the policyholder seeks. Regardless of the reasons for changing, attention to detail is crucial when changing carriers to ensure that employees get the benefits and services the policyholder now expects.

Most insurance companies are set up for new customer acquisition. However, recent studies suggest that customer retention should play a bigger role in profitability.[1] Simply put, the cost of acquiring a new customer, with the quote and installation phases, is more costly to the insurer than retaining an existing customer.

The following areas of the group life/AD&D program can potentially be impacted by a change in carriers:

- Eligibility for coverage

- Consistency in coverage for insureds

- Benefit levels

- Service types and levels of service

- Plan administration

Eligibility

The eligibility waiting period is usually not an issue when changing carriers. Employees who are in the process of satisfying the eligibility waiting period customarily have that time credited towards satisfying the eligibility waiting period under the new carrier. There may be differences administratively when it comes to how and when the newly eligible employees are added to the billing. In most cases, these differences are readily resolved.

Occasionally, the underwriter will waive the remainder of the eligibility waiting period for those in the process of satisfying it so that these employees can become insured on the new carrier's effective date. The idea is to lessen the eligibility tracking burden for the policyholder. The risk of death on these newly eligible employees is significantly less than that of having a medical, dental, or short-term disability claim. Newly hired employees, in this instance, would have the advantage of having a reduced eligibility waiting period because of change in carriers. However, if these employees are enrolling in a contributory plan, their 31-day enrollment window starts on the effective date of the new policy. In the flurry of activity when changing carriers, the policyholder may not be cognizant of the need to get the enrollment materials to these new employees right away. If they try to enroll after the 31 days, they will be considered late entrants.

Late Entrant Eligibility

The handling of *late entrants* wanting to enroll in a life plan other than a Section 125 plan can vary by carrier. Some plans will not allow a late entrant to attempt to enroll in a contributory plan. Other plans may allow a late entrant to enroll at some specified time, such as within two weeks prior to the start of a new plan year. Still other plans may allow a late entrant to apply for enrollment at any time. Regardless of the situation, late entrants must have their evidence application approved before entry into the plan.

Section 125 plans customarily allow late entrants to enroll during the annual enrollment period or upon a change in family status. Unless the underwriter authorizes an open enrollment, late entrants must have their evidence application approved before being allowed to enroll in the life program.

Previously Denied Coverage

Carriers vary in how they treat applicants whose evidence of good health was previously denied. In most cases, these evidence applications are for late entrants who want to enroll in the life plan or for an insured who requests coverage for amounts in excess of the Guaranteed

Issue (GI) limit. The protocol for handling a subsequent reapplication of evidence may not be specifically stipulated in the group contract. Practices regarding reapplication run the range of:

- Reapplication is allowed at any time for immediate reconsideration.

- Reapplication is allowed after a certain period of time.

- Reapplication is allowed during an annual enrollment or upon a change in family status.

- No reapplication is considered after an initial denial.

At change in carrier, the new carrier will typically apply its own reapplication rules. In most cases, the new carrier will allow a reapplication of a previously denied applicant according to the new carrier's rules. However, this is not always the case. Because this issue may not be explicit or clear in the group life contract, it is worthwhile for the producer to inquire of the new carrier the protocol regarding previously denied evidence applicants. This inquiry is best done in the presale process so that there are no surprises later. A favorable answer may be a selling point for the new carrier. In addition, the policyholder should be aware if reapplication practices will present additional administrative duties on the part of the policyholder under the new plan.

Consistency in Coverage

The most important element in a successful transition is to ensure that no insured person loses coverage or benefits solely because of the change in carriers, assuming this was the policyholder's intent. This concept is commonly known as "no loss/no gain"; where employees do not lose coverage or benefits nor do they become entitled to richer benefits. However, the employer has the option of reducing benefits or making certain classes of employees ineligible. If the benefit levels are lower and no loss/no gain applies, employees usually receive the lesser benefits of the new plan rather than what they would have received under the prior carrier.

One of the greatest concerns of producers and policyholders when switching carriers centers around employees who are not actively at work on the new policy effective date. The concern is that an employee will no longer be covered under any extensions of the prior carrier nor will the employee be eligible for coverage under the new carrier since he or she won't be able to satisfy the actively at work requirement. The situation most commonly associated with this potential gap in coverage is with an employee who is absent due to sickness or injury on the policy effective date. The crux of this issue lies in the uncertainty about the duration of the employee's absence. Is the absence a temporary, short-term event or is the employee disabled and beginning to satisfy the waiver of premium elimination period? The majority of employees who are absent on the new policy effective date are not disabled.

Most life contracts require an employee to have satisfied the actively at work requirement on the day before the new policy effective date to be covered under the new policy or to be actively at work on the effective date of the policy. In the RFP process, many producers request that the new carrier be willing to waive the actively at work requirement for those who are absent so that no employee is left without coverage due to the carrier change. The RFP may stipulate the actively at work provision be waived only for employees affected by the change in carrier, or it may require that the actively at work requirement be excised altogether. Most underwriters are hesitant to completely waive this fundamental risk management provision in the contract for a number of reasons, including:

- The insurer may be forced to take on liability which is, by rights, the liability of the prior carrier.

- Waiving the actively at work requirement for a select set of employees is an untenable precedent to establish. The question becomes: Is the actively at work requirement completely excised from the contract going forward, or is it waived only at the onset of the policy for those impacted on the new policy effective date?

Most carriers have a continuation of coverage provision for employees who are not actively at work. The provision typically allows employees to be covered for up to 12 months from the last day worked. A life claim or waiver of premium claim for a person on continuation sometimes requires the prior and successor carriers investigate for clarity and agreement on whose liability it is. The intent is to cover employees who:

- have a temporary short-term absence and who will soon be back to work;

  - The provision allows the employees to have continued coverage assuming they remain employed and provided premiums continue to be paid on their behalf. Most employees on continuation of coverage fall into this category, since most absences are of a short duration.

- are disabled employees whose absence is expected to be long term and who may eventually qualify for waiver of premium;

  - While relatively infrequent, it is this situation which presents the greatest risk for an insured losing coverage because of change in carriers.

  - The provision allows the employees to have continued coverage provided premiums continue to be paid on their behalf.

  - If it is clear that a disabled employee is unlikely to return to work, the employer may have to terminate the employee to make room for another to take his/her place. Then the issue becomes whether this disabled person meets the contractual definition of "employee."

Gaps in Coverage

There are numerous situations in which an insured could "slip through the cracks" upon a change in coverage. Below are a few representative examples. For each example, assume a change from Carrier A to Carrier B with a policy effective date of 3/1/13. Assume also a standard waiver of premium (to age 60) provision with standard "no loss/no gain" language in the new policy.

Example 1

A 62-year-old employee is disabled on 11/26/12, the same day she last worked. She cannot qualify for waiver of premium, because she is older than the waiver limiting age. She does, however, qualify for a continuation of coverage for up 12 months because the policyholder considers her still to be an employee. Assuming she remained out of work and the premium continued to be paid, she could potentially retain life coverage until 11/25/13 had no change in carrier occurred. Because the coverage under Carrier A ended 2/28/13 (continuation extensions typically apply only if the policy remains inforce) and she could not meet the actively at work requirement for Carrier B, her life coverage ended on 2/28/13. Carrier B is not obligated to pick up her coverage. This is a situation where a person's coverage was affected by a change in carriers since the continuation ceased when Carrier A's policy terminated on 2/28/13.

Example 2

A 37-year-old employee is disabled on 11/12/12, the same day he last worked. He could potentially qualify for waiver of premium after completing a 9-month elimination period on 8/12/13 under Carrier A, assuming the employer continued to pay the premiums during the elimination period. The employer is forced to replace the employee on 1/15/13 and officially terminates him on that date. The employee's coverage ends on 1/31/13, the end of the month for which the last premium was paid for the employee. The employee dies on 5/23/13 before qualifying for a waiver of premium under Carrier A.

The disabled employee was never covered under Carrier B, because he could not meet the actively at work requirement. Unfortunately, he was terminated and died before qualifying for the waiver of premium under carrier and went past his 31-day conversion privilege window (1/31/13–3/2/13) under Carrier A. This person died without coverage. Had no change in carrier occurred and if the employer had continued to pay the required premium under the continuation provision, Carrier A would have been liable for the claim.

Example 3

A 28-year-old employee has bronchitis causing her to be absent from work 2/27/13–3/4/13. This example perhaps exemplifies the most common potential gap in coverage due to change in carrier. Most employees who are absent from work on the effective date of the new policy are out due to a temporary sickness or accident. The continuation of coverage provision is designed to cover this event, but it ceased to exist for her after the Carrier A policy terminated on 2/28/13.

She was not actively at work to be covered under Carrier B on the 3/1/13 new policy effective date, so she was effectively without coverage 3/1/13–3/4/13. When she returned to work on 3/5/13, coverage commenced under Carrier B.

Solutions to Gaps in Coverage

Carriers are aware of these situations and have developed different responses to establish consistency of coverage when a policyholder switches carriers. Many insurers offer an enriched or enhanced continuity of coverage provision that can be added to the policy. This enrichment allows employees who were insured on the day before the new policy effective date to be covered under the new insurer up to the level of coverage they would have had if no change in carrier occurred. The enrichment typically recognizes the lesser of the benefits that would apply if there is a difference between Carrier A's and Carrier B's policy. This enrichment is usually offered at little or no additional premium.

Most insurers encourage individuals who may be out of work for an extended period or who potentially may qualify for waiver of premium to convert to individual coverage under the conversion privilege. The advantages of doing this are:

- The person will have some type of life insurance coverage if a change in carrier occurs and neither carrier covers him or her.

- If neither carrier recognizes or approves the waiver of premium request, the person will have coverage without being required to submit evidence of good health. If a person has a potentially disabling condition, he or she may have great difficulty obtaining individual life coverage without evidence of good health.

- If the person is approved for the waiver of premium, the carrier will typically refund the conversion premium paid during the elimination period.

Had an enriched continuity of coverage provision been in Carrier B's policy in Example 1, the 62-year-old employee may have had coverage extended until 11/25/13 under what would have been provided under Carrier A's continuation of coverage provision, provided there was a similar continuation under Carrier B and provided the premiums continued to be paid during the extension. The employee was insured on the new policy effective date with the enriched no loss/no gain, so she was eligible for continued coverage under Carrier B. After her continuation was exhausted, she likely was entitled to have individual coverage under the conversion privilege under Carrier B.

Had an enriched continuity provision been in Carrier B's policy in Example 2, the 37-year-old disabled employee could have been covered on Carrier B's policy, since he was insured on the day before the effective date. He could have been covered until 11/11/13 (12 months) under the continuation of coverage provision, provided Carrier B had a similar provision and premiums were paid.

However, his coverage under Carrier B would have been terminated, because under the continuation of coverage provision, the employer terminated him on 1/15/13 and was no longer remitting premium payments on his behalf after 1/31/13. Whether a change in carrier occurs or not, it is essential for the policyholder to continue to remit premiums for employees under the continuation of coverage provision if the intent is to continue to cover them. In this example, the employer had ceased to pay premiums for the disabled employee and had effectively ended his coverage.

It is important to note that if the employee had died within the 31-day conversion privilege window (1/31/13–3/2/13), it is likely that Carrier B (under an enriched continuity provision) would have paid the claim under the assumption that he otherwise would have converted all of his coverage. The claim amount would have been the lesser of what would have been paid under Carrier A or Carrier B.

Had the employee not died, he may well have qualified as a waiver of premium claimant. Theoretically, he would have been the liability of Carrier A, since his disability occurred while covered under Carrier A's policy. However, if Carrier A had refused to acknowledge liability, then Carrier B would have been responsible for his waiver claim. Carrier B would have approved his waiver coverage amount for the lesser of what he would have received under either Carrier A or Carrier B.

The enriched continuity of coverage provision was truly designed for the type of situation faced by the 28-year-old employee in Example 3. She had a minor absence and was unable to meet the actively at work requirement. She technically would have been covered under the continuation of coverage provision under an enriched no loss/no gain provision. If she had died in a car accident on 3/2/13, her claim would have been payable under Carrier B's policy. However, it is important to note that the life amount paid would have been the lesser of what her beneficiaries would have received under Carrier A or Carrier B.

Regardless of the methods used to avoid gaps in coverage due to a change in carriers, it is a best practice to obtain a list of employees who are known to be disabled and likely to qualify for waiver and make them known to the new carrier. A list of employees who may not be actively at work on the effective date of coverage would also be useful. This would allow the new carrier to have greater clarity on how these employees will be covered.

Returning to Work While on Waiver of Premium

Most waiver of premium provisions have a total (any occupation) disability definition. Most group disability carriers urge claimants to return to work whenever and however possible. Although infrequent, the situation can arise where a waiver of premium claimant attempts a return to work, but is unable to sustain the effort. Depending on the life insurer's contract language, working while disabled for any amount of time may disqualify the waiver claimant, since he or she no longer meets the contractual definition of total disability.

Some carriers have begun to address this incongruity in their language while others have not. Some carriers allow up to a 5- or 15-day return-to-work trial period before the claimant is no longer considered disabled and qualified for life waiver of premium. Older life contracts may not have this provision. If a return-to-work trial period is important to the employer and if there are claimants who may potentially be affected, this important detail should be explored during the RFP process.

Benefit Levels

Most life/AD&D contracts are comparable, having many of the same policy provisions. There can be differences, however, in how the particulars of the policy language are applied, which can make a difference in benefit payments or even eligibility for benefits.

ADEA Age Reductions

ADEA age reductions can vary with different carriers, not only in the schedules themselves but also in the manner in which the reductions are applied. Some carriers apply the reduction percentages to the original amount whereas others apply the reduction percentages to the already-reduced amounts. Figure 14-1 provides an example comparing the two reduction methods. Assume coverage amounts are rounded to the next highest $500.

Figure 14-1. Two Methods of Applying ADEA Age Reductions			
Pre-Reduction Amount		**Reduction Applied to Original Amount**	**Reduction Applied to Reduced Amount**
		$100,000	$100,000
ADEA Reduction Schedule			
Age			
65	35%	$65,000	$65,000
70	50%	$50,000	$32,500

Waiver of Premium

The waiver of premium provision is an area where carriers are likely to have many different versions. If a producer is unclear as to how a carrier's waiver provision would work at various ages and in varying situations, it is prudent to ask the carrier's rep to walk through a series of scenarios. Is the person eligible for waiver at a given age? If so, what is the elimination period? Is the definition of disability a totally disabled version?

Death Benefit Only

Some insurers offer a Death Benefit Only (DBO) provision. The DBO arrangement provides coverage for disabled employees as long as the employer continues to carry them on the coverage roster (and pays premium for them), but after case termination the insurer has no further obligation to cover the disabled employees. The DBO arrangement is substantially different than a waiver of premium provision and usually has a reduced price tag attached to it. When changing carriers, most policyholders request a continuation of the DBO arrangement in the RFP.

In the rare event the DBO policyholder wants to switch to Carrier B with standard waiver of premium and no loss/no gain provisions, it is imperative that the policyholder understand that there may be a substantial number of employees who may lose coverage on account of the change in plan and in carriers.

Guaranteed Issue Limit

The Guaranteed Issue (GI) limit will be clearly stated in the current policy and any RFP specifications if the case is out for bid. The way in which the GI limit is applied on an ongoing basis may not be stated. The frequency of employees or dependents submitting evidence of good health, therefore, can vary by carrier. Distinguishing the carrier differences can be ferreted out with the following questions:

- After initially exceeding the GI limit on account of an earnings increase, how often must the employee submit evidence thereafter when having another increase in earnings?

- In a plan in which the employee can choose a multiple of earnings and a particular multiple puts the employee over the GI limit, what happens if the employee further increases the multiple at a later time? Is a multiple of 1 or 2 increases allowed without evidence, or is evidence required with each increase no matter the size?

Service Types and Levels of Service

In the RFP process, differences between carriers' types and levels of service are often overlooked because of the seemingly straightforward nature of group life/AD&D insurance. However, there can be services that a policyholder has come to expect under the current carrier that are not offered or that are provided in a different fashion by the successor carrier. Policyholders may attach a great deal of importance to some of these services, so it is well worthwhile to investigate the details of the service offerings of prospective insurers and how they are administered.

Sometimes carriers provide services within the structure of their life/AD&D program that are not readily apparent. Details of some services may not even appear in the contract. For example, many carriers offer an Employee Assistance Program (EAP) as part of the life/AD&D

package. Since EAP plans vary widely in levels of service, investigating the differences by carrier is a worthwhile endeavor, particularly if the policyholder has had employees utilize EAP services through the previous life program. Additional add-on services include:

- Travel assistance

- Will preparation and estate planning

- Funeral planning services

- Beneficiary designation management

These and other add-on services are discussed in detail in Chapter 13. An important consideration in comparing carriers' services is that of cost. It is incumbent upon the producer to question whether or not a particular carrier's add-on services are included in the quoted rate or if they are options at additional charge. A complete understanding of all of the services a carrier provides is pivotal in helping the policyholder to make the choice in carrier that best suits the policyholder's needs.

Plan Administration

The details of how the life plan is operated on a day-to-day basis are documented in the administration manual the insurer issues to the policyholder. Although it is not standard practice, it can be a good investment in time to compare the prior carrier's administration manual to the new carrier's administration manual, particularly if the policyholder is switching carriers on account of daily service and/or administrative concerns. Differences in administrative practices between the carriers can be addressed and ameliorated before the effective date of the new policy or very shortly thereafter.

There are a number of ways in which the insured's birthday causes a change in age bracket and rate in a case that is step-rated. For example, does the change in age bracket occur:

- On the first day of the month in which the insured's birthday takes place?

- On the first day of the following month in which the insured's birthday takes place?

- On the first day of the calendar year in which the birthday occurs?

- On the policy anniversary date of the year in which the birthday occurs?

Another difference that may exist between carriers' billing practices is the way in which new employees are added to the monthly billing statement as well as when former employees are deleted. Figure 14-2 provides examples of how these are handled.

Figure 14-2. Differences of When Additions and Deletions Appear on Billing Statements	
Adding New Employees to Coverage	**Terminating Employees from Coverage**
• 1st day of the month in which employee enrolled	• Last day worked
• 1st day of the month following the month in which the employee enrolled	• Last day for which premium contributions provided coverage following termination
	• Last day of the month in which termination occurred

While these details may appear minor to some, they become very important in the claims process. When adjudicating a life claim, the insurer will often check to ensure that the proper premium was reported and paid for the claimant. The policyholder's clear understanding of the potential differences in the new carrier's billing process is vital for smooth billing and claims administration.

Common Notice

Some carriers offer a common notice provision that can apply if the policyholder has group Long-Term Disability (LTD) accompanying the life/AD&D policy. It is a practice whereby the information provided by the claimant and insurer related to an LTD claim is reused in processing a waiver of premium submission. The claimant is relieved from having to submit a separate waiver of premium claim.

The service is designed to cut down on forms and paperwork so that administration of the group plan is easier for all involved. If reducing time and man hours in group plan administration is important to a policyholder, knowing how the competing carriers handle a claim that could cut across lines of coverage is worth investigating.

Key Takeaways

- As with any switch in brand, the new provider is not likely to have precisely the same product and services as the predecessor.

- The most important element in a successful transition between carriers is to ensure that no employees lose coverage or benefits to which they were otherwise entitled had no change in carrier occurred.

- It is essential for the policyholder to continue to remit premium payments for employees under the continuation of coverage provision if the intent is to continue to cover them.

- The conversion privilege can become an essential provision in helping to protect insureds from losing coverage on account of a change in carrier.

- When adjudicating a life claim, the insurer will often check to ensure that the proper premium was reported and paid for the claimant.

- Carriers sometimes provide services within the structure of their life/AD&D program that are not readily apparent and may not even appear in the contract language.

- It can be a good investment in time to compare the prior carrier's administration manual to the new carrier's administration manual, particularly if the policyholder is switching carriers on account of daily service and/or administrative concerns.

- Regardless of the reasons for changing carriers, attention to detail is crucial to ensure that employees get the benefits and services expected.

Endnotes

1. McLauchlin, Jay, "Proactive Intervention: An Analytics Approach to Group Policy Plan Retention", *LIMRA's MarketFacts Quarterly* Spring 2010,(Windsor, CT: LL Global), p. 46.

Appendix A

IRS Section 79 Group-Term Life Insurance

http://www.irs.gov/govt/fslg/article/0,,id=110345,00.html

Group-Term Life Insurance

Total Amount of Coverage

IRC section 79 provides an exclusion for the first $50,000 of group-term life insurance coverage provided under a policy carried directly or indirectly by an employer. There are no tax consequences if the total amount of such policies does not exceed $50,000. The imputed cost of coverage in excess of $50,000 must be included in income, using the IRS Premium Table, and are subject to social security and Medicare taxes.

Carried Directly or Indirectly by the Employer

A taxable fringe benefit arises if coverage exceeds $50,000 and the policy is considered carried directly or indirectly by the employer. A policy is considered carried directly or indirectly by the employer if:

1. The employer pays any cost of the life insurance, or

2. The employer arranges for the premium payments and the premiums paid by at least one employee subsidize those paid by at least one other employee (the "straddle" rule).

The determination of whether the premium charges straddle the costs is based on the IRS Premium Table rates, not the actual cost. You can view the Premium Table in the group-term life insurance discussion in Publication 15-B.

Because the employer is affecting the premium cost through its subsidizing and/or redistributing role, there is a benefit to employees. This benefit is taxable even if the employees are paying the full cost they are charged. You must calculate the taxable portion of the premiums for coverage that exceeds $50,000.

Not Carried Directly or Indirectly by the Employer

A policy that is not considered carried directly or indirectly by the employer has no tax consequences to the employee. Because the employees are paying the cost and the employer is not redistributing the cost of the premiums through an insurance system, the employer has no reporting requirements.

Example 1 -All employees for Employer X are in the 40 to 44 year age group. According to the IRS Premium Table, the cost per thousand is .10. The employer pays the full cost of the insurance. If at least one employee is charged more than .10 per thousand of coverage, and at least one is charged less than .10, the coverage is considered carried by the employer. Therefore, each employee is subject to social security and Medicare tax on the cost of coverage over $50,000.

Example 2 - The facts are the same as Example 1, except all employees are charged the same rate, which is set by the third-party insurer. The employer pays nothing toward the cost. Therefore there is no taxable income to the employees. It does not matter what the rate is, as the employer does not subsidize the cost or redistribute it between employees.

Coverage Provided by More Than One Insurer

Generally, if there is more than one policy from the same insurer providing coverage to employees, a combined test is used to determine whether it is carried directly or indirectly by the employer. However, the Regulations provide exceptions that allow the policies to be tested separately if the costs and coverage can be clearly allocated between the two policies. See Regulation 1.79 for more information.

If coverage is provided by more than one insurer, each policy must be tested separately to determine whether it is carried directly or indirectly by the employer.

Coverage for Spouse and Dependents

The cost of employer-provided group-term life insurance on the life of an employee's spouse or dependent, paid by the employer, is not taxable to the employee if the face amount of the coverage does not exceed $2,000. This coverage is excluded as a de minimis fringe benefit.

Whether a benefit provided is considered de minimis depends on all the facts and circumstances. In some cases, an amount greater than $2,000 of coverage could be considered a de minimis benefit. See Notice 89-110 for more information.

If part of the coverage for a spouse or dependents is taxable, the same Premium Table is used as for the employee. The entire amount is taxable, not just the amount that exceeds $2,000.

Example 3 - A 47-year old employee receives $40,000 of coverage per year under a policy carried directly or indirectly by her employer. She is also entitled to $100,000 of optional insurance at her own expense. This amount is also considered carried by the employer. The cost of $10,000 of this amount is excludable; the cost of the remaining $90,000 is included in income. If the optional policy were not considered carried by the employer, none of the $100,000 coverage would be included in income.

Appendix B

IRS Publication 15b Employer's Tax Guide to Fringe Benefits

Section on Group Life & Accidental Death and Dismemberment Coverage.

Introduction

This publication supplements Publication 15 (Circular E), Employer's Tax Guide, and Publication 15-A, Employer's Supplemental Tax Guide. It contains information for employers on the employment tax treatment of fringe benefits.

Comments and suggestions. We welcome your comments about this publication and your suggestions for future editions. You can write to us at the following address:

Internal Revenue Service Business
Forms and Publications Branch
SE:W:CAR:MP:T:B
1111 Constitution Ave. NW, IR-6526
Washington, DC 20224

We respond to many letters by telephone. Therefore, it would be helpful if you would include your daytime phone number, including the area code, in your correspondence. You can email us at *taxforms@irs.gov. (The asterisk must be included in the address.) Please put "Publications Comment" on the subject line. Although we cannot respond individually to each email, we do appreciate your feedback and will consider your comments as we revise our tax products.

1. FRINGE BENEFIT OVERVIEW

A fringe benefit is a form of pay for the performance of services. For example, you provide an employee with a fringe benefit when you allow the employee to use a business vehicle to commute to and from work.

Performance of services. A person who performs services for you does not have to be your employee. A person may perform services for you as an independent contractor, partner, or director. Also, for fringe benefit purposes, treat a person who agrees not to perform services (such as under a covenant not to compete) as performing services.

Provider of benefit. You are the provider of a fringe benefit if it is provided for services performed for you. You are the provider of a fringe benefit even if your client or customer provides the benefit to your employee for services the employee performs for you. For example, you are the provider of a fringe benefit for day care even if the day care is provided by a third party.

Recipient of benefit. The person who performs services for you is the recipient of a fringe benefit provided for those services. That person may be the recipient even if the benefit is provided to someone who did not perform services for you. For example, your employee may be the recipient of a fringe benefit you provide to a member of the employee's family.

Are Fringe Benefits Taxable?

Any fringe benefit you provide is taxable and must be included in the recipient's pay unless the law specifically excludes it. Section 2 discusses the exclusions that apply to certain fringe benefits. Any benefit not excluded under the rules discussed in section 2 is taxable.

Including taxable benefits in pay. You must include in a recipient's pay the amount by which the value of a fringe benefit is more than the sum of the following amounts.

- Any amount the law excludes from pay.

- Any amount the recipient paid for the benefit.

The rules used to determine the value of a fringe benefit are discussed in section 3.

If the recipient of a taxable fringe benefit is your employee, the benefit is subject to employment taxes and must be reported on Form W-2, Wage and Tax Statement. However, you can use special rules to withhold, deposit, and report the employment taxes. These rules are discussed in section 4.

If the recipient of a taxable fringe benefit is not your employee, the benefit is not subject to employment taxes. However, you may have to report the benefit on one of the following information returns.

If the recipient receives the benefit as:	Use:
An independent contractor	Form 1099-MISC
A partner	Schedule K-1 (Form 1065)

For more information, see the instructions for the forms listed above.

Cafeteria Plans

A cafeteria plan, including a flexible spending arrangement, is a written plan that allows your employees to choose between receiving cash or taxable benefits instead of certain qualified benefits for which the law provides an exclusion from wages. If an employee chooses to receive a qualified benefit under the plan, the fact that the employee could have received cash or a taxable benefit instead will not make the qualified benefit taxable. Generally, a cafeteria plan does not include any plan that offers a benefit that defers pay. However, a cafeteria plan can include a qualified 401(k) plan as a benefit. Also, certain life insurance plans maintained by educational institutions can be offered as a benefit even though they defer pay.

Qualified benefits. A cafeteria plan can include the following benefits discussed in section 2.

- Accident and health benefits (but not Archer medical savings accounts (Archer MSAs) or long-term care insurance).

- Adoption assistance.

- Dependent care assistance.

- Group-term life insurance coverage (including costs that cannot be excluded from wages).

- Health savings accounts (HSAs). Distributions from an HSA may be used to pay eligible long-term care insurance premiums or qualified long-term care services.

Benefits not allowed. A cafeteria plan cannot include the following benefits discussed in section 2.

- Archer MSAs. (See Accident and Health Benefits.)

- Athletic facilities.

- De minimis (minimal) benefits.

- Educational assistance.

- Employee discounts.

- Lodging on your business premises.

- Meals.

- Moving expense reimbursements.

- No-additional-cost services.

- Transportation (commuting) benefits.

- Tuition reduction.

- Volunteer firefighter and emergency medical responder benefits.

- Working condition benefits.

It also cannot include scholarships or fellowships (discussed in Publication 970, Tax Benefits for Education).

Employee. For these plans, treat the following individuals as employees.

- A current common-law employee (see section 2 in Publication 15 (Circular E) for more information).

- A full-time life insurance agent who is a current statutory employee.

- A leased employee who has provided services to you on a substantially full-time basis for at least a year if the services are performed under your primary direction or control.

Exception for S corporation shareholders. Do not treat a 2% shareholder of an S corporation as an employee of the corporation for this purpose. A 2% shareholder for this purpose is someone who directly or indirectly owns (at any time during the year) more than 2% of the corporation's stock or stock with more than 2% of the voting power. Treat a 2% shareholder as you would a partner in a partnership for fringe benefit purposes, but do not treat the benefit as a reduction in distributions to the 2% shareholder.

Plans that favor highly compensated employees. If your plan favors highly compensated employees as to eligibility to participate, contributions, or benefits, you must include in their wages the value of taxable benefits they could have selected. A plan you maintain under a collective bargaining agreement does not favor highly compensated employees.

A highly compensated employee for this purpose is any of the following employees.

1. An officer.

2. A shareholder who owns more than 5% of the voting power or value of all classes of the employer's stock.

3. An employee who is highly compensated based on the facts and circumstances.

4. A spouse or dependent of a person described in (1), (2), or (3).

Plans that favor key employees. If your plan favors key employees, you must include in their wages the value of taxable benefits they could have selected. A plan favors key employees if more than 25% of the total of the nontaxable benefits you provide for all employees under the plan go to key employees. However, a plan you maintain under a collective bargaining agreement does not favor key employees.

A key employee during 2011 is generally an employee who is either of the following.

1. An officer having annual pay of more than $160,000.

2. An employee who for 2011 is either of the following.

    a. A 5% owner of your business.

    b. A 1% owner of your business whose annual pay was more than $150,000.

Simple Cafeteria Plans

After December 31, 2010, eligible employers meeting contribution requirements and eligibility and participation requirements can establish a simple cafeteria plan. Simple cafeteria plans are treated as meeting the nondiscrimination requirements of a cafeteria plan and certain benefits under a cafeteria plan.

Eligible employer. You are an eligible employer if you employ an average of 100 or fewer employees during either of the 2 preceding years. If your business was not in existence throughout the preceding year, you are eligible if you reasonably expect to employ an average of 100 or fewer employees in the current year. If you establish a simple cafeteria plan in a year that you employ an average of 100 or fewer employees, you are considered an eligible employer for any subsequent year as long as you do not employ an average of 200 or more employees in a subsequent year.

Eligibility and participation requirements. These requirements are met if all employees who had at least 1,000 hours of service for the preceding plan year are eligible to participate and each employee eligible to participate in the plan may elect any benefit available under the plan. You may elect to exclude from the plan employees who:

1. Are under age 21 before the close of the plan year,

2. Have less than 1 year of service with you as of any day during the plan year,

3. Are covered under a collective bargaining agreement, or

4. Are nonresident aliens working outside the United States whose income did not come from a U.S. source.

Contribution requirements. You must make a contribution to provide qualified benefits on behalf of each qualified employee in an amount equal to:

1. A uniform percentage (not less than 2%) of the employee's compensation for the plan year, or

2. An amount which is at least 6% of the employee's compensation for the plan year or twice the amount of the salary reduction contributions of each qualified employee, whichever is less.

If the contribution requirements are met using option (2) above, the rate of contribution to any salary reduction contribution of a highly compensated or key employee cannot be greater than the rate of contribution to any otheremployee.

More information. For more information about cafeteria plans, see section 125 of the Internal Revenue Code and its regulations.

2. FRINGE BENEFIT EXCLUSION RULES

This section discusses the exclusion rules that apply to fringe benefits. These rules exclude all or part of the value of certain benefits from the recipient's pay.

The excluded benefits are not subject to federal income tax withholding. Also, in most cases, they are not subject to social security, Medicare, or federal unemployment (FUTA) tax and are not reported on Form W-2. This section discusses the exclusion rules for the following fringe benefits.

- Accident and health benefits.

- Achievement awards.

- Adoption assistance.

- Athletic facilities.

- De minimis (minimal) benefits.

- Dependent care assistance.

- Educational assistance.

- Employee discounts.

- Employee stock options.

- Group-term life insurance coverage.

- Health savings accounts (HSAs).

- Lodging on your business premises.

- Meals.

- Moving expense reimbursements.

- No-additional-cost services.

- Retirement planning services.

- Transportation (commuting) benefits.

- Tuition reduction.

- Volunteer firefighter and emergency medical responder benefits.

- Working condition benefits.

See Table 2-1 for an overview of the employment tax treatment of these benefits.

Table 2-1. Treatment Under Employment Taxes			
Type of Fringe Benefit	*Income Tax Withholding*	*Social Security and Medicare*	*Federal Unemployment (FUTA)*
Accident and health benefits	Exempt,[1,2] except for long-term care benefits provided through a flexible spending or similar arrangement.	Exempt, except for certain payments to S corporation employees who are 2% shareholders.	Exempt
Achievement awards	Exempt[1] up to $1,600 for qualified plan awards ($400 for nonqualified awards).		
Adoption assistance	Exempt[1,3]	Taxable	Taxable
Athletic facilities	Exempt if substantially all use during the calendar year is by employees, their spouses, and their dependent children and the facility is operated by the employer on premises owned or leased by the employer.		
De minimis (minimal) benefits	Exempt	Exempt	Exempt
Dependent care assistance	Exempt[3] up to certain limits, $5,000 ($2,500 for married employee filing separate return).		
Educational assistance	Exempt up to $5,250 of benefits each year. (See Educational Assistance, later.)		
Employee discounts	Exempt[3] up to certain limits. (See Employee Discounts, later.)		
Employee stock options	See Employee Stock Options, later.		
Group-term life insurance coverage	Exempt	Exempt [1,4] up to cost of $50,000 of coverage. (Special rules apply to former employees.)	Exempt
Health savings accounts (HSAs)	Exempt for qualified individuals up to the HSA contribution limits. (See Health Savings Accounts, later.)		
Lodging on your business premises	Exempt[1] if furnished for your convenience as a condition of employment.		

Table 2-1. Treatment Under Employment Taxes (Cont'd)

Meals	Exempt if furnished on your business premises for your convenience.		
	Exempt if de minimis.		
Moving expense reimbursements	Exempt[1] if expenses would be deductible if the employee had paid them.		
No-additional-cost services	Exempt[3]	Exempt[3]	Exempt[3]
Retirement planning services	Exempt[5]	Exempt[5]	Exempt[5]
Transportation benefits(commuting)	Exempt[1] up to certain limits if for rides in a commuter highway vehicle and/or transit passes ($120, but see the Caution on page 1), qualified parking ($230), or qualified bicycle commuting reimbursement6 ($20). (See Transportation (Commuting) Benefits, later.)		
	Exempt if de minimis.		
Tuition reduction	Exempt[3] if for undergraduate education (or graduate education if the employee performs teaching or researchactivities).		
Volunteer firefighter and emergency medical responder benefits	Exempt	Exempt	Exempt
Working condition benefits	Exempt	Exempt	Exempt

1. Exemption does not apply to S corporation employees who are 2% shareholders.
2. Exemption does not apply to certain highly compensated employees under a self-insured plan that favors those employees.
3. Exemption does not apply to certain highly compensated employees under a program that favors those employees.
4. Exemption does not apply to certain key employees under a plan that favors those employees.
5. Exemption does not apply to services for tax preparation, accounting, legal, or brokerage services.
6. If the employee receives a qualified bicycle commuting reimbursement in a qualified bicycle commuting month, the employee cannot receive commuter highwayvehicle, transit pass, or qualified parking benefits in that same month.

Accident and Health Benefits

This exclusion applies to contributions you make to an accident or health plan for an employee, including the following.

- Contributions to the cost of accident or health insurance including qualified long-term care insurance.

- Contributions to a separate trust or fund that directly or through insurance provides accident or health benefits.

- Contributions to Archer MSAs or health savings accounts (discussed in Publication 969, Health Savings Accounts and Other Tax-Favored Health Plans).

This exclusion also applies to payments you directly or indirectly make to an employee under an accident or health plan for employees that are either of the following.

- Payments or reimbursements of medical expenses.

- Payments for specific injuries or illnesses (such as the loss of the use of an arm or leg). The payments must be figured without regard to any period of absence from work.

Accident or health plan. This is an arrangement that provides benefits for your employees, their spouses, their dependents, and their children (under age 27) in the event of personal injury or sickness. The plan may be insured or noninsured and does not need to be in writing.

Employee. For this exclusion, treat the following individuals as employees.

- A current common-law employee.

- A full-time life insurance agent who is a current statutory employee.

- A retired employee

- A former employee you maintain coverage for based on the employment relationship.

- A widow or widower of an individual who died while an employee.

- A widow or widower of a retired employee.

For the exclusion of contributions to an accident or health plan, a leased employee who has provided services to you on a substantially full-time basis for at least a year if the services are performed under your primary direction or control.

Special rule for certain government plans. For certain government accident and health plans, payments to a deceased plan participant's beneficiary may qualify for the exclusion from gross income if the other requirements for exclusion are met. See section 105(j) for details.

Exception for S corporation shareholders. Do not treat a 2% shareholder of an S corporation as an employee of the corporation for this purpose. A 2% shareholder is someone who directly or indirectly owns (at any time during the year) more than 2% of the corporation's stock or stock with more than 2% of the voting power. Treat a 2% shareholder as you would a partner in a partnership for fringe benefit purposes, but do not treat the benefit as a reduction in distributions to the 2% shareholder.

Exclusion from wages. You can generally exclude the value of accident or health benefits you provide to an employee from the employee's wages.

Exception for certain long-term care benefits. You cannot exclude contributions to the cost of long-term care insurance from an employee's wages subject to federal income tax withholding if the coverage is provided through a flexible spending or similar arrangement. This is a benefit program that reimburses specified expenses up to a maximum amount that is reasonably available to the employee and is less than five times the total cost of the insurance. However, you can exclude these contributions from the employee's wages subject to social security, Medicare, and federal unemployment (FUTA) taxes.

S corporation shareholders. Because you cannot treat a 2% shareholder of an S corporation as an employee for this exclusion, you must include the value of accident or health benefits you provide to the employee in the employee's wages subject to federal income tax withholding. However, you can exclude the value of these benefits (other than payments for specific injuries or illnesses) from the employee's wages subject to social security, Medicare, and FUTA taxes.

Exception for highly compensated employees. If your plan is a self-insured medical reimbursement plan that favors highly compensated employees, you must include all or part of the amounts you pay to these employees in their wages subject to federal income tax withholding. However, you can exclude these amounts the employee's wages subject to social security, Medicare, and FUTA taxes.

A self-insured plan is a plan that reimburses your employees for medical expenses not covered by an accident or health insurance policy. A highly compensated employee for this exception is any of the following individuals.

- One of the five highest paid officers.

- An employee who owns (directly or indirectly) more than 10% in value of the employer's stock.

- An employee who is among the highest paid 25% of all employees (other than those who can be excluded from the plan).

For more information on this exception, see section 105(h) of the Internal Revenue Code and its regulations.

COBRA premiums. The exclusion for accident and health benefits applies to amounts you pay to maintain medical coverage for a current or former employee under the Combined Omnibus Budget Reconciliation Act of 1986 (COBRA). The exclusion applies regardless of the length of employment, whether you directly pay the premiums or reimburse the former employee for premiums paid, and whether the employee's separation is permanent or temporary.

De Minimis (Minimal) Benefits

You can exclude the value of a de minimis benefit you provide to an employee from the employee's wages. A de minimis benefit is any property or service you provide to an employee that has so little value (taking into account how frequently you provide similar benefits to your employees) that accounting for it would be unreasonable or administratively impracticable. Cash and cash equivalent fringe benefits (for example, use of gift card, charge card, or credit card), no matter how little, are never excludable as a de minimis benefit, except for occasional meal money or transportation fare.

Examples of de minimis benefits include the following.

- Occasional personal use of a company copying machine if you sufficiently control its use so that at least 85% of its use is for business purposes.

- Holiday gifts, other than cash, with a low fair market value.

- Group-term life insurance payable on the death of an employee's spouse or dependent if the face amount is not more than $2,000.

- Meals. See Meals, later.

- Occasional parties or picnics for employees and their guests.

- Occasional tickets for theater or sporting events.

- Transportation fare. See Transportation (Commuting) Benefits, later.

Employee. For this exclusion, treat any recipient of a de minimis benefit as an employee.

Group-Term Life Insurance Coverage

This exclusion applies to life insurance coverage that meets all the following conditions.

- It provides a general death benefit that is not included in income.

- You provide it to a group of employees. See The 10-employee rule, later.

- It provides an amount of insurance to each employee based on a formula that prevents individual selection. This formula must use factors such as the employee's age, years of service, pay, or position.

- You provide it under a policy you directly or indirectly carry. Even if you do not pay any of the policy's cost, you are considered to carry it if you arrange for payment of its cost by your employees and charge at least one employee less than, and at least one other employee more than, the cost of his or her insurance. Determine the cost of the insurance, for this purpose, as explained under Coverage over the limit, later.

Group-term life insurance does not include the following insurance.

- Insurance that does not provide general death benefits, such as travel insurance or a policy providing only accidental death benefits.

- Life insurance on the life of your employee's spouse or dependent. However, you may be able to exclude the cost of this insurance from the employee's wages as a de minimis benefit. See De Minimis (Minimal) Benefits, earlier.

- Insurance provided under a policy that provides a permanent benefit (an economic value that extends beyond 1 policy year, such as paid-up or cash surrender value), unless certain requirements are met. See Regulations section 1.79-1 for details.

Employee. For this exclusion, treat the following individuals as employees.

1. A current common-law employee.

2. A full-time life insurance agent who is a current statutory employee.

3. An individual who was formerly your employee under (1) or (2), above.

4. A leased employee who has provided services to you on a substantially full-time basis for at least a year if the services are performed under your primary direction and control.

Exception for S corporation shareholders. Do not treat a 2% shareholder of an S corporation as an employee of the corporation for this purpose. A 2% shareholder is someone who directly or indirectly owns (at any time during the year) more than 2% of the corporation's stock or stock with more than 2% of the voting power. Treat a 2% shareholder as you would a partner in a partnership for fringe benefit purposes, but do not treat the benefit as a reduction in distributions to the 2% shareholder.

The 10-employee rule. Generally, life insurance is not group-term life insurance unless you provide it to at least 10 full-time employees at some time during the year.

For this rule, count employees who choose not to receive the insurance unless, to receive it, they must contribute to the cost of benefits other than the group-term life insurance. For example, count an employee who could receive insurance by paying part of the cost, even if that employee chooses not to receive it. However, do not count an employee who must pay part or all of the cost of permanent benefits to get insurance, unless that employee chooses to receive it. A permanent benefit is an economic value extending beyond one policy year (for example, a paid-up or cash-surrender value) that is provided under a life insurance policy.

Exceptions. Even if you do not meet the 10-employee rule, two exceptions allow you to treat insurance as group-term life insurance.

Under the first exception, you do not have to meet the 10-employee rule if all the following conditions are met.

1. If evidence that the employee is insurable is required, it is limited to a medical questionnaire (completed by the employee) that does not require a physical.

2. You provide the insurance to all your full-time employees or, if the insurer requires the evidence mentioned in (1), to all full-time employees who provide evidence the insurer accepts.

3. You figure the coverage based on either a uniform percentage of pay or the insurer's coverage brackets that meet certain requirements. See Regulations section 1.79-1 for details.

Under the second exception, you do not have to meet the 10-employee rule if all the following conditions are met.

- You provide the insurance under a common plan covering your employees and the employees of at least one other employer who is not related to you.

- The insurance is restricted to, but mandatory for, all your employees who belong to, or are represented by, an organization (such as a union) that carries on substantial activities besides obtaining insurance.

- Evidence of whether an employee is insurable does not affect an employee's eligibility for insurance or the amount of insurance that employee gets.

To apply either exception, do not consider employees who were denied insurance for any of the following reasons.

- They were 65 or older.

- They customarily work 20 hours or less a week or 5 months or less in a calendar year.

- They have not been employed for the waiting period given in the policy. This waiting period cannot be more than 6 months.

Exclusion from wages. You can generally exclude the cost of up to $50,000 of group-term life insurance from the wages of an insured employee. You can exclude the same amount from the employee's wages when figuring social security and Medicare taxes. In addition, you do not have to withhold federal income tax or pay FUTA tax on any group-term life insurance you provide to an employee.

Coverage over the limit. You must include in your employee's wages the cost of group-term life insurance beyond $50,000 worth of coverage, reduced by the amount the employee paid toward the insurance. Report it as wages in boxes 1, 3, and 5 of the employee's Form W-2. Also, show it in box 12 with code "C." The amount is subject to social security and Medicare taxes, and you may, at your option, withhold federal income tax.

Figure the monthly cost of the insurance to include in the employee's wages by multiplying the number of thousands of dollars of all insurance coverage over $50,000 (figured to the nearest $100) by the cost shown in the following use the employee's age on the last day of the employee's tax year. You must prorate the cost from the table if less than a full month of coverage is involved.

Table 2-2. Cost Per $1,000 of Protection For 1 Month

Age	Cost
Under 25	$ .05
25 through 29	.06
30 through 34	.08
35 through 39	.09
40 through 44	.10
45 through 49	.15
50 through 54	.23
55 through 59	.43
60 through 64	.66
65 through 69	1.27
70 and older	2.06

You figure the total cost to include in the employee's wages by multiplying the monthly cost by the number of full months' coverage at that cost.

*Example.*Tom's employer provides him with group-term life insurance coverage of $200,000. Tom is 45 years old, is not a key employee, and pays $100 per year toward the cost of the insurance. Tom's employer must include $170 in his wages. The $200,000 of insurance coverage is reduced by $50,000. The yearly cost of $150,000 of coverage is $270 ($.15 x 150 x 12), and is reduced by the $100 Tom pays for the insurance. The employer includes $170 in boxes 1, 3, and 5 of Tom's Form W-2. The employer also enters $170 in box 12 with code "C."

Coverage for dependents. Group-term life insurance coverage paid by the employer for the spouse or dependents of an employee may be excludable from income as a de minimis fringe benefit if the face amount is not more than $2,000. If the face amount is greater than $2,000, the entire amount of the dependent coverage must be included in income unless the amount over $2,000 is purchased with employee contributions on an after-tax basis.

Former employees. When group-term life insurance over $50,000 is provided to an employee (including retirees) after his or her termination, the employee share of social security and Medicare taxes on that period of coverage is paid by the former employee with his or her tax return and is not collected by the employer. You are not required to collect those taxes. Use the table above to determine the amount of social security and Medicare taxes owed by the former employee for coverage provided after separation from service. Report those uncollected amounts separately in box 12 on Form W-2 using codes "M" and "N." See the Instructions for Forms W-2 and W-3 and the Instructions for Form 941.

Exception for key employees. Generally, if your group-term life insurance plan favors key employees as to participation or benefits, you must include the entire cost of the insurance in your key employees' wages. This exception generally does not apply to church plans. When figuring social security and Medicare taxes, you must also include the entire cost in the employees' wages. Include the cost in boxes 1, 3, and 5 of Form W-2. However, you do not have to withhold federal income tax or pay FUTA tax on the cost of any group-term life insurance you provide to an employee. For this purpose, the cost of the insurance is the greater of the following amounts.

- The premiums you pay for the employee's insurance. See Regulations section 1.79-4T(Q&A 6) for more information.

- The cost you figure using the Table 2-2.

For this exclusion, a key employee during 2011 is an employee or former employee who is one of the following individuals. See section 416(i) of the Internal Revenue Code for more information.

1. An officer having annual pay of more than $160,000.

2. An individual who for 2011 was either of the following.

   a. A 5% owner of your business.

   b. A 1% owner of your business whose annual pay was more than $150,000.

A former employee who was a key employee upon retirement or separation from service is also a key employee.

Your plan does not favor key employees as to participation if at least one of the following is true.

- It benefits at least 70% of your employees.

- At least 85% of the participating employees are not key employees.

- It benefits employees who qualify under a set of rules you set up that do not favor key employees.

Your plan meets this participation test if it is part of a cafeteria plan (discussed in section 1) and it meets the participation test for those plans.

When applying this test, do not consider employees who:

- Have not completed 3 years of service,

- Are part-time or seasonal,

- Are nonresident aliens who receive no U.S. source earned income from you, or

- Are not included in the plan but are in a unit of employees covered by a collective bargaining agreement, if the benefits provided under the plan were the subject of good-faith bargaining between you and employee representatives.

Your plan does not favor key employees as to benefits if all benefits available to participating key employees are also available to all other participating employees. Your plan does not favor key employees just because the amount of insurance you provide to your employees is uniformly related to their pay.

S corporation shareholders. Because you cannot treat a 2% shareholder of an S corporation as an employee for this exclusion, you must include the cost of all group-term life insurance coverage you provide the 2% shareholder in his or her wages. When figuring social security and Medicare taxes, you must also include the cost of this coverage in the 2% shareholder's wages. Include the cost in boxes 1, 3, and 5 of Form W-2. However, you do not have to withhold federal income tax or pay federal unemployment tax on the cost of any group-term life insurance coverage you provide to the 2% shareholder.

Appendix C

Useful Life Insurance Web Sites

Website	Location	Content	Using the information
American Council of Life Insurers	www.acli.com • http://www.acli.com/Consumers/Life%20Insurance/Pages/Default.aspx • http://www.acli.com/Tools/Industry%20Facts/Life%20Insurers%20Fact%20Book/Pages/Default.aspx	Information on the life insurance industry. • Information for consumers on life insurance • Industry information as presented in the Fact Book	-RFP generation -Explanation of contract and other terms -Evaluating competitive landscape
Bureau of Labor Statistics (BLS)	www.bls.gov	Content on employee benefits and how widespread various coverages are.	-Planning life enrollment, esp in comparing life to other group benefits -Allows producer to demonstrate popularity of life compared to medical, dental, disability. -Benchmarking client's plan against other plans

Internal Revenue Service (IRS)	www.irs.gov • http://www.irs.gov/app/picklist/list/formsPublications.html • http://www.irs.gov/govt/fslg/article/0,,id=110345,00.html	Information on taxes and employee benefits. • Publication 15b contains information about Section 79. Publication 15a addresses taxation of disability benefits. • Addresses Section 79	-Assist in design and structure of client's group life plan -Formulating the right questions for tax advisers Understanding how to account for Section 79 imputed income.
The Life & Health Insurance Foundation for Education (LIFR)	www.lifehappens.org	Useful information about life insurance and disability insurance. The website has calculators to help consumers determine the amount of insurance.	-Can be used to direct employees to educate themselves on life coverage and for use in an enrollment campaign.
U. S. Department of Labor (DOL)	www.DOL.gov • http://www.dol.gov/compliance/guide/index.htm • http://www.dol.gov/elaws/fmla.htm • http://www.dol.gov/elaws/userra.htm	Information on many aspects of labor law. • ERISA • FMLA • USERRA	-Plan compliance information -Assist in design and structure of client's group life plan
U. S. Equal Employment Opportunity Commission (EEOC)	www.eeoc.gov • http://www.eeoc.gov/laws/types/age.cfm	Information on labor practices. • Specific information on age discrimination.	-Assist in design and structure of client's group life plan -Compliance on government reporting

National Association of Insurance Commissioners	http://search.naic.org/search?q=group+life&btnG=Search&site=NAICAffiliates&client=default_frontend&output=xml_no_dtd&proxystylesheet=default_frontend	General information on life coverage -Tips and considerations -Terms -New bulletins and updates	-Provide client with background information about life insurance to make better-informed decisions

Glossary

Accelerated death benefit: This contract provision enables a terminally ill employee or dependent to receive a portion of proceeds from their group life plan while still alive. The concept is to provide claims funds to a person who very likely has extraordinarily high medical expenses. (This term is also known as a *living benefits option,* and an *advanced death benefit.*)

Age Discrimination In Employment Act (ADEA): Federal law enacted in 1967 that protects workers age 40 and older from discrimination due to age in employment practices and benefits. Applies to employers with 20 or more employees.

Annual enrollment: Typically occurs in a Section 125 Plan each year during a specified period. The annual enrollment is designed to allow currently enrolled participants to re-evaluate their needs and make different benefit selections. In group life coverage, if an individual opts for a level of coverage greater than the Basic Annual Earnings multiple increment allowed or in excess of the G.I., the individual may have to submit evidence of good health in order to obtain the higher levels of coverage. An annual enrollment may or may not be an open enrollment. (This term is also known as *open enrollment.*)

Anti-selection: Actuarial term used to describe the phenomenon in which a person who may potentially have a known condition or impending claim chooses to attempt to enroll in the group insurance program. It is akin to purchasing homeowners insurance while the house is on fire. (This term is also known as *adverse selection,* and *selection.*)

Assignment of benefits: This policy provision allows employees to assign their legal interest in the group life and AD&D (loss of life) policy to another person. That person now has all the rights and privileges the employee had under the policy including the right to name the beneficiary or to exercise the Conversion Privilege. (This term is also known as *assignment,* and *absolute assignment.*)

Attending Physician's Statement (APS): Documentation provided by the applicant's physician or consulting physician to the insurer in support of an evidence of good health application. The documentation may cover a wide range of data and is used to help the insurer to determine if the applicant will be approved for coverage or not. (This term is also known as a *physician's statement.*)

Basic life: Is typically non-contributory group life insurance coverage provided by the employer. In general, basic life schedules are modest with the employee having few, if any, options or choices in amount of coverage.

Beneficiary: Legal term used to describe the recipient of group life and/or AD&D benefits in the event of a claim. In some states, employees are prohibited from naming the policyholder (employer) as the beneficiary of claim proceeds.

Blending: The process used in a rate evaluation in which the results of the experience analysis and manual rate and combined together to yield one rate. (This term is also known as *melding*.)

Booklet/certificate: A booklet certifying group coverage is ostensibly issued to each employee covered under the group policy. The booklet is a legal document which describes in detail the benefits to which the certificate holder is entitled as well as essential policy information such as how to file a claim, appeals of denials, and eligibility requirements. In today's technologically advanced environment, most booklet/certificates are available to employees online. (This term is also known as *Cert, booklet, certificate,* and *handbook*.)

Claim stabilization fund: A financial vehicle that is part of the group insurance arrangement similar to a policyholder "bank account" with the insurer. Policyholders are able to leave surplus premiums on deposit with the insurer in an interest-bearing account that can be used to pay future premiums or other plan costs. (This term is also known as *claim stabilization reserve, premium stabilization reserve* or *fund, premium deposit account, premium reserve fund,* and *special fund*.)

Common notice: A practice whereby the information provided by the claimant and physician related to an LTD claim is re-used in processing a waiver of premium submission. The claimant is relieved from having to submit a separate waiver of premium claim.

Common premium: A premium that has been adjusted to reflect what the paid premium would have been historically had the current rate been in place during the entire experience base. The paid premium and constant premium will be identical if the current rate were in place for that period of time. (This term is also known as a *constant premium*.)

Composite rates: Premium rates that are charged based on one rate that applies to a class or the entire group.

Contributory: A group insurance plan in which the insured pays for a portion of or all of the premium. (This term is also known as *contrib,* and *supplemental*.)

Conversion privilege: A group life policy provision which enables an insured whose group term coverage is terminating to convert to an individual life policy without having to submit evidence of good health to the insurer. The group insurer offers the individual policy to the insured who decides whether or not to convert.

Credibility: The believability of the historical experience data. The predictive value of the data is typically assigned a percentage and applied in the formula rating process.

Death Benefit Only (DBO): Type of group life insurance contract in which the insurer pays only for death claims. There is no premium of waiver provision and disabled employees would have their claims paid only in the event of their death while the contract is inforce.

Decline to Quote (DTQ): Process in which the case underwriter does not issue a proposal in response to a Request for Proposal. (This term is also known as *no quote*, and *quote declination*.)

Deferred effective date: A requirement that is a standard group contract provision which requires employees to be actively at work before coverage or increases in coverage can take effect. (This term is also known as an *active full-time requirement*.)

Department of Labor (DOL): Federal agency that administers employment laws that affect employee benefits including ERISA, ADEA, FMLA, USERRA.

Direct billing: Method of plan administration in which the insurer takes the lead role in operating the day-to-day non claim functions of the group benefits program. This method is usually reserved for smaller policyholders. (This term is also known as *direct accounting, home office accounting,* and *list billing*.)

Discretionary clause: This policy provision states that the insurer has the sole authority and discretion to interpret the language and provisions in the policy. Their discretion applies to how the contract language affects the benefit payments and operation of the plan. This provision arises out of ERISA in which only a "plan fiduciary" may interpret the plan.

Elimination period: The period of time commencing from the initial date of disability to contractually stated period (usually 6 or 9 months) that a disabled employee must wait before qualifying for waiver of premium. In most cases, the disabling condition must be continuous and be totally disabling. (This term is also known as a *waiting period*, a *benefit waiting period*, and a *qualifying period*.)

Employment Retirement Income Security Act (ERISA): Federal law enacted in 1974 to protect and provide some measure of security to employees who have health and welfare benefits. This law is administered by the Department of Labor and has a far reaching affect on benefit programs.

Expatriate: A U.S. based employee working for an American company who works abroad. (This term is also known as *ex-pat*.)

Family Medical Leave Act (FMLA): Federal law enacted in 1993 that provides workers with leave of absence for specific health and family situations covered in the law itself. Applies to employers with 50 or more employees in a 75 mile radius.

Fiduciary: Arising out of ERISA, a fiduciary is anyone who has discretionary authority over a benefit plan covered under ERISA. Fiduciaries have specific duties as outlined in ERISA.

File Policy Language: Process required by most states of every insurer conducting group life business in their state. Most states require insurers to submit their contract language and policy forms and application to the state for review and approval prior to issuance of the contract language. Filing the language is a consumer protection mechanism for insureds who would be covered under the group life contract.

Flex-funding arrangement: A premium payment arrangement for the policyholder to have the protection and services provided through a traditional life plan yet paying for claims only as they surface. Rather than paying a full monthly premium, the policyholder remits only the amount needed for expenses to administer the plan plus monthly claims. (This term is also known as a *cost plus arrangement.*)

Form 5500: Annual report required by ERISA in which a group policyholder reports the basic financial information of a benefit plan. (This term is also known as *5500*, and an *annual ERISA report.*)

Formula rate: Underwriting term used to describe the standard process for conducting a rate analysis. The formula establishes the rate applying the insurer's underwriting guidelines and protocols before any discounting or adjustments are applied. (This term is also known as a *start rate.*)

Grace period: The amount of time from the date that premium is initially due until the last day the insurer will accept the premium to keep coverage active. It is a required statutory provision and enables the policyholder to collect any premium contributions from covered employees and remit the premium to the insurer.

Grandfathered: Term used to describe the underwriter's acceptance of insureds whose coverage and/or rates may be outside of the current contractual arrangement for all other employees. This special arrangement is an accommodation by the insurer to allow the insureds to have benefits offered by the prior insurer(s).

Guaranteed Issue (GI): The threshold amount of group life coverage for which an insured qualifies without being required to submit medical evidence. It is "guaranteed" since the coverage amount is not subject to an evaluation of the insured's health related to the coverage. (This term is also known as a *non medical maximum.*)

Health Insurance Portability and Accountability Act (of 1996) (HIPAA): The HIPAA Privacy Rule provides federal protections for personal health information held by covered entities and gives patients an array of rights with respect to that information. HIPAA is balanced to permit the disclosure of personal health information needed for patient care and other important purposes.

Hold harmless agreement: Arrangement in which the policyholder relinquishes the insurer from any responsibility for claims or other liability that may emerge after the policy has terminated.

Imputed income: Amounts of group life insurance over $50,000 that are attributable to IRC Code Section 79. Essentially, these are amounts of coverage subject to federal taxes. The amount of tax is determined by taking the amount of insurance over $50,000 face amount and multiplying by a rate factor that has been established by the IRS. These are called Table I rates.

Incurred But Not Reported (IBNR): The reserve need established by the insurer to account for unrevealed liability and/or reserves needed to pay for claims after the contract has terminated. (This term is also known as *reserves*.)

Independent Medical Exam (IME): An examination required of a person by the insurer conducted by a disinterested, neutral third party. In effect, it is a second opinion regarding the diagnosis and prognosis of the person being examined and typically occurs when the initial physician exam is inconclusive or contested by the patient. If the initial medical data is unclear or inconclusive, a third party may be needed to help interpret the data. IME's may also be used when a rejected applicant requests reconsideration.

IRC Code Section 79: Internal Revenue Service Code which makes group life insurance amounts over $50,000 taxable as income.

IRS Section 125: Internal Revenue Service (IRS) code allowing group benefit plans to have certain tax-advantaged status and mechanisms for the benefit of the enrolled employees and their dependents. A key advantage is to allow employees to contribute towards premium with "pre-tax" dollars which effectively increases the purchasing power of the contribution. (This term is also known as a *125 Plan*, a *cafeteria plan*, and a *flexible benefits plan*.)

Late entrant: An individual who was previously eligible to enroll for coverage but did not do so. Subsequently, they want to enroll in the benefits program having gone past their enrollment window of opportunity. Underwriters view late entrants as higher than usual risks because they want coverage now when previously they didn't.

Letter of credit: A financial arrangement in which a lending institution, typically a bank, backs and guarantees payment for a liability which the policyholder may take on with the insurer.

Life years: The average number of lives covered in the plan in a year or portions of a year. If multiple years of experience are used, the underwriter will add up the average lives for each year being considered.

McCarran-Ferguson Act: Federal law enacted in 1945 that exempts insurance from federal regulations. Enables states to regulate insurance.

Medical evidence: A requirement of the insurer that applies to individuals seeking to enroll into the group program or to qualify for amounts in excess of the Guaranteed Issue limit. In order to qualify, the individual must apply for coverage by submitting documentation and possibly submit to physical examination to prove that the applicant is deemed healthy enough for the coverage. Based on the evidence presented, the insurer determines whether or not the applicant qualifies for the coverage. Generally, the medical underwriting in individual life is more comprehensive than group life. This term is also known as *evidence, evidence* of *good health, evidence* of *insurability, medical underwriting,* or *underwritten coverage.*

Multiple Employer Welfare Arrangement (MEWA): An employer welfare benefit plan established to provide benefits to the employees of two or more employers. There are numerous arrangements that can fit the definition of a MEWA as defined by ERISA. MEWA's are often used as a platform for the employers who are in the MEWA to obtain group coverage. (This term is also known as a *multiple employer trust.*)

National Association of Insurance Commissioners (NAIC): Association of state insurance commissions who regulate the insurance industry. The NAIC enables state insurance regulatory authorities to work together to make state regulation more consistent across the states.

Non contributory: When group insurance premium is wholly paid by the policyholder/employer. The insureds are not required to contribute towards the cost of coverage. (This term is also known as *non contrib.*)

Non participating plan: Regardless of the financial result of the case at year's end, the policyholder is not eligible to participate in a potential refund process. (This term is also known as *non par,* and *pooled.*)

North American Industry Classification System (NAICS Code): A system established by the U.S. government to categorize businesses. Originating in 1997, this 6-digit system was designed to replace the previous SIC Code system. This replacement was intended to more accurately reflect the nature of American and North American businesses.

Open enrollment: An open enrollment is typically a type of annual enrollment. Rules requiring evidence for late entrants or for increases in basic annual earnings multiple increments are often relaxed.

Participating plan: A plan which enables a policyholder to participate in the financial outcome of the group plan and be eligible for a potential refund from the insurer. (This term is also known as *par*, and *experience-rated*.)

Participation: Term applied to the enrollment level, it describes the number of employees who actually enroll in the program as compared to the number who are eligible to enroll.

Permissible loss ratio: The loss ratio which establishes the adequacy of the current rate. It is typically the inverse of the expenses needed to run the case. If a case's expenses were 27 percent, the Permissible Loss Ratio would be 73 percent. (This term is also known as an *acceptable loss ratio*, a *desired loss ratio*, or *target loss ratio*.)

Portability: Enables an insured whose group life coverage is terminating to take the coverage with them. They port the coverage without being actively employed as a condition of continued coverage. Ported coverage's greatest advantage over the conversion privilege is that it is typically less expensive although restrictions apply. (This term is also known as *port*.)

Principal sum: In AD&D coverage, this is the amount to be paid to the beneficiary in the event of death or the amount to be paid to the employee for physical loss due to a covered accident. (This term is also known as an *indemnity sum*, and an *indemnity amount*.)

Producer: Term used to describe the person(s) and/or organizations who represent the Plan Sponsor or policyholder (typically the employer) to insurers in obtaining group insurance for the policyholder. (This term is also known as a *consultant*, or *agent*.)

Professional Employer Organization (PEO): An organization which provides businesses with staff. The PEO recruits, screens, and solicits businesses to match the talent and skills of those employees they have engaged to various business entities. The PEO typically is provided a commission or service fee when one of their employees is employed by the business. Most PEO employees are used by the business on a temporary basis and are often not considered full-time employees for group insurance coverage. (This term is also known as *professional employment agency*, or *staff leasing agency*.)

Pyogenic Infection: Some carriers make reference to pyogenic infection in their AD&D exclusions. A pyogenic infection is an invasion by and multiplication of pathogenic microorganisms in a bodily part or tissue, which may produce subsequent tissue injury and progress to overt disease through a variety of cellular or toxic mechanisms.

Rate guarantee: The period of time for which the insurer guarantees the premium rates to the policyholder. The rate guarantee is subject to conditions such as continued and timely premium payment, unchanged contractual agreements, and no significant changes to the employee census.

Reinsurance: The process by which one insurer takes out insurance from another insurer to limit its financial risk in the event of unforeseen circumstances. There are a number of arrangements in which the two insurers can establish an agreement. (This term is also known as *insurer stop loss*.)

Request for Proposal (RFP): The bid put together by the producer on behalf of the policyholder to solicit bids from insurers. The request details conditions, contract and service requirements that must be met by the successful insurer. (This term is also known as *bid specifications*.)

Schedule of benefits: The page in the group master policy or in the booklet certificate which specifically identifies the schedule or benefit formula or calculation that applies to an individual insured's coverage amount. The schedule of benefits typically describes minimum eligibility requirements for coverage as well. (This term is also known as *the schedule*, or *plan of insurance*.)

Self-administered: Method of plan administration in which the policyholder takes the lead role in operating the day-to-day non-claim functions of the group benefits program. This includes functions such as creating a monthly bill and tracking and updating enrollment. (This term is also known as *self-reported and self-accounting*.)

Shock claim: An underwriting term used to describe a claim of such high severity that it is considered aberrant and is very unlikely to occur in such magnitude again during the rate projection period.

Situs: Refers to the state from which the group contract will be issued. Frequently, it is the headquarters of the policyholder's company, but does not necessarily have to be. A situs state's regulations and mandates related to the group contract typically take precedence over other regulations jurisdictions.

Social Security Normal Retirement Age (SSNRA): The 1983 COBRA Omnibus Bill replaced the traditional Social Security retirement age of 65 with a "normal'" retirement age based on year of birth. Many carriers have adopted SSNRA as the termination of a disabled insured's waiver of premium rather than age 65.

Special Investigative Unit (SIU): An organization employed by or subcontracted to the insurer to investigate potentially fraudulent or questionable claims. (This term is also known as a *fraud unit*.)

Standard industry classification: A system established by the U.S. government to categorize businesses. Originating in the 1930's this 4-digit system has been used by group insurers historically to generate life manual rates. (This term is also known as *SIC code*.)

Step rates: Premium rates that are charged based on the employee's age. Typically, the insurer charges based on 5 or 10 year age brackets. (This term is also known as *age-bracketed rates*.)

Summary Plan Description (SPD): A documentation requirement established under ERISA. An SPD is a plain language explanation of the plan of benefits. It explains the benefits provided and the rights and responsibilities of the plan sponsor and participants.

Supplemental life: Typically group contributory coverage where the employer provides the platform enabling the employee to make choices about amount of group life coverage. It usually augments the amount of coverage provided under a basic life plan. Most coverage amount options are based on a multiple of annual earnings. (This term is also known as *voluntary life*, or *optional life*.)

Table I rates: Government provided rates with which an employer determines the imputed income on amounts of group life insurance over $50,000 in face value.

Term coverage: Life insurance coverage for a stated period of time – the "term". The insured has no investment or accrual component. At the end of the term of coverage, coverage terminates.

Uniformed Service Employment and Re-employment Rights Act (USERRA): Federal law enacted in 1994 to provide employment and benefit rights to National Guard personnel and Military reservists recalled to active duty.

Volume of insurance: Amount of coverage (face amounts) on an aggregate basis of all amounts of life insurance coverage in the class or the group. If all insureds were to have a claim, it is the amount of claim dollars the insurer would have to pay. (This term is also known as *volume*, *amount of insurance*, or *amount of coverage*.)

Voluntary products: While there are a variety of meanings attached to "voluntary" life products, for the purpose of this book, it is defined as a group insurance product in which the insured pays 100% of the premium. (This term is also known as *contributory, employee-pay-all*, and *supplemental*.)

Waiver of premium: A life policy provision in which a qualified disabled insured may continue coverage, without further premium payments after completing an Elimination Period of 3 to 9 months (varies by contract) and meeting the definition of disability found in the contract. (This term is also known as *waiver, premium waiver*, and *PW*.)

Worksite products: Individual insurance products sold to employees in the workplace.

Index